# ALL THE RAGE

# All the Rage

## A PARTIAL MEMOIR IN TWO ACTS
## AND A PROLOGUE

# BRAD FRASER

DOUBLEDAY CANADA

Doubleday Canada and colophon are registered trademarks of Penguin Random House Canada Limited

LIBRARY AND ARCHIVES CANADA CATALOGUING IN PUBLICATION

Title: All the rage / Brad Fraser.
Names: Fraser, Brad, 1959- author.
Identifiers: Canadiana (print) 2021013206X | Canadiana (ebook) 20210132205 | ISBN 9780385696371
   (hardcover) | ISBN 9780385696388 (EPUB)
Subjects: LCSH: Fraser, Brad, 1959- | LCSH: Gay dramatists—Canada—Biography. | LCSH: Gay liberation
   movement—Canada. | LCSH: Gays—Canada—History. | LCSH: Gays—Canada—Social conditions. | CSH:
   Dramatists, Canadian (English)—Biography. | LCGFT: Autobiographies.
Classification: LCC PS8561.R294 Z46 2021 | DDC C812/.54—dc23

Cover design: Talia Abramson
Cover photograph: Raoul Josset
Back cover image: 123creativecom/Pixaby

Printed in Canada

Published in Canada by Doubleday Canada,
a division of Penguin Random House Canada Limited

www.penguinrandomhouse.ca

10 9 8 7 6 5 4 3 2 1

Penguin
Random House
DOUBLEDAY CANADA

*For Braham Murray, Iris Turcott, Kate Newby,*
*Spencer Schunk and everyone who*
*lost someone to AIDS*

## AUTHOR'S NOTE

THIS BOOK IS A WORK OF MEMORY. It has been acquitted to the best of my recollection, which is freakishly good.

Names have been changed in certain cases to forestall possible social or legal repercussions.

Many people who have played profound roles in my life are not mentioned herein. Some might be offended, some might be relieved. Either way, we know what we shared, and perhaps those stories will be told another day.

This memoir was written with the assistance of the Ontario Arts Council.

# PROLOGUE: BASTARD BORN

MY MOTHER HAD BEEN SIXTEEN for three weeks when I was born in 1959. My father was eighteen. They'd met at a dance less than a year earlier. They were two sides of the same coin. Wes was the loud, manipulative bully; Sharon was the quiet, passive-aggressive controller. Neither was what the other needed but they were both what the other wanted. Both had quit school before completing the ninth grade.

Wes Fraser was born and raised in Gainford, Alberta, sixty miles west of Edmonton on the way to Jasper. His father, Fred, was a farmer whom the census listed as a half-breed (Scottish and Cree). Fred's mother was a Metis woman who lived in St. Albert, a suburb of Edmonton. She was the last in a long line of Metis women married to Frasers who came to the new country as trappers. Wes's mother, Margaret, the first white woman in the Canadian arm of the Fraser line, was of English descent.

Together Fred and Margaret homesteaded in northern Alberta and had four surviving children. Fred would later replace their sod-roofed dwelling with the four-sided sun-blackened pine-board house that was the closest thing I knew to a home in my childhood, as we often stayed there or lived in the one room shack constructed behind the house. My paternal grandparents doted on me as a child and I loved them both, but particularly Grandpa, who called me Monkey Face and would often take me with him in the truck when he had to run errands. Grandpa collected and sold scrap metal—the yard and fields were littered with dead vehicles and farming equipment he would haul away from other farms. When I was very young there were horses, cows, pigs and chickens, but later he got rid of everything but the horses, which were used to take tourists from the nearby town of Seba Beach on trail rides during the summers.

The house was without running water and electricity until 1970 and was just far enough off the road not to have a phone. (Grandpa considered the extra fee for a connection exorbitant.) They cooked on a wood stove and churned their own butter. Water was hand-pumped into buckets and hauled to the house, heat came from a pot-bellied coal heater, and light was provided by coal-oil lamps and candles. There was a smell of animals, outhouses, fresh-baked bread, newly mowed hay and overturned earth. Children ran wild and screamed as loud as they wanted, as did adults, although usually for other reasons. Some of the best and the worst memories of my early life are contained in that house and the acres of bush, fields and sloughs around it.

My mom, Sharon Briscoe, came from the comparatively cosmopolitan city of Edmonton, Alberta's capital. She was the fifth child in a family that grew over two decades to eleven. Sharon's father, Ernie, was a carpenter and then an administrator in the Alberta carpenters' union for most of his career. His own father had deserted his Jewish wife and children after relocating to Alberta. Sharon's mother, Mary, was from southern Alberta. She was in her teens when her family moved on a horse-drawn wagon to Edmonton, where she was quickly married off to my grandfather.

By the time I was born Sharon's parents resided in the Bonnie Doon neighbourhood. Six of their kids were by then married with kids of their own, and only my two slightly older uncles lived with them. Compared with the Frasers' farm, the Briscoe home—a bungalow like any other in a working-class neighbourhood—was palatial. And it had running water and an indoor bathroom.

I did not feel the same love from these grandparents as I did from my father's side. The Frasers were emotionally volatile, physically tender or violent, and predatorily loving. The Briscoes were self-contained and emotionally distant. Fraser gatherings always ended in physical or emotional violence. Briscoe gatherings ended with relief and no contact. Adding to the requisite teenage drama of an unwanted pregnancy, my father's family despised my mother and my mother's family despised my father.

Before long they were dating and Wes was taking her out to the farm on weekends. Given the ignorance and fear of sex that permeated both families, it's no surprise that Sharon was quickly knocked up.

Contrary to the custom of the day, my father, for reasons known only to him, did not immediately marry my pregnant mother. Instead she was shipped off to one of those institutions that existed in the fifties to help young women deal with the stigma and challenges of an unwanted pregnancy. Wes would bring up doubts about my paternity a few times in my later life, planting an always-nagging seed of uncertainty in my mind. However, if he'd truly believed I wasn't his son, then why did he marry Sharon and legally adopt me a few months after I was born? They were joined together at Edmonton City Hall and spent their wedding night in sleeping bags on the floor of Sharon's parents' unfinished basement. I slept in a makeshift cradle, probably a milk crate or cardboard box, beside them.

I think Mom was deeply affected by her time in that home for unwed mothers. Any unpleasantness that had happened in her earlier family life, and in her encounters with other boys and Wes, she hoped would be alleviated through me. I believe even in the womb she meant me to be her saviour. From birth she expected me to be the agent of her growth and liberation. I was showered with love and affection. I was told I was special. I was also a male she could finally control.

I remember being in the living room of our grandparents' farmhouse. It was just me and an older male cousin—someone my siblings and I were often left with while the adults were out drinking. His pants were open, his hard, pink cock sticking out. "Bradley, come here and suck on this." Always an accommodating child, I did what he asked. It was a fun game, though he said that I could never tell anyone about it. Sometimes, when we were staying at the farm, he'd slip into bed with me late at night and do things I was too tired to remember. After being protected for decades by his family, who loved nothing more than blaming us children for his victimization, this cousin was finally sent to jail for raping an infant. I was molested by other babysitters throughout my childhood. Not all of them were men.

Even if my parents or other adults had suspected any of this, I wouldn't have been able to communicate properly what was happening; they gave me no vocabulary to discuss such things. My parents were not communicators. There was no teaching from them. They had no ability to think critically and were driven only by emotion and instinct. I'd learned it was horrible to be yelled at or smacked, but it was even worse to be subjected to the cold, silent treatment they both resorted to for whatever transgression I'd unwittingly committed. Throughout my life people have remarked on how perceptive I can be, sometimes bordering on psychic. This is the result of having parents who demand you read their jumbled minds even as a toddler. I would eventually become most adept at it with all kinds of people.

Other than the farm and the shack, our lives were lived in an endless succession of rental properties. My father found the cheapest place he could, my mother cleaned it thoroughly, and we resided there for anywhere from a few weeks to a few months before we were inevitably evicted for non-payment of rent.

My mother gave birth to three other children—I have two sisters and a brother, all of us just barely two years apart. The experiences of my childhood are not necessarily those of my siblings, and their stories are not mine to tell.

Wes worked a variety of menial jobs in the early years, and we moved back and forth between Gainford and Edmonton. Then one day when I was five I fell asleep in Edmonton and woke to find myself in the main-floor suite of a rundown three-storey house, my mother scrubbing the floors and my father off drinking with his buddies. We were now living in Calgary. There my parents established the pattern for the rest of their marriage: Wes worked out of town from Monday through Friday and came home on weekends.

I was playing on the front porch one summer day when I heard a sound I'd never heard before: a kind of scream that didn't sound human but didn't quite sound mechanical either. I looked over the banister. A car with three people in the front seat had sped around the corner and had slammed on the brakes before they hit an elderly native woman who was crossing the street. I can vividly remember the look of horror on their faces when the car collided with the woman and she rolled up the hood into the windshield before rolling back into the street with a dull thud.

I ran into the house. My parents were drinking in the kitchen with the couple who lived upstairs. I screamed, "Mommy! Daddy! Mommy!"

I breathlessly described what I'd seen. They looked at me skeptically. My father said, "You better not be making this up."

I pointed at the front door and begged them to go look. All four adults moved to the door and saw the woman lying in the street. With exclamations of shock they all rushed out to the street. I was completely forgotten. I know the elderly woman lived because my father showed me the article in the paper the next day, but no one expressed the slightest concern about how I might've been affected by what I'd witnessed. Tellingly, as I grew up, I had little interest in learning how to drive.

A short time after this I woke up in a small white two-bedroom house back in Edmonton; another decaying neighbourhood, another couple of days working the street to make friends, something I'd become handy at by this point.

We had a Christmas tree of our own that year—until then we'd always spent Christmas with grandparents and enjoyed their tree. I got a bike it took me months to learn to ride. (I was not then what you'd call physically gifted and was said to be a whiny child.)

One of the few things my father did with me was take me to movies. My siblings were all too young, so on the occasional Saturday afternoon he'd tell Sharon he was taking me to a matinee and we'd drive to the nearby Avenue Theatre to see whatever was playing. I remember most of these movies quite vividly and used to parse them for some clue to anything Wes might have been trying to communicate to me at the time, but, in the end, they were just whatever was playing.

This was me and my father being together in the way he was most comfortable with. Silent. Focused on something else. I could feel his hulking presence beside me, hear his breathing, and smell his odour of cigarettes and a pleasing hint of BO. This was probably the only place I ever felt comfortable with him. When we were with the family or other people he was never shy about telling me what to do or criticizing me but the second we were alone together he would shut down. I always felt this was because I was doing something wrong.

Later that summer my father made a momentous announcement. We were moving, and this time it wasn't one of those go-to-sleep-in-one-place-and-wake-up-in-another moves. This one was planned and announced well in advance. My father had landed a permanent job with a road construction company and we were moving to B.C. For an extended family who had never been more than a couple of hundred miles from where they were born, this was big news. Since my dad's brother, Don, had also gotten a job with the same company, we wouldn't be leaving alone. Sharon and Don's wife, Janet, were close, and their three kids were our closest cousins. My father's sister Margaurite (fondly known as Aunt Pug for her upturned nose) and her family would join us a few months later.

We would spend the next five years living mostly on the side of what later became known as the Highway of Tears—Highway 16, running from Prince George to Prince Rupert—as my dad helped to build the final stretch of the Trans-Canada Highway. Wes mostly worked in remote areas and would usually spend Monday to Friday at a man camp. Sharon hated this schedule, as it left her responsible for the kids for the entire work week, and she'd insist we live close enough to wherever his current camp was for him to be able to return home whenever possible. Consequently we moved even more frequently than we had in Alberta.

I couldn't wait to start school. In the past couple of years I'd become aware that older people could do this thing called reading, which was what happened when you understood those black marks all over everything. I knew there was a whole other world of stories and information out there that came with being able to read and I was impatient to discover it. And I learned fast. When I was told books were actually written by people, I was gobsmacked. The idea that people made their livings telling stories fascinated me, and I decided then that's what I would do.

The first few months in B.C., while we were living in Vanderhoof, went well, but over the next two years I would attend five different schools in four different mining towns. By the second grade I was starting to have meltdowns in class because every school seemed to be teaching something new.

We were visiting Aunt Pug and Uncle Harvey in Endako when my parents mentioned we would soon be moving back to Vanderhoof from Lake Kathlyn. Aunt Pug said, "I will not allow you to make that boy switch schools again. What kind of education do you expect him to get?"

My parents shrugged. Neither of them had much regard for education.

Aunt Pug said, "Bradley, do you want to finish school here?"

I nodded, but not quickly enough to offend my parents. I knew if I offended them they'd say no on principle.

And so it was decided I would finish grade two in the two-room school house that served grades one to six in Endako while living with Aunt Pug and Uncle Harvey. I slept on the couch in the living room where their mean little chihuahua would curl up between my legs and snarl and bare his tiny needle teeth every time I moved, waking me up. My aunt and uncle's long-term rental house was old and small, but it felt like a real home rather than a temporary motel room in a journey to nowhere. They didn't drink much, they rarely left their children alone, and they weren't constantly fighting. For the first time I realized there were other ways to live than the one I'd come to think of as normal. My trips to see my family on the weekend made me even more aware of the differences.

While other kids had neighbourhoods made up of streets and houses, my neighbourhood was created by pop culture. My favourite TV shows and the popular songs on the radio did not vanish when we switched towns; nor did the spinning comic racks in every corner store featuring my best friends, Superman, Batman and Wonder Woman. My father refused to let me bring my comics along whenever we moved. This was long before the idea of collecting comics was heard of, and the only reason I wanted them was because I would read them until they eventually fell apart. But he'd say "no room" and toss them into the trash.

I read everything I could get my hands on. Wes was never shy about leaving *Playboy* and other men's magazines around the house, along with the gorier twenty-five-cent, black-and-white magazine-size horror comics that were sold alongside them. I devoured every word. No concerted effort was ever made to keep such material away from the children. No one ever explained that some things could be less constructive to read than other things, so I had no parameters and mentally hoovered up the shit with the gold. I was genuinely shocked when I was at the homes of other kids and realized their parents controlled what they read.

My parents never talked to me about sex, but you don't live in circumstances such as ours without being aware of every moment of your parents' sex lives or domestic conflict, and besides, almost everything they read seemed to be about sex.

Just before I started the third grade we rented a farm about half an hour outside of Smithers, B.C., a small alpine town. It was a working farm, huge and sprawling, with a well-built two-storey Dutch farmhouse and loads of outbuildings, meadows and forested areas. There was even a stream that ran beside the barnyard and down a hill to disappear into a culvert that ran under the road. It was a paradise for four wild kids and the two family chihuahuas, Lady and Chico—my dad bred them to sell the puppies and was more demonstrably loving with them than with any of his family—but not so much for my mother, who was once again isolated and required to feed various livestock.

I often felt guilty because I preferred the time Wes was away from home to when he was with us. By this time he'd intimidated me into submission. He was always unhappy with me because I wasn't masculine enough. I wasn't particularly effeminate, but I was sensitive and creative as well as slight of build. I was sad when animals were hurt or I heard about bad things happening to other people and I cried when my favourite cousins and aunts left after a visit. I was forever getting in trouble for playing with dolls. Things did not improve when I explained to Wes that I wasn't playing with them but making them better clothes. I loved to sew and was quite good at it. I was always making my sisters new outfits for Barbie, as well as detailed houses I crafted from shoeboxes and smart furniture I'd cut out of cardboard and carefully glue together.

Doing this sort of thing was what made me happiest. What I experienced when I was drawing, painting or crafting was similar to what happened when I was reading comic books or novels. I lost any awareness of where I was or how time worked and existed in a blissful, suspended state where I wasn't negotiating the dangerous world of adults and the ruthless world of children. I could be made happy by so many simple things: a paint-by-numbers set, an Aurora monster model kit, half a dozen comic books, a packet of Plasticine, two Faber-Castells and a couple sheets of paper. Yet my parents would continually give me baseball mitts, plastic weapons of war, cars and the like in an attempt to change, and control, my troublesome true nature.

Even at school I was shamed for my interest in the arts rather than the rough-and-tumble world of developing physical violence and intimidation boys of my generation were expected to indulge in. My lack of ability in gym class often got me called a sissy and a fruit. In grade three, when my order from the Scholastic Book Club, *Little Women*, was called out for pick up the class laughed at me. I wasn't picked on as much as the other gender-ambiguous kids were but, by the time I was in high school, when someone wanted to attack me they did it by calling me a fag. I was also insulted for my appearance, mostly my mouth. Liver-lips was number one, with Bucky, for my spaced, bucked teeth, number two. From the beginning of school I'd been made aware of my dental deficits and problems with my teeth have been consistent throughout my life. Good-looking kids are always told they are good-looking, kids who are not good-looking are always told they are not.

We were eventually evicted from the idyllic farm when our hard-core Christian landlords discovered my father had been slinging beer in the bar of the Bulkley Hotel on weekends during the previous winter, when he was traditionally laid off and we lived on his unemployment. We kids were shipped to our Grandparents Fraser for a few weeks that summer. When we returned we now lived in town, in the Smithers version of the other side of the tracks, which was right next to the train tracks because the only thing on the other side was wilderness.

My first year in Smithers had seen less bullying than the previous two years, when I'd been the new kid every few months, which guaranteed being bullied on its own, and by the time we moved into town I had a couple of friends from class to hang with. For the first time I had sleepovers and spent time with other families, and I became even more aware of how odd my family was.

When I got home my mother would never ask how it'd been but I'd tell her anyway, extolling the beauty of the other home, the deliciousness of the food, the friendliness of the parents. Sharon would shoot me an irked look and say, "You don't have it so bad here."

This was a favourite line of reasoning for my parents. As long as there were people who were worse off than us, we were okay. We weren't starved, beaten or violently raped like the children of some of our parents' friends and acquaintances. We might exist on processed food and bad cooking but at least there was usually some kind of food in the fridge. We might have only gotten a couple of outfits of clothes a couple of times a year but we were appropriately if cheaply dressed for the seasons and usually had someplace to live.

One day my mother was kneading dough for bread. Baking was the one culinary category she had some skill in. I looked up from the paper bag I was drawing on with a pencil that I'd sharpened with a knife because we were the kind of household where something as practical as a pencil sharpener was considered exotic and asked, "Why can't we ever live in nice houses?"

Without looking up she said, "There's nothing wrong with this house."

I put the pencil down. "I mean a house with a nice yard and garage and a lawn and that."

"We can't afford it."

"How come the men Daddy works with all have trailers of their own and we don't?" Most of Wes's peers owned trailers that they moved from town to town so they had consistent homes for their families in various trailer courts.

Sharon gave me a hard look and said, "Because they can afford it." And the conversation was over.

The truth was my parents' entertainment budget—their love of partying—kept us poor. Given a choice between paying bills or going out three nights a week, there was no choice.

I came home from school one day and could tell from the way Sharon was sitting at the kitchen table intensely smoking that something was wrong. When I asked she said, "Aunt Janet is gone."

I had no idea what she meant. "Gone where?"

"She took the kids and left. No one knows where they are."

Something atom-bomby went off in my ten-year-old head. This made no sense. Why would members of our family suddenly disappear without telling us? Especially Aunt Janet and her kids. "Why?"

"She got tired of Don beating her."

"Will we ever see them again?"

She stubbed her cigarette out with extra vigour. "Nope."

This moment was also the start of my mother treating me as if I was her friend because she had no idea how to make appropriate friends. Eventually she would tell me things about my father and her marriage that she had no business telling me, and which I didn't want to know. But I knew she needed me so I never complained.

That next summer, when we returned to the house by the tracks after another extended summer holiday in Alberta, the doors were padlocked and there was a large poster telling everyone we'd been evicted for non-payment of rent.

Wes immediately found another dump behind a gas station right where the highway and Main Street intersected. It was slowly sinking into the swamp that Smithers was built on. My siblings and I immediately dubbed this "the flooded house." I was more embarrassed by this house than any place we'd lived in and I never had friends over. Not that many of my friends ever wanted to come to my house anyway. They were all terrified by Wes's loud, mean-spirited "joking" and weirded out by Sharon's concentrated indifference.

One day Sharon was washing the dishes and I was drying them when she said, "Your father and I are thinking about splitting up. He's going to live at the Bulkley Hotel and I'm going to live here. We'll try that."

I began to cry. This was my worst nightmare. I was convinced we would disappear from the larger family just like Aunt Janet and her kids. Sharon said, "Quit crying. It might not happen." Then she gave me a hard, warning look and said, "Don't say a thing to the other kids."

They didn't split up and she never mentioned this again but I lived in fear of a divorce announcement at any minute for months.

As summer arrived and Wes continued to come home, my terror of the potential separation decreased and my stress-induced psoriasis cleared up. After some bumpy spots, finishing the school year was a lot of fun. I had a close group of four male friends and we spent hours having adventures around town on our bikes. (I'd shamed my parents into buying me a cheap discarded bike from a richer friend as an early birthday gift.) I was riding home after one of these adventures when I saw a truck outside the house loaded with our belongings. I threw my bike down in the gravel parking pad, leaped over the eternal puddle in front of the bottom stair and raced into the kitchen, where my mother was seated on a wooden crate, smoking and drinking Coke from the bottle.

"We're moving?"

She nodded casually, licked a piece of tobacco off her bottom lip, caught it on a fingertip and flicked it away. I threw my head into her lap and cried. After a moment she pulled me away by my arm and said, "Your dad took the kids for ice cream. Go wash your face so he won't see you like this."

"I don't want to move," I protested. "I have friends here!"

"You'll make friends in Merritt."

"Where's Merritt?"

"The Okanagan."

I said, "I don't want to go to the Okanagan."

"No one gives a shit what you want," said my father as he walked through the door with the other kids in tow, their faces shiny with smears of dried ice cream. "Now get in the truck." And then, like he could read my mind: "I threw the comics away."

In Merritt we moved into a one-bedroom motel suite, but at least this one was downtown, not on the highway, so we could explore the dusty town. Just before school started, the two-bedroom suite next to the motel owner's apartment came open and we moved out of the cramped one-bedroom. Instead of sharing a single bed, head to toe, as my sisters did across from us, my brother and I went to sleep in our parents' bed until they were ready to retire, when we were moved to the hide-a-bed in the living room. Not the best living conditions, but I have rarely been happier than I was sitting in the living room on a Saturday morning, eating Honeycomb and watching hours of cartoons through the miracle called Cablevision which expanded our TV viewing from the single-channel world we'd known in the north.

My parents decided I was now old enough, at twelve, to babysit my siblings. They'd always held me responsible for anything negative or stupid my siblings did, and this just continued that process. Now I was my mother's best friend and surrogate as well. Wes resented our closeness and would make fun of it from time to time.

Mom enrolled us in a free town-sponsored summer day camp, where I met the first people from India I'd ever seen. I'd met other people of colour because my mother's brother had married a Black woman in the early sixties, which created a great deal of friction in both the Briscoe and Fraser families, each of which had their own racist/anti-racist contingents. Despite my father's Metis heritage, he wasn't at all above using the crudest epithets for any other race. Sharon was the voice of reason here, proclaiming endlessly that "all people are equal" even as she gave me the stink-eye for bringing a Chinese boy home after school. This split in attitudes would be reflected in their children.

One weekend Wes didn't come home. This was a rare experience but not entirely unknown, as the company sometimes demanded overtime.

The next Friday when I got home from school, Sharon was scrubbing the floor in the entranceway and crying. I asked her what was wrong. She shook her head.

"Where's Dad?"

She dropped her rag in the bucket and put her head in her hands, sobbing without reservation now. A chill ran through me. "Did he leave us?"

She nodded, her chin trembling.

"Why?"

"I don't know." She stood, pulling down the legs of the jean cut-offs she always wore around the house, grabbed the bucket and went into the tiny kitchen. Tears were leaking out of my eyes. I was shaking.

"Mom—"

"Go out and play with the other kids." She threw the bucket into the sink and disappeared into the bedroom, slamming the door.

I realized we were living Aunt Janet and Uncle Don's story in reverse. My father had left us.

At first Sharon was too stubborn and embarrassed to admit to the few friends she had that anything was wrong. We ate through everything in the house. She borrowed money from a few friends, but we didn't associate with the kind of people who ever had extra money, so that was short-lived. I began to have uncontrollable crying jags in class and to lash out at the resulting jibes in a way that lost me the few friends I had. At night I'd lie in bed and listen to Sharon talk to her girlfriends on the phone and quickly pieced together that Wes had abandoned his family for a woman in Williams Lake they called the Amazon, and he had no intention of returning. My siblings were no longer buying Mom's explanation of continuing overtime and everyone was getting scared.

The local grocer, who we'd run credit with each week until Dad showed up on the weekend and paid the bill, refused an extension after three weeks. When we'd been two days without food mother finally threw herself at the mercy of a couple she knew and admitted we'd been abandoned. They took her to the appropriate office for emergency welfare. Eating again, Sharon got a job at the big supermarket and paid off the grocer's bill. I did everything I could to distract my brother and sisters from our father's absence while escaping into comic books, cartoons and bike rides whenever possible.

And then everything changed again with a late-night ringing of the telephone.

I heard my mother answer the call. She listened for a long time, asked a few hurried questions and hung up. She opened the bedroom door. "Bradley, come out here." I pulled my pants on and went into the living room.

"Grandpa Fraser died tonight."

I began to cry.

My father's father had loved me in a way his son couldn't. I'd always felt valued and protected with him. We'd last seen him only a few months earlier when my father had decided at the last minute that we were going home for Christmas.

Everyone was there except Aunt Janet and her kids. On Christmas Eve we all sat around the pot-bellied stove in the living room of the old farmhouse singing Christmas carols, my pedophile cousin playing a sweet guitar, while outside bloated snowflakes sifted down from a brittle Alberta night sky.

The day we were leaving, Grandpa'd pulled me aside, given me a whisker rub on my smooth cheek, pointed at the eyeglasses I'd started wearing the year before and said, "Don't read so much. It'll ruin your eyes," before hugging me for the final time.

The day after the phone call, Wes returned without explanation and took us on a dangerous drunken drive back to Gainford for his father's funeral. When we got home he and my mother had many intense, hushed arguments in their bedroom at night. I could hear the murmured accusations and counter-accusations. Wes was particularly incensed when he learned Sharon had gone out with another man while he was shacked up with another woman in Williams Lake. We still had two and a half months of school but as soon as it was done he moved us back to Gainford and the farm.

The house was in terrible shape. Mice and spiders came out of the floors and walls. A huge colony of bats had taken up residence in the attic. Initially we were terrified whenever a bat flew out and we'd scream for our parents to save us. After a couple of months we'd just grab a plastic tennis racquet, kill the thing and take it outside to the garbage. This was not the idyllic retreat I recalled so fondly from my childhood. It was a badly built, ugly old house with ratty furnishings, even by the low standards of the community, and I hated living there.

My parents never explained why we'd moved to Alberta, but I suspect Wes was trying to get us as far away from his girlfriend as he could. It seemed to make him more miserable when he was with us. He became even more authoritarian than before. I'd be lying on my bed reading when I'd hear him yell my name. I'd have to hike downstairs to see what he wanted, which was usually for me to change the TV channel for him or to get him another beer. We'd all been taught our place. His comfort was everything. Ours meant nothing. My resentment shimmered and began to take form. I was growing tired of being afraid.

The most positive experience of this period was Dave Haugen, my seventh-grade teacher, fresh out of university and hungry to make his mark as a teacher. For one English class he assigned us to write the most descriptive paragraph we could. I was reading *Dracula* at the time and let my obsession with horror movies take over. I wrote a paragraph that started "There on the bed lay Jude, her throat torn open as if by some savage animal, her breasts splattered with blood" and went on in the purplest Victorian-flavoured prose to depict the murder scene in a manner that was part Bram Stoker and part Harold Robbins.

Mr. Haugen was so impressed he read the entire paragraph to the class, who were equal parts disgusted and intrigued. When he was done he set the page on my desk, looked me in the eye and said, "You should think about being a writer."

Mr. Haugen's positive influence was countered by my father's growing strangeness. My penis was growing, and I'd discovered it was one thing that could give me some pleasure in a life often bereft of it. But our living situations did not allow any privacy for a kid becoming an adult. The bathroom was my sole refuge, and I'd often rub one out while sitting on the shitter or taking a bath. But Wes, for whatever inscrutable reason, had decided it would be hilariously funny if he pulled the door open when I was bathing—there was no lock—to throw a glass of cold water on me while the rest of the family stood behind him and watched, laughing. This happened a number of times and each time it was humiliating. But it was presented as just a joke, as Wes's abuse and manipulations often were.

It was also at the farm that I got my first exposure to queer lit, which I suppose makes an ironic sense as it was also the place where I first learned to suck cock. The bookcase in the living room contained maybe thirty or forty books, and I'd perused them all looking for parts I could wank to—I was already an expert at skimming until I found the dirty bits—but three of them had tangible effects on me.

They were: Carson McCullers's *Reflections in a Golden Eye*, Thomas Hal Phillips's *The Bitterweed Path* and James Kirkwood's *Good Times/Bad Times*. Each of these books is now recognized as a queer classic. Each of them forced me to look beyond the dirty bits and consider the entire story. It was revelatory. Although I still didn't have a name for what I might be—I certainly didn't feel like a fag or a sissy—I saw myself in these books where same-sex love was never stated but the themes were clear. Where had these books come from? The only committed reader in the family besides me was Wes. Were these his books? Had he read them?

Most of what he read was soft-core porn, and each of these books was marketed using their promise of taboo sexual content as a hook. Though I only realized they were queer classics over a decade later, it's interesting to consider the possibility that Wes was reading these books at the same moment his eldest son was discovering his own sexuality.

One day I was hanging out with school friends on the beach at Seba, the summer town two miles from the farm, when I met a girl from Edmonton. When we were introduced she asked me, "Are you related to Lorrie Fraser?" I nodded eagerly—"She's my cousin"—and gave her a quick update on my search for Aunt Janet. On her next trip to Seba she gave me Lorrie's address, and when I returned home I triumphantly told my mother what I'd done. Sharon made me swear not to tell anyone. Janet had disappeared for a reason and mom was sure she didn't want any Frasers finding her.

The next opportunity she had, my mother loaded us into the car and drove into Edmonton, where we were happily reunited with our lost cousins. I think Aunt Janet was less than pleased, but she welcomed us in and we all caught up on the intervening years. As we left, everyone promised they wouldn't betray her whereabouts.

Around the same time my father had to take a couple of sudden trips to B.C. that were not explained and usually lasted the entire weekend. Because we had no phone, he'd deliver the news of his absence in a call to our neighbours, who then conveyed the message to us. Sharon knew he was seeing the Amazon again, and her seething resentment was like a toxic gas.

One Friday morning, just as Wes was leaving for work he announced he wouldn't be home until Sunday night. Sharon said nothing, but I could tell from the way her eyes contracted that something profound was going to happen. He didn't look at us when his ride arrived and he walked out the door.

The second he was gone Sharon told us all to throw some clothes into paper bags because we were leaving. We kids didn't protest; we didn't beg to stay. Sharon got us into the car, and with Janet's help we had an apartment and emergency supplies within a few days. We'd had to give up our dogs. Happily, though, an elderly couple at the SPCA, on seeing the family's distress, adopted them immediately.

Going to school in the big city was intimidating. Kids there were a lot more aggressive than kids where I'd lived. Also, the student body was more diverse. I constantly felt self-conscious and inferior, but as my hair grew out and I got some bell-bottom pants, I began to feel like less of a freak.

I'd been at junior high for three weeks when I came home one day and saw Wes's canary-yellow Acadian parked in front of our apartment building. My sisters and brother were gathered at the open car door. Wes had his arms around them. I walked past slowly. Our eyes met. He didn't hold a hand out to me or in any way invite me into the tableau.

Sharon was at the sink doing dishes. I asked how he'd found us. She told me he'd hired a private investigator. I said, "You're taking him back."

She didn't look at me, just nodded.

I walked into the bedroom I shared with my brother and closed the door.

At first Sharon and Wes's reconciliation was a lot of fun. They bought a ton of seventies furniture on credit from Woolco and swore to dedicate themselves to their family. Wes even took me to a couple of movie matinees—no conversation, of course. But within a few months they were feuding again.

That's when the beatings started.

The first time, he and Sharon were fighting in the living room after we kids had gone to bed, and I went out to make sure she was okay. Wes said, "Get back in your room."

I said, "No."

Wes had rarely hit us. His emotional manipulation and intimidation were enough to keep his family in line. He had never hit my mom.

He hit me instead.

And he enjoyed it. I could feel it as the energy of that pleasure in his hand became the pain in my face. It was a hard, open-palmed slap he knew wouldn't leave a mark. I felt like my jaw had separated from my skull. Sharon screamed for him to stop. Wes said, "Go back in your room."

I said, "No."

He hit me in the face from the other side, same meaty, open palm. He called me a faggot. My eyes lost focus. I fell against the wall. I knew if I tried to defend myself it would just be worse. He pushed me into my bedroom and I fell onto the bed, helplessly listening to their resumed shrill conflict, feeling like the most terrible child in the world.

Later he came in, sat on the edge of the bed, put his hand on my shoulder and told me he hadn't wanted to do that but I had to behave. He hugged me and, oddly, through my bruises, I felt closer to him than I'd ever been.

The beatings weren't about my behaviour; they were about keeping me in line and subservient to his will. And I was having none of it anymore. I refused to behave the way he wanted me to. I didn't swear at him or talk back, I just continued to say no when he would order me to do something he could easily do himself. It took a lot of courage-summoning for me to do it. I'd spend hours telling myself it was only pain. Pain always went away eventually.

When he beat me a third time my mother threatened to hit him over the head with a frying pan. This just increased the abuse. When she called the cops, two of them showed up and I watched as my father gaslighted us all as he became that other, easygoing person he performed in public. He convinced the cops it was just a minor domestic disturbance and he was disciplining his son. They assured him he had every right to do what he was doing, and left.

Wes and I were alone in the apartment the next time we got into it. At one point he picked me up, threw me down on the tile-on-cement floor and kicked me a few times. I wasn't unconscious, but I couldn't move or see right. After a moment he stopped and stood staring down at me. Then he helped me to my feet, took me out to the car and drove to the nearest hospital, where I was diagnosed with a concussion.

My father sat on the one chair in the ER. I sat on the examination table. The doctor stood in the doorway and asked, "How did this happen?"

I looked at my father expectantly. He smiled at the doctor. "He fell down the stairs."

The doctor looked from me to Wes. They shared a look. The doctor nodded and left the room. I loathed them both.

Even after that there was one more beating. This time when he slapped me I laughed at him.

He slapped me again.

I laughed and said: "You're beating up a kid. Your son. You're nothing but a fucking bully. You're pathetic."

He hit me again but his eyes were shiny and wet.

I'd stopped laughing. Now I spoke casually. "You can beat me until I'm dead. I don't care. You're a mean asshole and a terrible father and I never want to be like you in any way. I never will." Then I laughed again, feeling a kind of power I'd never known in my life.

Wes looked stunned, and then he kind of reached for me as if for a hug. I sneered at him and went to the bathroom to wash my bleeding lip.

These beatings did not figure into Sharon's decision to finally leave Wes a few months later. It was over for good after a night out with a group of people from the apartment building, when Wes hit on one of her single-mother friends.

We moved into a city-subsidized housing development in Beverly, on Edmonton's outmost eastern edge. The townhouse had three bedrooms, one bathroom, a galley kitchen with an eating area, and an unfinished basement with modern laundry machines. We even had a patch of lawn out front.

Sharon worked a series of jobs—factory shift worker, store clerk, cocktail waitress—all of which she quit the second she got bored. Between jobs we lived on welfare. She made it clear she would no longer be cleaning up, cooking meals or washing clothes for us but neglected to teach any of us how to do those things ourselves. She made little effort to get us to school on time or take part in parent/teacher meetings. She didn't look at any of my report cards after I completed grade nine. She discovered the singles scene and spent much of the week sewing new outfits to wear to events where she met many men.

Meanwhile, I worked a variety of part-time jobs in the evenings in order to keep myself in stylish clothes, smokes, records and comic books.

In Beverly I made friends. If I wasn't exactly popular, I wasn't exactly unpopular either and was pleased to be invited to parties and to hang out with the various groups of people I intersected with. I wasn't a jock, I wasn't a nerd, I wasn't a drama kid, but I knew people from each of these groups and circulated among them with as much comfort as one can feel at that age. I went out with girls and obtained a number of furtive hand jobs while necking in basement rec rooms or the back seats of cars at drive-in theatres. However, much as I liked these girls, I secretly knew I was more sexually interested in boys. As I got older there were drunken experiences with other guys, also mostly furtive hand jobs, which would never be spoken of afterwards.

As a student at Eastglen High I was mostly indifferent. The one thing all of my teachers could agree on was that I was imaginative and had a facility for expressing myself through writing that was beyond my years.

I had developed a sharp tongue and a dark sense of humour that could be merciless. I had an unerring talent for finding someone's most vulnerable point and attacking it if I had to in order to protect myself, which I was far too quick to do. Like all kids that age I was fucked up but not nearly as fucked up as I should've been considering my upbringing. Somehow in all of that conflict I'd learned to parent myself, to look out for my own best interests and, most impossibly of all, to maintain some degree of self esteem.

Why was I so different from my family? Was I not my father's son? Was it the queerness? It made me feel like a freak, but there was a kernel underneath making me feel strength in my differences. That kernel of whateverness somehow kept me from the precipice of despair I sometimes teetered at in those days.

I had lost any fear of adults and if I respected one it was because they had earned it. I had a quick mind and a great vocabulary and I enjoyed pointing out the flaws in their arguments or their biases. I didn't speak to them like a mouthy teenager; I spoke to them as another adult. Among my peers I was known as the guy who wasn't afraid to tell the group something could be wrong even if they all believed it to be right.

By the end of the eleventh grade I was in deep academic trouble, having spent most of my time hanging out in the smoking pit with my friends or at home watching afternoon movies in the empty house.

Paradoxically, I wanted desperately to graduate from high school. Very few people in my extended family had done so, and no one in my immediate family. It was important to me because I didn't want a life anything like the life I'd come from. The problem, though, was most of my classes were so damn boring. I'd read all the assigned material, but the teachers' summations of it put me to sleep or caused endless, compulsive doodling. To their credit, a number of my teachers recognized the problem and would help me out with one-on-one tutoring or more challenging assignments, but to little effect. Still, I knew that if I wanted to avoid the trap of my background and class, I would have to make some dramatic changes to my life.

Like most gay people of my generation, my true character, narrative and life did not emerge until I left my upbringing and my family behind, which was not as profoundly difficult for me as it was for others, since my family had already been shattered.

I knew that my upbringing had instilled a tremendous anger within me and that if I didn't find a way to channel that anger constructively it would end up directed at those around me or myself. I also knew it would trap me in the world I came from. Creative activities had always been the best way for me to channel my negative emotions and I knew my salvation would be with them. I also knew what I'd been taught was love didn't seem like love at all, and I had developed some serious questions and ideas about the many meanings, often negative, that word can have.

Thankfully, something was about to happen that would facilitate the change I craved. Something that my life to that point had made me uniquely qualified for.

ACT ONE

Les Enfants
Terribles

# PART ONE

# TWO PARIAH AT A BUS STOP IN A LARGE CITY LATE AT NIGHT

MY NASCENT ADULT playwright/activist/artist self was born the moment the house lights went down in a small theatre at Victoria Composite High School in Edmonton, Alberta, in 1976. I was seventeen.

The show was *Philemon*, a little-known musical by Tom Jones and Harvey Schmidt, who had also written one of off-Broadway's longest-running twentieth-century shows, *The Fantasticks*. It starred a friend from junior high school who persuaded me to attend. Its highly theatrical, suggestively minimalistic production style, coupled with the haunting, sometimes infectious score, transported me in a way I'd never been transported before. By the time the lights came up at the end and we had all burst into rapturous applause, the trajectory of my life had been irrevocably changed. Within a week I decided to leave Eastglen High and transfer to Vic Comp to attend their Performing Arts program.

Switching high schools would take me away from Beverly and the close friends I'd made there. A few were supportive, but there was a sense of betrayal, that I was becoming snooty and artistic. We came from a world of shop stewards, shift workers at the nearby industrial plants and oil refineries, bus drivers and rail workers, waitresses and store clerks, alcoholic fathers and bitter passive-aggressive mothers; a world of quiet emotional and sexual abuse numbed by the joys of suburban alcoholism, bullies, gangs, cliques and bar fights. I wanted a world of glamour and excitement.

When I registered at Vic I did something I'd always wanted to do but had never quite found the courage for at any other school I'd attended: I registered as Brad (rather than Bradley) Fraser. I was determined to become someone else, and becoming Brad was the first step in my transformation. It upset Sharon when I refused the name she'd given me but I stuck to my guns. Brad wasn't her best friend.

My first-year class convened in a large rehearsal room with gleaming (for two days) black floors and huge windows set high up on the wall. We had two teachers, Billy Bob Brumbalow, a flamboyant Texan who was cagey about his sexuality, as teachers had to be in those days, and Don Pimm, a Burl Ives lookalike who assaulted many young women throughout his career as a teacher with impunity, as they did in those days. The class itself was two-thirds female. We were the usual assortment of oddballs, freaks and beautiful people that drama schools attract. We were "drama kids," smart, talented, glib, needy and highly annoying.

Mornings were devoted to academic credits in such classes as English and History of Theatre, and afternoons were spent in the rehearsal room or stage area, learning stagecraft. We studied Laban movement—plenty of walking through Jell-O and allowing your body to be a pulsating beat—breathing exercises, rudimentary Alexander Technique, a bit of fencing, stage movement, articulation, period technique, acting, makeup and scene study. The program was a lot harder than I'd expected, and swanning around in tights made me self-consciously aware of how graceful and coordinated I was not. I often struggled to learn lines for scenes and would get in trouble for paraphrasing in performance. Over the first three months of the program nearly half of the students would drop out.

The year before, I'd started working part-time at the Fred Astaire Dance Studio in downtown Edmonton as a telephone salesman. The studio was about as tawdry faux-glamorous as anything in seventies Edmonton could be. It also had a dodgy rep. A year earlier, a crusading radio reporter by the name of Eddie Keen—heard daily on 630 CHED, the most popular local teeny-bopper station—had exposed a viper's nest of corruption and fraud that involved many sad, lonely people signing contracts for expensive lifetime dance lessons without really knowing what they were getting into. I remember something slightly homophobic about these reports even before I knew what homophobia was. The suggestion that the male dancers involved were all gigolos or "worse" (code for gay) and the women were all prostitutes seemed rather unfair.

At this point in my life "homosexuality" was a clinical word that was only just beginning to be bandied about publicly. It was usually depicted as something perverted and insane.

It's erroneous to say there were no gay role models or icons at the time. Such well-known personalities as David Bowie, Elton John, Charles Nelson Reilly, Paul Lynde and Liberace were widely assumed to be gay without ever copping to it, and much-loved regardless.

But it was the people who dared to identify themselves as gay who fascinated me. I remember reading about Tennessee Williams's notorious coming-out interview with Dick Cavett and thought it was incredibly brave. When football player Dave

Kopay came out in a controversial and bestselling autobiography in 1977, all of the stereotypes started to fall apart in my mind. If a football player could be gay, then anyone could be gay.

There was also the Anita Bryant controversy around that time. The former beauty queen turned orange juice shill spoke out against one of the earliest gay-rights bills, and when she was pied in the face on national TV, it was my first exposure to that level of public hatred and gay defiance. I already knew that many people still considered being gay a mental illness, despite its having been dropped from the foremost guide to mental disorders a few years earlier, but I was shocked to learn there were still many places where it was illegal to be gay, or to try to meet other men in the streets and invite them for sex.

As a student in the Performing Arts, or PA, program I was often offered free tickets to preview live shows at the few theatres in town, most of them new. I went to each of them eagerly, as I wouldn't've been able to afford it otherwise. The shows I remember most vividly from that time were the few that were set in Canada, because there was something very novel then—and now—about seeing Canadian culture being offered to Canadians.

The most profound theatre experience I had was at the Citadel Theatre, during its inaugural season in the new brutalist space that squats over a formerly seedy part of downtown, sitting five rows away from the stage for a dress rehearsal of a play called *Equus*, by Peter Schaffer. This play about a conflicted psychiatrist trying to find out why a teen boy would gouge out the eyes of six horses, and its imaginative and theatrical staging, would influence me deeply. The image of the six muscular men in skin-tight costumes, stylized horse heads and platform hooves was disturbing and erotic, as was the nudity in the show. The acting of the entire company was exceptional. I was transported beyond myself into a kind of eternal present tense that I have pursued ever since.

Later in the year, we prepared for the Edmonton Kiwanis Music Festival, a province-wide celebration and competition of not only music but the best performers and debaters from Alberta high schools. I chose a monologue from *Equus* in which Alan Strang—the boy who blinded the horses—tries to explain where his fascination with horses might have come from. The piece is loaded with horny horse/man imagery, and for the first time I didn't struggle to learn the lines. On the day of the presentation I spent the last half-hour before my entrance circling the dressing room, speaking my lines over and over again, faster and faster, until they became thoughts that came without effort. When I was called to the stage I was hot with a kind of simmering power that filled me to bursting when I started the scene.

Three minutes later I finished and bowed my head. When I looked up, the other students were staring at me, dumbfounded. I knew I'd nailed it. I could feel it in my heart. I'd been confident in a way I hadn't ever felt before, in control, but also involved. Not self-conscious the way I'd felt in all of my earlier acting exercises and scenes. The students applauded long and hard and I knew they meant it. If you know how snatchy theatre students can be, you'll know what an accomplishment that was.

I went into the competition confident, cocky and ready to show the world just how special I was and left with the much-coveted best actor citation for my monologue.

We broke for the summer. Most of my fellow students would vanish from my life for good. After the Fred Astaire Dance Studio ultimately closed, I got a job at the Roxy Theatre on 124th Street. I was an usher who wore a wilted yellow polyester blazer. I took tickets and policed the theatre for drinkers, smokers, talkers and people who put their feet on the seats.

In my spare time I wrote scenes, short one-acts, silly vignettes— I was fucking around with language, exploring ideas, trying to reproduce characters I saw on the bus or at work, banging at my portable Smith-Corona late into the night and chain-smoking. Most of the short plays I wrote were based on works we'd explored in school, absurdist moments modelled after Pirandello, poetic, melodramatic moments after O'Neill, florid, horny moments after Williams. This was where writing as a habit started for me.

The start of the second year of the PA program was not as momentous as the first, but I did make a new friend. Hilda Jurgens arrived in Edmonton from Ottawa via Montreal after a nightmare divorce between her parents. Her mother, along with her mom's new live-in boyfriend, packed up her three high-school-age kids and dragged them across the country for a new start in Edmonton.

Hilda was a hefty girl, sharp and smart, with a mass of carrot-orange hair that made her stand out in any situation. She, like me, had a love of pop culture, a gift for language and a delight in laughing and making others laugh. She took an instant shine to me, and even though I could tell she was nursing a crush that wasn't reciprocated, we started hanging out. A few months later I would get her a job at the Roxy, ensuring we'd spend even more time together.

A large part of my day was spent on public transit, where reading was the only thing that passed the time. I knew the chances of my actually going to university were slim, so I was always researching what university students were reading in their literature classes and then finding books from the syllabus in the Wee Book Inn, a used bookstore next to the Roxy.

My discovery of plays had happened a few years earlier with a late-night television viewing of *Who's Afraid of Virginia Woolf?*. Black-and-white, claustrophobic and using dialogue with a rhythm and drive I'd never encountered in film, this movie was somehow different from the ones I knew. Shortly after watching and being absolutely devastated by it, I discovered the Katharine Hepburn/Ralph Richardson version of *Long Day's Journey into Night*. After making the connection between these films and the plays they were based on, I realized that plays were like movies, just with a lot more talking. This was the beginning of my exploration of both mediums that would fascinate me for the rest of my life.

I started work on a one-act play. It was called *Two Pariah at a Bus Stop in a Large City Late at Night* and was a complete rip-off of Albee's *Zoo Story*. A precocious, perhaps brain-damaged teen encounters a middle-aged man one night in a park and they have a mutually revealing, vaguely intimate encounter that affects them both. Derivative indeed, but there was an authenticity to both characters' voices that saved the piece when Phil—my straight best friend at Vic—and I presented it as my final project. The class was appreciative, and Billy Bob and Don urged me to keep writing.

I'd entered the play in the Alberta Culture Playwriting Competition, which was one of a number of new cultural programs the provincial government was sponsoring. While I waited for a response, my time in high school was wrapping up. I walked away with most of the awards at the Kiwanis festival again, was awarded the Eva O. Howard Award for top drama student at Vic Comp, won another award with a group of three or four other people for being the top arts students in the city and then, a few days before my graduation, I won in the student category of the provincial playwriting competition.

This sudden smattering of honours made me a minor celebrity for a few weeks. A reporter from the *Edmonton Journal* interviewed me. They even sent a photographer to the school to take pictures of me in the one-acts we were doing at the time.

Mom responded to all this with her usual indifference. When I hinted that I might like to go to my graduation and awards night if I had a bit of money for the clothes, she snapped, "Don't expect anything from me." In the end I worked instead and never heard any of the kind and supportive words that were spoken of me that night by my teachers and fellow students.

One of the rewards of winning the playwriting competition was four weeks at the legendary Banff School of Fine Arts as the student member of the Playwrights Colony. All expenses were covered and there was a weekly stipend to keep things interesting. I couldn't wait to go. I hoped this trip would change my life.

The Banff Centre is an artists' colony and corporate retreat in the Rocky Mountains. Artists in disciplines ranging from the dramatic to the conceptual met over the summer months for intensive training and exploratory sessions in one of the most beautiful settings on earth. The Playwrights Colony was a program designed to encourage the writing of new Canadian plays for all the new theatres springing up across the country. I found most of the people in the colony stuffy. They were an earnest, academic crowd writing talky plays about coal mine strikes and incest on prairie farms and self-conscious, unfunny Toronto comedies.

It was here I heard of the Stratford Festival for the first time as well as new-work pioneers in Toronto like the Tarragon, Factory and Theatre Passe Muraille. I also learned about two playwrights who were hot on the international scene that year: Tom Stoppard, whose *Travesties* was making the rounds in theatres, and Joe Orton, thanks to an excerpt from an upcoming biography I read in a big-time magazine. The story of his death at the hands of his male lover a decade earlier fascinated me.

Thankfully there were two people in the colony who kept me from feeling like the only David Bowie among a coterie of Gordon Lightfoots.

Paul Reynolds was the first out gay person I ever knew. He was a stage manager at the time, trying to work his way to being a director, which was his role in the colony. He was dryly witty and candidly raunchy, but also intelligent and kind (to me if not everybody else).

Jack Piper was in the acting company, while also appearing in a sappy two-person musical he performed in an improvised ball-room/theatre at the beautiful Banff Springs Hotel. He had a swarthy Middle Eastern look I found irresistible. He also had a quick wit and, although he was engaged to a woman, seemed very comfortable in the company of men. Sometimes, while he was reading someone's play, his eyes would lock on mine across the table and he would smile conspiratorially as if to say, "We both know how boring this is." That intimate sparkle in his eyes would give me an instant erection that took ages to subside.

One solitary evening, out of boredom I ended up in the school's bar shortly after it opened. A small black-and-white TV propped on a side stand announced the Canadian television premiere of *The Apprenticeship of Duddy Kravitz*, adapted from the novel by Mordecai Richler. Two and a half hours and four beers later, I was genuinely moved by the film and feeling vulnerable when Paul Reynolds turned up, looking as stricken as I felt.

He looked relieved to see me, replenished my Labatt's Blue, bought himself a Dubonnet and joined me at my table.

I asked, "How are you?"

He pursed his lips and gave me a dry, one-sagging-eyelid look. "Bad night."

"What happened?"

He rolled his eyes upward "Jack Piper's fiancée arrived."

"So?"

Paul leaned in and whispered, "Darling, I've been sleeping with Jack since we got here."

I tried to look sympathetic but I was jealous as fuck. I wanted it to be me who was involved with Jack Piper. "And now?"

"Now I am once again replaced by a woman. It's an old story. Ignore me."

I laughed.

Paul squinted at me and said, "And what about you, young man? I still really have no idea if you're gay or not."

I picked at the label on my beer bottle and looked away. This was the first time someone had asked me this point blank. "Pretty sure I'm gay," I said, "but I've done some stuff with girls too."

We had more drinks. We talked. He was the first person I'd ever met who could talk about being gay openly and honestly. When I mentioned my squeamishness about the idea of anal sex, he laughed and explained that most North American men are raised to be tight-assed and afraid of the anus, but, if you knew how to keep yourself clean, it could be just as sensitive and important as any other sex organ. These were seismic things to learn in a world that offered no sexual education at all to queer kids.

After we'd closed the bar and stumbled back to my room as we both seemed to know we would, after we'd kissed clumsily and stripped, his soft body up tight to my lean, hunched one, after he'd gone down on me while apologizing for not being able to get it up himself, after he'd made my cock feel better than it had ever felt before and slurped back every drop of my jizz, I knew I'd had my first truly gay encounter. Everything I learned in Banff that summer was secondary to my experience with Paul Reynolds.

# PART TWO

# WITH LOVE FROM YOUR SON

ON MY RETURN TO EDMONTON I soon found a job as a directory assistance operator. It was shift work, and I could trade shifts, allowing me time to write and audition.

The Walterdale Playhouse was Edmonton's first live theatre and today is one of the oldest amateur theatre groups in the country. It was founded by a group of culture-hungry academics and frustrated artists in 1959. They generally did the imperialistic American/British fare that dominated the elitist idea of what should be produced in theatres at the time: plenty of Coward, Simon and Shaw—and, to their credit, the occasional latest play of controversy, with varying degrees of success. They held open auditions for every show and anyone was welcome.

I was frustrated that there were few parts for a young man of my age and type in most of the work they did, but I made a point of showing up to read for anything that might vaguely fit. I got to know people around the theatre and before long I was helping out backstage, being invited to the occasional party and becoming a member of the club.

Some months later at a show, a children's trifle a friend was acting in, I was pulled from my bored theatre stupor when three men dressed as rats danced onto the stage. As they started singing some off-key nonsense about how badass they were, the entire audience straightened up, tittering. The reaction had nothing to do with their performance and everything to do with the fact they were wearing light-coloured tights without the appropriate undergarments, making their bouncing genitalia visible to everyone.

In the coming months one of these rats became a very important person in my life, and another became the first man I seduced.

The man I seduced, Patrick, was the eldest of the rats, a "mature" fellow in his early thirties, short and cute with a beard and a sweet smile. During the obligatory phone call to a friend in the cast to thank her for the invite to the show, I managed to wheedle his number out of her by claiming I was doing a report on children's theatre for some paper or other.

Nanoseconds after hanging up I was on the phone to the actor, complimenting him on the brilliance of his performance. Seconds after that I'd scheduled an appointment to interview him in his apartment a few days later.

Patrick was an excellent host. Whether he bought my story or whether he was humouring me I have no idea to this day. He was making dinner while we talked and I pretended to take notes, then at some point I ran out of questions, he ran out of answers, and we ended up naked in his bed.

An hour later I was stumbling out of his apartment a little light-headed but grateful. We'd see one another again over the next few months, and although he taught me some really important things about sex, our chemistry was rooted in friendship more than lust, and we were both fine with that.

Meanwhile my mother emancipated herself and announced she was getting her own apartment with my youngest sister. At eighteen it was time for me to move on. I was resentful and argued that I needed another year at home to decide whether I would go to university or not. Sharon was unmoved.

A few months later Phil, my best friend from PA, and I found a two-bedroom apartment on the seedy edge of downtown and furnished it with what we'd had in our bedrooms and donations from family and friends.

By then I was working on another play that would be called *With Love from Your Son*. It was something I'd been pecking away at since Banff. Late at night, sometimes in the morning before I'd go to work, weekend afternoons when nothing was happening, I'd be rattling my new electric typewriter, bought with my prize money from the Alberta Culture Playwriting Competition, churning out the story of a troubled young man who sells his cock to a mother-obsessed gay dude in order to buy medicine for the troubled guy's sick father. It was a cliché-ridden potboiler only a young man with a strong sexuality and little experience could think was original. I finally typed a cleanish draft and sent it off to the playwriting competition, this time in the adult category. It would be months before the results were announced.

A friend from PA had recently started in the Technical Theatre course at Grant MacEwan Community College in Edmonton. I'd met a number of her fellow students at a party and liked them a lot. A handsome guy named Cam and I had hit it off, taunting one another with our version of witty banter. Cam had moved from Vancouver a year earlier looking for the promise Alberta offered to so much of the rest of the country at that time. We all wanted to be actors but were settling for this technical theatre thing until we could figure out a way to get famous. That night had ended in a drunken blackout and I hadn't seen him since.

Desperate to be part of something again, I signed up to join the class in January, for the second semester. I went to part-time status at the phone company when school started, which allowed me to handle rent and expenses, just.

Another guy joined the class at the same time. His name was Randy Sandowski and he was one of the three well-hung rats from the kid's show. Randy had met the class at earlier social functions and seemed to know most of them much better than I did. Neither of us was particularly friendly toward the other, even though we were often paired together on projects, being the new kids. I found him a little too John Travolta in manner and dress, which was very eighteen months ago at the time. He would later say he found me patronizing.

Most members of the class were also involved with the Walterdale Playhouse, either helping out technically or hoping to win a part and get onstage. There were auditions for *The House of Blue Leaves* by John Guare, and everyone had decided to go and watch even if we weren't auditioning. I arrived late and quietly took a seat in a row right behind Randy, Cam and Dee—a beautiful dark-haired woman from class with a gravelly voice and a raucous laugh.

Someone was reading onstage so there was not time for me to make my presence known. When the reader finished, Dee leaned into Randy, oblivious to me right behind them. "So, what do you think of the class?" she asked.

Randy said, "It's great. I like almost everyone."

She smiled conspiratorially. I could tell they'd probably fucked. "Who don't you like?"

Randy said, "Brad."

Before Dee could respond or he could elaborate I leaned forward and loudly cleared my throat. They both looked back at me, turned white and swallowed guiltily.

Luckily, the next reader then took the stage, so they had an excuse to turn away before any of us could say anything. I watched the backs of their necks turn red and was thankful they couldn't see the look in my eyes. Not because I was mad, but because I was hurt.

A couple of days later Randy and I were teamed in an electronics class to learn how to solder wire when the instructor approached and took the soldering iron out of my hand to illustrate a point, saying, "Whenever you're soldering, make it a habit to—"

I cut him off. "If soldering ever becomes habitual with me, I'll kill myself."

The instructor gave me a dirty look and departed. Randy doubled over with laughter; hand over his nose to hide the snot he just blew out of one nostril.

Cam and Randy were close, but Cam and I had also developed a friendship, so it was natural the three of us would end up hanging out together. One night they dropped by the apartment after cruising around for something to do and coming up short. We were having a hammered discussion about sex, as we often did, while I sketched Randy posing for me in his underwear and leather jacket, wearing my straw fedora. Cam watched over my shoulder.

The talk this time was about the morality of getting head. Did the sex of the other person matter if all you were going to do was come in their mouth? Did letting a guy suck your cock make you gay? Randy was surprisingly democratic in an old-world way. "Who cares who it is as long as someone's sucking your cock?" Cam didn't care. I told them about my blow job from Paul Reynolds in Banff. Neither was sure how to react.

The three of us would skip classes to go and drink beer at the Saxony Hotel all afternoon or do poppers while watching two showings of *The Rocky Horror Picture Show* back to back. Our partying was getting out of control, and the first thing to suffer was school. Lectures on lighting gels and costume history were increasingly less seductive. We'd missed so many classes that on our way to the bar one afternoon, Cam finally said, "If we miss this class we can never go back." We shared a concerned look and then went to the bar anyway. That was the end of our time in the Technical Theatre course.

Also, there was something happening between Randy and Cam, a palpable curtness. They were like a couple who're really getting to know one another once the glamour has worn off. We were each a year apart, Cam at twenty, me in the middle at nineteen, and Randy at eighteen. We were all about the same height and had similar builds, although Randy, who'd been working out with weights since high school, had a beefy, muscular chest and shoulders we both envied. Cam was more willowy and lighter in tone. I was the skinny one with the dark hair and pale skin.

One afternoon Cam and I were at Edmonton City Centre shopping for clothes at Big Steel or Black Sheep, and he brought up the conversation we'd had about blow jobs. He told me he often sucked cock, usually guys he met by hitchhiking around the city when he was drunk late at night.

I was a bit agog, not that Cam was a cocksucker, which I'd surmised ages ago, but that he was telling me so unabashedly. He was dating a girl at the time, although I only remember her dimly. He'd admitted they'd had some good sex. "So you're bi," I said. He looked at me intensely without smiling and said, "Maybe. You?" I shrugged. We both laughed. Nervously bisexual.

Then Cam and Randy had a falling-out that proved permanent. The details are unknown to me, but I do remember that the climactic event in the demise of their friendship was Cam coming home one night to find Randy fucking Dee in his bed. Apparently he'd given Randy keys to his coffin-sized basement bachelor suite for nights when Randy was too drunk to drive. After that Randy just stopped showing up. Cam was heartbroken but also spiteful.

This was also when Cam and I went to Flashback for the first time.

By the time I was in Vic Comp I had heard about Flashback, a gay bar then on the western end of Jasper Avenue underneath the Hot Box Restaurant. I was dying to go, but it was a private members' club, so even when I turned eighteen I couldn't get in without a member—members being gay people. I didn't know any gay people, so it was a Catch-22.

It was Cam who finally came through, after he landed a stylist apprenticeship at Hair by Michael. The titular Michael, who was a straight guy with a family and a very successful shop, naturally employed a number of gay men, and one of them was to leave Cam's name, plus a guest's, at the door.

We fretted all week about our outfits. I'd found an amazing pair of high-heeled pointy-toed disco shoes that looked great with my high-waisted pants and button-down white shirt, my hair carefully blown into a nearly-over-one-eye Bryan Ferry bang. Cam's hair had a certain Morgan Fairchild thing going on and his pants were tighter than mine.

The club had moved to an alley just off 104th Street and 103rd Avenue, a fifteen-minute walk from my place. We climbed the loading dock stairs that led to the entrance, but just as I reached to open the door, Cam put his hand on mine and said, "Let's not go in?"

I looked at him in shock. "What? Why not?"

He said, "What if we're gay?"

I said, "Oh Cam, don't be stupid."

We laughed and went through the door.

We were nervous and excited, taking in every detail of the place: the antique signs over the rustic wooden bar, the pinball and rudimentary video games flashing against one wall, in the next room a recessed lounge with a bar-level backgammon table and matching stools, the main room with its bi-level dance floor and tacky Christmas lights on a patio-lattice ceiling.

A fragrance permeated the place, so much so that for a few months afterwards I wondered if gay men had a sac of something in their butts that was broken the first time they were fucked and made them smell this way for the rest of their lives. Then I discovered it was Aramis cologne, as integral to a gay man's identity at the time as opening that extra button on your shirt.

Cam said, "Wanna dance?" I smiled and said, "Sure!" There was something thrilling about walking up those three steps to the dance floor without people even noticing. I was dancing with another guy, feeling self-conscious but free too, safe in a way I'd never imagined during my teen years.

Cam smiled at me. I smiled at him.

We were totally gay.

That night, after the best time of our lives to that point, Cam left with a silver-haired gentleman who often appeared in high-end underwear advertisements, and I went home with a smiley shorter guy who was incredibly hot.

He shared an apartment in a high-rise on the river valley hill on the south side of downtown with a big girlfriend who also hung out at the bar. I was nervous and clumsy. We kissed and sucked each other's cocks for a while, but when he wanted me to fuck his ass my dick wilted and I made a hasty retreat, ashamed that, despite all my related reading, I had no idea how to fuck another guy. All my experience so far had been frottage and oral.

As I would learn the next day over excited glasses of Coke in my kitchen, Cam got royally fucked by the silver daddy and wasn't at all self-conscious about his enjoyment of it. I confessed my failure with my guy and my qualms about butt-related complications. Cam shrugged and laughed his snatchy laugh. "I don't think about that," he said. "I just wash up really well and relax when he's sticking it in." His eyes narrowed as he looked at me across the table. "I could show you if you want."

We went to my bedroom and stripped down, stretched out on the single bed I'd brought from the townhouse and kissed passionately until our cocks were rock hard. His cock was uncut, which was new to me. He said, "Got any lube?" I only had Vaseline. He was okay with that but mentioned K-Y worked better. I smeared some over my cock while he put some on his ass and his dick, then guided me in.

I said, "You're good at this."

He said, "Yeah." This was the first of the many times I would fuck Cam over the next decade or so. While he had a crush on me in those early days, I never felt romantically about him, but we would end up being fuck buddies in the truest sense of the term.

Cam and I went to Flashback every weekend. We tried going during the week a few times, but it was dead. We shopped on our lunch breaks for impractical and uncomfortable shoes, pleated pants and collarless shirts for the next weekend's revels. Le Château was the go-to place for club wear, perfectly straddling that line between threatening punk and much more palatable new wave.

Cam met a thirty-year-old hairdresser and was immediately deeply in love. He would move in with Lorne weeks after their first meeting.

We also learned about the dangers of hanging out at gay clubs.

One night Cam was busted at the club when we stepped out onto the loading dock to smoke a joint and two cops appeared out of the shadows. The only thing that saved me was that Cam was holding the joint and had the weed in his sock. I had nothing on me. It would take him years to be pardoned for these charges so he could travel without restrictions.

People were bashed all the time on their way in and out of the club. Drag queens were regularly beaten by cab drivers, and a friend who went to PA a few years after me was punched in the face when he stepped onto the loading dock to have a smoke. All of the exploitation and violence made us more careful, but it didn't keep anyone at home in fear.

Later that spring *With Love from Your Son* won the adult category of the Alberta Culture Playwriting Competition. It was my first attempt at a full-length play and was as ambitious as it was naive. I'm sure it won the award for my sharp dialogue, rather than anything original. I got a nice bit of prize money and was invited back to Banff for a workshop and staged reading of my play—thankfully only for a week this time.

The first prize that year included a production of the winning script at a new theatre in town. This was very exciting, as I was desperate for a professional production, but after a couple of meetings about the play I felt little connection with the artistic director who would be at Banff to direct the workshop and could see that he was uncomfortable with the sexual material. Then he told me that they were going to produce the second-place play and not *With Love from Your Son*, as my script "wasn't quite right" for their audience—even though they had no audience at all. This would be the first of many times my work was passed over for something less successful but also less "controversial", meaning less gay. It hurt every time it happened.

A few nights before I was due to take the bus to Banff, Cam persuaded me to go to the local bathhouse, the Pisces Health Spa, for the first time, even while he was shacked up with Lorne. We were both drunk and I was dying to see one of these places I'd only read about, mostly in porn mags—a place devoted to nothing but sex. It was my greatest dream and my greatest fear combined.

The guy behind the window glanced at our ID, took our cash and leered at us like the chickens we were. Just inside was a snack bar, so we decided to grab a quick snack before going further. We were immediately confronted by a deranged-looking hippie dude with long black hair and a skinny, hirsute body. Looking about as high as a person can look, he said, "If you boys want some fun tonight, Kinky's in room 201," then whipped off the towel he was wearing around his waist and shook his generous cock at us. The guy behind the window yelled, "Kinky, you know you can't do that shit where we serve food." Kinky laughed and scampered off into the darkened corridors that branched out from the snack bar. "He has a nice cock," said Cam as he scarfed down the last of his fries, and then we ventured into the hallways beyond to see what was what.

What we found was a series of cubicles facing each other across a series of corridors. One fairly large space was the dark room for those who wanted completely anonymous sex, and another was occupied by a hot tub, steam room, sauna and bathroom area. We'd gone on a weeknight and so the place was only mildly busy. Cam disappeared into someone's room almost immediately.

After wandering the corridors and peering into rooms containing horny men I felt no sexual attraction to, I spent most of the night sitting in the room of a soulful hairy young guy, chatting. Nothing happened, but I did give him my number. Although I wouldn't know it until Banff, he'd given me something too. Finding the treatment for crabs at a small-town drugstore was most embarrassing—but I did manage to do it.

Reaction at the Banff workshop to the public reading of my play was vaguely disapproving while acknowledging my potential if I'd just give up the gay shit. People were encouraged to leave written reactions anonymously, and the one that stayed with me the longest was the one which said, "We're not all sad, angry mama's boys, you know." That was my first inkling that being gay might be about what *I* was actually experiencing rather than what popular media told me it was.

Paul Reynolds, who was back that year although we'd had little time to spend together, was not encouraging about the script but assured me I'd write better someday and urged me to look him up if I was ever in Toronto, where he was relocating to work at the Shaw Festival. I was confused. Canada had a Shaw Festival? I'd never heard of it. The idea that Canada had a festival celebrating the, in my estimation, most boring playwright of all time appalled me, although I assured Paul I would look him up if I ever got out there.

The other significant development that summer was Randy Sandowski coming back into my life. Ever since his break with Cam he'd been AWOL, but when I got home from Banff, Phil informed me Randy had called a couple of times.

Cam, whose absolute immersion into gay life had left me a bit uncomfortable, had also started experimenting with drag. While I was all for guy/guy sex, this alternative sexuality/gender business left me a bit confused, so I pulled away from Cam. After years of being called a fag and a fairy as a child, I still felt I had to prove my masculinity, whatever my sexual preferences.

Randy and I became best friends that summer. It began with our shared sense of humour, our love of the irreverent and our delight in dissecting the most sacred of cows as cruelly as possible. There was literally nothing we would not say to one another.

I took him to Flashback for his first time. Cam was there, seated in a booth near the door. He stood as we walked by, smiling in his sweet snatchy way, saying, "Hey, girls." Randy smiled back, barely concealing his disgust. I cheek-kissed Cam, waved at the others at the table and ushered Randy to the bar.

In 1979/80 I did various duties on five of the eight shows in the Walterdale season. I started out by designing the set for and playing a small part in *The Prime of Miss Jean Brodie*.

It was during auditions for this show that I met Kate Newby. A compact woman with dark hair, pale skin and a tough edge, I found her highly attractive. The day we met she was dressed in a man's antique white shirt, the high-waisted, pleated jeans that were popular at the time and ballet pumps. I was impressed with her reading. We flirted a bit that night and by the end of the run we were dating. Although I was beginning to identify as gay, I still liked to go out with women and found some of them genuinely physically attractive.

Walterdale was getting interesting in that period, thanks to an eccentric and talented Romance Languages professor named Vivien Bosley, a British expat who was the artistic director of the theatre. Despite coming from the country that blessed us with most of the plays Walterdale produced, Vivien was much more interested in taking chances with some Canadian shows.

We got on well, and shortly after the announcement that I'd won the Alberta playwriting competition for the second time, she asked me if I'd be interested in writing something for the following season. I immediately said yes and started thinking about what kind of play I'd like to write. She gave me no guidelines, and neither did anyone else at the theatre.

The next year became a whirlwind of rehearsals, writing and job-hopping. I got bored at the telephone company and left to work at a graphic arts store where my friend Hilda from PA was employed. I hated the nine-to-five hours but the people were fun and I was quite good at selling the merchandise, which I had experience with.

During that period I saw a play that left a lasting impression. Michael Cristofer's *The Shadow Box* was crucial to what would come later in my writing career and life, not just for its fearless look at a difficult subject—three familial units coming together at a hospice for the terminally ill—but also for its fragmented use of choral techniques in the dialogue to advance the story and enhance the mood. The structure was both commercial and poetic. I'd read it before seeing it, thankfully, because the production I saw never quite came together theatrically in the way the script demanded.

I was partying every night of the week. Randy and I were insatiable when it came to accruing experiences, fucking people—he women and me mostly men—and drinking. We'd both been indifferent to drugs when we met, but at a friend's urging I ended up doing acid one night at Flashback and had a great time doing it. It wasn't long before I persuaded Randy to try it too. We danced, laughed our heads off and alienated almost everyone we met with our abrasiveness.

We were still high long after the club closed and we ended up driving to Borden Park, across from the exhibition grounds, a place I knew as a child, and climbing the back of the bandshell, venturing right out to the edge high above the ground. We sat there, legs dangling over nothingness, talking quietly, luxuriating in one another's presence, feeling what we both knew was a unique sort of love.

There came a time in my early club-going life when I learned an important lesson. If you take drugs to have a good time, when you can't find drugs you have a really shitty time. For a few months Randy and I wanted to do acid, or MDA, or anything really, whenever we went out. And on those nights when we couldn't find drugs, we had a shitty time. Eventually we found a happy medium, limiting the drug nights to a couple of times of month. We spent late nights and early mornings restlessly roaming the city in whatever car he had at the time looking for fun, looking for distractions, looking for adventure while Springsteen sang "Racing in the Street" on Randy's eight-track.

One day I walked into the Classic Bookshop in Edmonton Centre on my lunch break and there in "New Releases" were two shelves filled with a book that froze me on the spot and set my heart racing. It had a simple, elegant black cover with a high-contrast white font that read *Gay Plays: The First Collection*. I bought it immediately. I still have that copy, hard-thumbed and much loved. I don't necessarily feel the same way about the individual plays in this brilliant anthology as I did then, but each of those scripts informed my philosophy on the art and the craft of writing a play and let me know I was part of a much larger movement. But more than that, they let me know gay people had a right to tell their stories as much as anyone else and could perhaps even make money at it.

Cam was reading Vito Russo's *The Celluloid Closet*, and I snatched it out of his hands the second he finished it. I'd always loved old films, and this brilliant book gave me an inkling of what gay history was and how it was often wiped out. I remember being particularly affected by seeing just how terribly gay people were depicted in popular media. We were either poofs, friendly eunuchs or, most common of all, villainous or evil. Russo's book offered me a way of understanding how the majority looked at us and gave me something to react against and respond to in my life and in my art for the rest of my days.

Also, I was often an asshole.

Vain without being attractive, narcissistic without having proven much, needy while often offering little in return, I loved to shock people by saying truly outlandish racist, misogynistic, homophobic, anti-everything things that made them laugh or cringe, sometimes both at the same time. The only thing that saved me from complete social rejection was the fact that when I was funny I was very funny and my targets were so wide-ranging and equally distributed that only the densest people would not get the edge of satire that informed my barbs. I was using prejudice to criticize prejudice in a way only a queer person who grew up in poverty could get away with.

Like most assholes I was secretly scared someone might see through me and find out just how low my self-esteem was, particularly when it came to my appearance and my attractiveness to other people. I was still battling those belittling voices of my childhood.

I decided to join a gym, hoping to address my terrible posture and body image, even if it couldn't address my dental issues. While my initial workouts were embarrassing I eventually got the hang of it and came to enjoy what I was doing.

Sadly, I eventually got too busy at the theatre to work out four times a week. When I finally returned to the gym, I found it had closed for good the day before.

———

I only did two shows in the 1980/81 season at Walterdale, but they both required more effort than everything I'd done in the previous season.

*Zastrozzi* was my introduction to the work of Toronto playwright George F. Walker. This dark, funny and very stylish play concerns a naive young man's attempt to escape the vengeance of the master criminal of Europe. It's expansive, challenging and has a great deal of style. I was cast as Verezzi, the god-obsessed near-idiot who is the object of the protagonist's obsession.

The show opened and we all had fun doing it. There was a small flash of controversy when during a couple of shows I left my underwear off for the sex scene in the first act. This was an act of defiance, because when the idea of fleeting nudity had been discussed in rehearsal the board somehow got word of it and sent back an edict refusing permission. My moment of protest only ended up making me wish I'd been blessed with one of those dicks that, even when it's cold and you're scared, still reads at the back of the house.

# Mutants set to premiere

## Novice debuts as playwright and director

### By KEITH ASHWELL

"In 25 words or less? The subject is . . . friendship."

Elaborating just a little more, 21-year-old Brad Fraser says his play, Mutants, to be staged at the Walterdale Playhouse from Jan. 27 to Feb. 7, is about "a portion of society that depresses me very much — my peer group."

It's a play that nearly didn't get its premiere, at least at Walterdale. In an unprecedented step, executive members read the script shortly before rehearsals began and hands were raised in horror.

It was the language.

With a brief, bland smile, Brad said: "I'm told the language is considered offensive. My position is it's colloquial. What people call offending words are not there for effect — I do nothing for effect, or, I try not to."

Not only will this be Brad's first performed play, it will also mark his debut as a director. (He has assisted, in Les Belles Soeurs, he's designed, for The Prime of Miss Jean Brodie, he's stage managed a Christmas show and he's acted in Shikata Ga Nai and Zastrozzi — all Walterdale productions.

His resume?

A graduate of the Victoria Comp performing arts class. Two-time winner of Alberta Playwrighting Competitions: in the 1977 high school competition for Two Pariahs At A Bus Stop In A Large City Late At Night; in 1978, in the adult full-length category for " . . . what did I call it? Oh! Oh, it'll come to me. I know I'll remember it."

Two summers in the Banff Playwrights' Colony. Varied theatrical experience (see above), freelance writing for CBC Radio and ACCESS and now, a full-time employee of a graphic-arts supply company.

Those award-winning plays have not been staged "and nor shall they ever be. They are the first two plays of a 17-and 18-year-old."

The Mutants began to be written last May, adding 10 hours work a week to his regular employment.

When it was finished it was "montrous. Its running time was seven hours at least. It was everything I've ever wanted to say about everything."

It is now of respectable dimensions — a first act of intended 65 minutes' performance, a second of 45.

Re-writing and cutting became less and less painful to the playwright. Now he says he's merciless with his script.

He admits there's an extreme danger in the

Brad Fraser

writer directing. University of Alberta drama graduate Stephen Heatley, himself a director, helped him workshop the play into a better form and helped him establish and sustain an objectivity about its performance.

As for the cast of nine who all play adolescents — "Their enthusiasm and professional more than compensate for lack of experience.

"These kids are really bleeding. They've worked four to five hours a night for me from Dec. 7 and we've only had Christmas Day, Boxing Day and New Year's Eve off."

Brad had no hesitation in caling himself "a rough and tough director" who doesn't fool around, who tells his cast abruptly when something is wrong.

How autobiographical is The Mutants? "To the extent that all the characters are an element of me."

How does his writing for females stand the test of being acted out? "Well, my second play had two women in it and they were both men. In this play the women's roles generally are working but there are, times when they lapse into cliche. I guess that's a matter of experience."

Ironically, for a young man who has no doubts and indeed unconsciously gives his audience the conviction that he will one day be totally involved in the world of theatre. Brad didn't see his first play until four years ago.

"I was a teenager who couldn't get to sleep who sat watching the filmed version of Who's Afraid Of Virginia Woolf at one a.m and who had to go to school in the morning.

"It just knocked me out." Almost immediately he began writing — Edward Albee a la Brad Fraser.

If his play gets a bad reception at Walterdale . . . "It won't really change things," he says with almost unnerving calm. And if it has a successful run . . . "It still won't. It'll be a long hard climb into professional theatre, but it will happen."

# PART THREE

# MUTANTS

AFTER A PROTRACTED REWRITE of *Mutants*—a title that came to me late in the writing and reflected my comic-book-outsider interest in Marvel's X-Men and those who are born unlike their parents—I decided to present the script to the board at Walterdale.

Stephen Heatley, to whom I'd been assistant director for Michel Tremblay's *Les Belles Soeurs* during the previous season, and who was named dramaturge on my show, responded positively a couple of weeks later. Vivien also thought it was much better than the previous draft, which they'd read months earlier, but that it still had far too much going on. No one else responded.

My roommate Phil, who had also gotten a job at the telephone company, and I decided it was time to go our separate ways, as he'd met the woman who would become his first wife. I roommate-surfed for a while, usually taking the extra bedroom in a friend's two-bedroom apartment for as long as was convenient to my host.

One night as I was primping in the bathroom before leaving for work, I heard the local news announcer say ". . . police bust at a local gay bathhouse . . ." I moved into the living room and stared at the television. There was footage of men being pulled from Pisces Spa in their towels and thrown into waiting paddy wagons. One of the men was Kinky, who yelled at the camera defiantly. I got a cold feeling in my stomach, realizing I could've easily been among them.

The complaint that launched the raid had apparently come from within the gay community—from a concerned citizen whose partner was stepping out on him. There had been bathhouse raids in Toronto four months earlier. There, almost all the 289 men charged as found-ins eventually had the charges dropped or dismissed. In Edmonton many men were ruined after they were advised, again by someone in the community, to plead guilty. In both cities men's lives were devastated because the cops and politicians didn't approve of their sex lives.

The long-term result of the police actions in both cities was to make their gay communities much more vocal and organized.

The phone rang one day and it was Vivien. A few other board members had finally read my play.

I said, "What did they think?"

Vivien said, "Oh, Brad, my darling, the response wasn't so great."

I was off balance. "Not so great?"

Vivien said, "They—well, they want to cancel the show."

I sat in a chair heavily. "What?"

Vivien informed me that six people had read the script, and while two of them had "enjoyed" it—I could hear by the italics in her voice that "enjoyed" meant accepted—the other four had been shocked by what they read and were now insisting the show be replaced with the usual night of one-acts.

I said, "What did *you* think of the play?"

There was a dry pause before she said, "It's difficult, Brad. I can't say I liked it and I can't say I disliked it. It's powerful. Challenging. I have to see what you do with it. I support your right to do it one hundred percent. I wouldn't've asked you otherwise."

"Thank you."

Vivien added, "I need you to fight for this, Brad. I need you to make them see your vision the way I have."

An emergency meeting of the entire board had been called for the next week. I was twenty-one years old and I was going into a meeting of university professors, teachers, professionals of all types, older, richer, better educated than me, many of whom wanted to kill the play I'd been focused on for a year.

Walking into that Walterdale meeting, I straightened my spine and rolled my shoulders back. Honestly, there was a side of me that loved incredible conflict against unfair odds. In these situations I got adrenalized—my mind became sharp and focused. Whatever might happen, I was not going to give up without a real fight.

Vivien chaired the meeting and kept everyone on point.

At first the objections were tentative: "the language is so vulgar," "it has no sense of hope," "I'm not sure all the theatrical conceits are working." Someone said that Jett, the gay character, was unnecessary, some said clichéd; some clearly didn't want any gay characters on their stage at all, despite earlier productions of *Boys in the Band* and *Tea and Sympathy*, both of which dealt with homosexuality.

I said, "Look, just over a year ago I was asked by the artistic director of this theatre to write a play. I was given no guidance and no directives, so I wrote the play I wanted to write. I showed that play to the artistic director, got feedback from the dramaturge, made it available to the board at each juncture—although none of them read it—and behaved in a most professional manner.

Now I've found out you want to cancel it. This is surprising to me and upsetting but I've done a lot of work and if you cancel my play I'll sue you." This was of course a bluff; I had neither the means nor the know-how to go down the lawyer road.

A lot of surprised faces stared back at me.

Judy Unwin, the AD before Vivien, stood up and said, "Brad has worked with us for years. He is as much a part of this theatre as any of us. We can't censor this boy. We can't."

It was a wonderful eleventh-hour appeal. The board then voted and I won, barely. The show would go ahead. I stood up, thanked them and left.

Outside the theatre I leaned against the wall, gulping in air, trying to slow my racing heart. I got myself together and flew down Whyte Avenue to my bus stop, triumphant.

Now to ensure I didn't fuck up.

Around this time I picked up a copy of *Omni* magazine and read a small squib in the news roundup about a rare cancer that appeared to be affecting gay men in certain parts of New York. I thought it was odd but didn't give it much more thought.

Friday nights at Flashback were quieter because they were gayer. The hordes of hets who flooded the place on Saturday were usually someplace else on Fridays, which meant the club was cruisier, so I always went. By this time I knew most of the employees and drag queens by name and greeted them as I checked the place out.

Then I saw the guy on the dance floor.

He was a medium-height, beefy, muscular man in his early thirties with thick dark hair and eyebrows, a perfect bulging ass and a generous basket. Stunning, intimidating, he resembled porn star Peter North more than a little bit. When the song ended he came off the dance floor and headed for the bar. I was always way too intimidated to speak to a guy I found hot, but this man was not shy. He gave me a bright smile and extended a thick-fingered hand. "Hi, I'm Benny," he said with a slight Texan twang that made him seem both exotic and familiar.

"I'm Brad."

"Can I buy you a beer?"

"You sure can."

We spent the rest of the night huddled together, talking.

He used my name just enough to invite trust but never so much as to arouse suspicion. He worked for a steel company and travelled all over the continent meeting with clients. He seemed the most perfect man I'd ever met. Even though many club-goers knew him and stopped to say hello or nodded greetings from across the room, that night I felt I was the only focus of his interest. By the time he got around to telling me he had a long-time, much younger lover at home, I would've forgiven him anything. He was also clear about the fact they had an open relationship.

He was the first man to fuck me. I was reluctant, as a few had tried before and I'd found it painful, but he knew what he was doing, how to get me to relax and open up. When he finally worked that fat dick into me I was amazed how good it felt. He started slow then went hard, bringing me to the first prostate orgasm I'd ever experienced. It left me shaking and out of breath. In all the many times I encountered Benny in the future, this was the only time he topped me.

I now understood why so many men were eager to get fucked. I would suggest it for all men regardless of their sexual persuasion. First of all, your prostate is located where it is for a reason. Secondly, the act of opening up sexually rather than being the penetrating partner can be quite freeing. And finally, between the right two people and under the right circumstances, it can be a hell of a lot of fun.

Benny dropped me at my apartment the next morning, giving me a wet kiss in the car, indifferent to the people walking by. I asked him if I'd see him again. He said he'd call me when he next came through town.

Knowing the relationship had no future, I put my broken heart behind me rather quickly. I had a show to open.

While the insecurities I felt at the time were acute, no one at the auditions for *Mutants* saw any indication. I came across as a confident, controlled director.

Hilda was playing caustic rebel Abra, which surprised no one since I'd written the part specifically for her, while the rest of the cast varied from people I'd worked with to people who had never been in a play before. A few days later, shortly after the first reading of the play in my apartment, the actor playing Jim, the lead, dropped out.

As luck would have it, Randy had just returned to town after an extended sojourn with his relatives in the north. It had been a few months since we'd seen one another and we made up for it by partying that night. Flashback, acid, endless beer and music, then we staggered out of the club into the desolation of downtown Edmonton at 4 a.m. Too high to drive, we wandered the empty streets and alleys.

In one of those alleys we found a fire-escape ladder at the rear of a four-storey brick building and climbed to the top, laughing but slightly freaked out as well. From the roof of the building we could see the bland, flat city spreading to the west, a spidery web of lights. The rest was obscured by the concrete-and-glass towers around us. I asked Randy if he wanted to play Jim in my play. He said he did.

Then he leaned against me as we sat on the ledge of the roof with our legs dangling over, just like we'd done at the Borden Park bandshell months earlier. It felt great to be back together.

It was a good thing we had that moment, because the next three months would test every relationship I had.

My idea of direction at that time was telling the actors exactly where to move, what to say and how to say it. Given the varied experience and talent level of the cast, this was probably not a bad thing, although certainly it is not what I'd do now.

I became obsessed with the show. After rehearsal and the usual beers with Randy, I'd go home and think about what we'd be doing the next day. The script was radically overwritten and the time it was taking me to block the play—to designate where actors should move on the stage—was overwhelming. On more than one night I dreamed of solutions to blocking problems I'd been wrestling with during rehearsal.

Early in the process I took the entire cast and crew to Flashback. They were all very excited. For most straight people a trip to a gay bar is like a trip to an amusement park.

This outing was the catalyst for art to begin imitating life, when the cast members began to morph into the people they were playing. The straight actor playing the main character's brain-damaged best friend came out as gay almost immediately upon arriving. All kinds of sexual shenanigans were going on between the cast and some of the crew. Randy broke a couple of hearts.

Even at that young age when temptation was the most urgent, I knew better than to fuck with people I worked with in the relatively powerful position of director. I've stuck to that rule ever since.

I also learned, as rehearsals became more intense, that my role and what I was required to do didn't really allow me to bond with the performers in the same way I was accustomed to as another actor. I was the guy in control. I was an outsider.

People got emotional. People got hysterical. And then people got truly miserable when a killer pukey/coughy/shitty flu struck us during the penultimate week of rehearsal, just before getting onstage to integrate the technical elements. After calling in sick to my day job at least once a week for the last two months because I was either too exhausted or hungover to go in, I now had to take an entire week off because I really was sick. My assistant director, a very skilled actor who'd been in *Zastrozzi*, stepped in to work sensitively with the actors at the exact moment they were all considering a rebellion against my control.

I couldn't bear to sit with the audience on opening night. Instead I listened at the door in the lobby until an usher shooed me up to the rehearsal hall, where I paced and listened to the show over the intercom. My words sounded tinny and fake through this device. Even the laughter—far more than I was expecting—sounded false.

Vivien, who'd already seen the show, appeared in the rehearsal hall wearing a chic camel-coloured ensemble, her riot of curly blonde hair writhing around her head as it always did. She said in her plummy English accent, "We're all very proud of you, Brad. This is an amazing accomplishment." Then she hugged me and I began to cry. She rocked me and patted my back until I could pull myself together and thank her for her support as the sound of applause blared from the speakers.

The reviews took days to come out and weren't the unbridled raves I'd dreamed of. The *Edmonton Journal* reviewer talked about my need to tame the theatrical devices raging in my system and bemoaned my merciless assessment of his generation. Alan Hustak, who had directed Zastrozzi, gave it a qualified thumbs-up on CBC Radio and referred to me as "an abrasive young talent." The university paper gave us a rave. This was my first experience with reviewers as a writer and director, and the mixed response would be a hallmark of my future career. Eventually a review would come out, written by U of A English professor Diane Bessai, that was both critical and constructive. It ran in the *Canadian Theatre Review* and helped to spread word of my show and my potential. Diane became one of my most astute critics and ardent supporters. I had many stimulating encounters with her over the years.

But those first reviews made me fucking miserable.

Unknown to me, attendance at the show had been building in the second week. Vivien told me they were amazed at the number of young people coming to a theatre known for catering mostly to the violet-rinse set. At Flashback people stopped me to say how blown away they'd been by the show. Stephen Heatley had me in to speak to one of his university theatre classes, and it was clear to me that most of the people in the class had been affected by it—even if they hadn't liked it.

On closing night I finally went back to see the show and was astounded by how the cast had claimed it. They were truly living within the framework of the play, and it was theirs now. Sitting among the audience, I finally felt proud of what I'd done, regardless of what anyone else thought about it.

I rewrote the play after that production but for all the wrong reasons. Instead of working to make it closer to what I'd hoped to write, I tried to integrate and answer everyone's criticisms. In doing so, and in cutting most of the profanity and sexually explicit material, I wrote for approval. No one who read the rewrite liked it. Everyone talked about how it had lost its rawness and spine. They were right.

Shortly after we closed, the actors went through their withdrawal depression, weeks after I'd gotten over mine. This crash is almost inevitable for anyone working on a show, partly because of the loss of creative activity and social interaction that comes with the theatre, and partly for being out of work again. I got a call from Gerry Potter, who'd recently founded Workshop West Playwrights' Theatre as artistic director. I knew Gerry from my first year at Banff. He told me Paul Thompson was in town, had seen the show and wanted to meet me.

I said, "Who the hell's Paul Thompson?"

Gerry filled me in. Paul Thompson is often credited with being one of the originators of collective creation, as it was known then, and was one of the founders of Theatre Passe Muraille. Today they call collective creations devised/documentary/verbatim theatre. It can take many forms but usually asks performers to also be writers, to do exhaustive research with authentic subjects, which they then share with the rest of the company to form some sort of theatrical presentation. The most successful have always had a strong director or writer behind the scenes to shape and curate the material.

I remembered reading in the papers about his collective show *I Love You, Baby Blue*, a collective lampooning sex in Toronto, after it was closed by the cops and the entire cast arrested for nudity and sexual content. The case was huge news across the country because it challenged Canada's obscenity laws and won. After closing to deal with the court case, the show reopened in a larger house and did enough business that Theatre Passe Muraille could rent its own building.

The immense success of Paul Thompson's next show is said to have bought the building. That show was *Maggie and Pierre*, about Canada's Prime Minister, Pierre Trudeau, and his wild-child wife, the former Margaret Kemper, bad girl and Rolling Stones enthusiast. It was co-created with, and performed by, one of Canada's most wonderful theatre-makers, Linda Griffiths, who played both Maggie and Pierre during the one-person show. It had just completed a successful national tour the year we did *Mutants*.

When I met Paul on campus for a coffee, I was confronted by a smallish, elf-faced man with a heavy white beard and plenty of white hair—an odd combination of hobbit and Gandalf. He was in his early forties then but I swear he looks the same forty years later as he did on that day in 1981. He had a chaotic energy, leaping from subject to subject, listening and not listening in equal parts.

He'd seen the show and was blown away by its intensity and the authentic performances he thought I'd drawn from the amateur cast. I asked him if he wanted to do the play in Toronto. He shook his head and told me it was a promising play but wouldn't fly there. "Let it go," he said. "It's your first play. Leave it behind. What are you working on now?"

The truth was I wasn't working on anything, as in addition to my day job I'd started working at a new gay bar called Boots 'n Saddle. But I lied and said I was well into the first act of a new play. Paul asked what it was about. I threw out an idea I'd been toying with for a while, about two boys in a mental home. One of them, a jock from a well-to-do family, had attempted suicide. The other, a smart-mouthed street hustler, had tried to kill someone. The hustler character also believed, perhaps truthfully, perhaps not, that he had the power of a werewolf.

Paul Thompson's eyes lit up. "When can I read what you've got?"

"Oh it's pretty rough right now," I said. "I'll need a few weeks to get the first act done."

He said, "Send it to me as soon as you're finished. I'll talk to the artistic director at 25th Street Theatre in Saskatoon. They've been doing some risky stuff."

We parted with a handshake, and I raced home to my type-writer to bring this bogus play into existence.

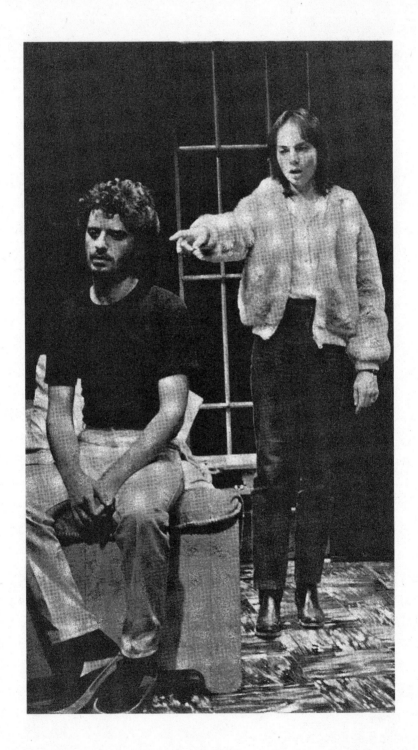

# PART FOUR

# WOLFBOY

IN THOSE EARLY DAYS I WROTE without a net. No outline, only a vague plan, a concept and a lot of fumbling around on the page. Such was my technique.

I was great at writing David and Bernie, the wolfboy and the jock. Annie, the ghost girl who haunts David, and even his rather one-dimensional father basically worked, but I'd decided to ape my love of *Equus* a little too closely and added a psychiatrist character who, like Dysart in that play, works to get the truth of the dramatic event from Bernie. And, just to increase my likelihood of failure, I'd decided the play would have a three-act structure in the classic mid-twentieth-century American way.

I banged out the first act in a couple of weeks. It was thirty pages of mostly interplay between David and Bernie, fun to write, and only hinting at the complications to come from the secondary characters. I didn't even bother to rewrite these first thirty-five pages before sending them off to Paul with only a cursory hand edit.

Around this time I met my first boyfriend, which was a great relief because Cam had been dumped by Lorne and found his own apartment and another boyfriend, while I'd had none.

My boyfriend worked as a cook on a ship in the Arctic Ocean for four weeks straight, then had ten days off to come home. When we met, he was in the last few days of this furlough and crazy to party. We left Flashback together that night and spent the next three days smoking pot, drinking beer, eating pizza and exploring one another. It was heaven.

When he returned to work on that ship at the North Pole, I spent the next four weeks missing him. I also wrote the second act of *Wolfboy* (which was then called *Die Lycanthrope*, my nod to *Die Fledermaus*, the opera that had been one of the inspirations for my hero Batman) and sent it off to Paul Thompson.

The boyfriend returned from the ship and we had a heartfelt reunion. Nothing is more endless at the age of twenty-two than a four-week separation from someone you desire and hope you love. Between my shifts at the bar and his catching up on his life, we didn't have time to truly reconnect until the weekend, and when we did it was an epic food/blow/sex party. He told me he loved me. I told him I loved him. Then we blacked out.

And after that? I wish I could remember. I know we saw one another a few more times but just kind of mutually lost interest. There was no big scene. No dramatic breakup. It was as if, after that night of partying, everything else was anticlimactic.

Paul Thompson contacted me after reading the first two acts of *Die Lycanthrope* and loving it. A short time later I heard from Andy Tahn, then artistic director of 25th Street Theatre. He also loved the play and wanted to produce it in the upcoming season. He sent me a telegram contract that I pored over exhaustively before signing the last page and sending it back. The play was contracted to open in mid-October, which was just a few months away.

Randy read every scene as it came out of my typewriter. We talked about the characters, their motivations, where it should go, what it all meant. I hoped he'd play the suicidal jock and I'd play the hustler. At Thompson's suggestion I added the part of a naive young nurse, Cherry (named after the *Cherry Ames* student nurse books my cousins had read as girls) for Hilda to play. Paul had loved Hilda in *Mutants* and thought she had a lot of promise.

A month and a half later I got on a commercial airliner for the first time to fly to Toronto to meet the director and some of the cast who would join me in Saskatoon. Layne Coleman, someone I had no familiarity with at all, had been hired to direct, and I was coming in for casting "approval" and to work with him on the third act.

I was excited. I'd taken a leave of absence from the gay bar, cashed in all my retirement benefits from the telephone company and art shop, and was flying to Toronto at someone else's expense with $400 in traveller's cheques carefully hidden in my carry-on.

Randy drove me to the airport that day. We didn't hug before I went through security because men didn't show affection to one another at that time, so we shook hands instead and looked into one another's eyes with excitement and fear. I'd tried to get him cast as Bernie but I don't think Paul thought much of his acting in *Mutants*, killing my dreams of us becoming a famous theatrical duo.

Layne picked me up at the airport with his girlfriend, Karen Woolridge, who was playing the ghost girl Annie. As we drove into the city I asked if the large body of water we were passing was the Atlantic Ocean. Karen barely managed not to roll her eyes as she said "Lake Ontario." I felt like a total hick.

I was deposited at the Waldorf-Astoria Hotel on Charles Street East, half a block from Church Street. Despite the elevated name, this was a theatrical hotel, cheap and relatively clean. It had a large room with a queen bed, bath and kitchenette. I'd packed my ginormous ghetto blaster into my hockey bag along with my favourite cassettes and most of my wardrobe, so I was set up for four days of hard work and hard fun.

After I unpacked I lay down on the bed for a snooze, and was just nodding off when something hit my chest. I opened my eyes and saw my first cockroach—sitting next to my nipple. It must have fallen off of the ceiling. I freaked out, flicked it across the room, grabbed a shoe and obliterated the roach, then called the front desk, outraged. "A cockroach just fell on my chest," I said in my most wounded voice.

There was a brief pause before the desk clerk said, "You're aware you're staying in downtown Toronto, right?" I thanked him dryly and hung up. My childhood amid vermin had not inured me to bugs.

After grabbing a burger at a McDonald's on Yonge Street I stocked up on some Stoned Wheat Thins and grapefruit juice from the Becker's, along with a dozen beers from the Beer Store that I stowed in the tiny fridge, and set out to discover gay Toronto. I'd done my research in the pages of *The Body Politic*, Canada's national gay publication which could be bought at any newsstand next to the porn and had a list of places I wanted to check out.

I headed south to St. Joseph Street and checked out Katrina's. It was obviously too early for much action and I think it was a Tuesday night, which holds little promise in any city to this day, but the DJ, a swarthy hot moustachioed white guy with a South African accent, took a shine to me and offered me some pot if I had someplace we could share it. I said my hotel was just a few blocks away. He turned the booth over to another guy and we headed back to my hotel room to get high. I couldn't believe how fast I'd gotten lucky.

As we smoked the joint, he perused my cassettes, which ranged from Lou Reed and Bruce Springsteen to Soft Cell and the Kingston Trio, and became decidedly less flirtatious. By the time we were high he could barely wait to get out of the apartment. I said goodbye and faced the hard realization I'd just been rejected for my taste in music.

Undaunted, I next went to Buddy's, in an alley off Gerrard Street, where I met a gaggle of friendly, middle-aged sweater queens and struck up a conversation about local bars. When one of them warned me against going to the Barn because of its "overt leather overtones" I decided that was probably the best place for me to check out.

The Barn was a small, hot bar with a tiny dance floor, great music and the most interesting group of characters you could find in Toronto on any night of the week. I found the "overt leather overtones" were mostly mild. In those days the Barn was above a piano bar with a geriatric clientele, but the club would eventually take over the entire building. It was cruisy, and the guys ranged over every physical type and age, skewing slightly toward the over-thirty set. This was the bar the glamour boys showed up at after an evening at the stand-and-model bars if they were serious about getting laid. This would remain my go-to bar in Toronto for the next twenty-five years. No matter where I'd been earlier, I'd almost always end up at the Barn for last call.

I was cruised a lot and was a bit intimidated by how aggressive an act it was at the Barn—none of the passive-aggressive "I'm cruising you/I'm not cruising you" I'd learned at the Edmonton bars. I alternated between being flattered and repulsed and, at the end of the evening, went back to my hotel with a hottish thirty-fivish hairy guy who was drunkenly friendly.

The next morning I grabbed a fast-food breakfast and walked to Theatre Passe Muraille, where the reading would be held. Gradually the cast arrived and I met the actors. Stuart Clow and Angelo Rizacos were cast as David and Bernie. Bob Collins had been cast as the abusive/regretful father, Karen Woolridge played David's dead friend Annie, and Jo Ann McIntyre was cast as Dr. Sherrot. Someone must have read in for Cherry, since we wouldn't see Hilda until we got to Saskatoon.

They read the first two acts. The David/Bernie scenes really sizzled. The David/Annie scenes were properly provocative, and the boys with the young nurse scenes were fun. But the Bernie and his father with Dr. Sherrot scenes, which were as plentiful as any other subplot in the play, were forced and derivative. Even worse, there was not yet a third act to end the play.

At the end of the reading everyone was complimentary and intrigued. Bob Collins, wearing a nearly floor-length coyote fur coat and an outback hat, said, "So what happens with this weird vampire kid and the jock? Do they fuck or what?"

That was exactly the dilemma I was wrestling with as I worked toward the end of the play. Did they fuck or what?

Layne and I went for something to eat after the reading and talked through the possibilities. Then I went back to the hotel and worked diligently through the next few days. I gave the material I'd already written a heavy edit based on that first day's reading—there's no better way to spot the overwriting in an early draft than to hear the words spoken aloud—and pushed into the third act.

I stopped writing late in the evening, when I'd head out for dinner and another gay bar to explore. After Edmonton with its three bars, the excess of choice in Toronto was overwhelming. I learned quickly that if they weren't interested in fucking with you, guys in Toronto bars had little interest in talking to you. The clone look had taken over, and everyone had a moustache and muscles packed into white wifebeaters and 501s. I had a moustache and bad posture. I was not immediately comfortable in these more competitive bars. It wasn't until after at least two beers and forty-five minutes that I'd stop feeling hideously self-conscious and relax a bit.

After checking out whichever bar was happening that night and sometimes picking up, sometimes not, I'd go back to the hotel and write until I couldn't keep my eyes open, finishing the final scene of the final act after two days. In that version David blew Bernie, leading to Bernie's realization that the whole relationship had just been an extended gay grooming. Bernie returned home with his father, and David started to howl like a wolf, then stopped, said "Fuck it," and walked off the stage. Blackout.

The ending didn't work for Layne at all. He said it was all fuck and suck and who-loves-who and not very exciting. And he was right. The ending was a bit of a queer ambush from a play that skirted the issue for most of its playing time. I had no idea of where to go and he could do little to help me.

Perhaps if I'd had an experienced queer dramaturge or director to help me find a way to fuse my sensibility, which was still very homoerotic without being homo-explicit, and my subject, which was the struggle for intimacy in a world that encourages only the most mundane kind of contact, things might've been different for *Wolfboy*, but such a person wasn't available to me at the time. That Layne was not that person is not his fault. He did everything with and for my flawed writing that he possibly could.

I skipped the bars that night to rewrite the third act. Ultimately I copped out with another total *Zoo Story* rip-off in which Bernie stabs David, which everyone was far more comfortable with— possibly because of its familiarity and reinforcement of the "dead fag in literature" trope I would strive so hard to change in future work. Ultimately I would end it with David drinking Bernie's blood and talking about eating his body, which did add a more original dimension to those hackneyed shenanigans.

For my last night in Toronto I visited the Club Baths, in a renovated Victorian mansion on Carlton Street. The club had a labyrinth of twisting hallways, hidden staircases and an outdoor pool that was already closed for the season. The possibilities were so overwhelming—the open doors, the invitations to sex, the many bodies in towels, the whispered come-ons—that I ended up retreating to my room to smoke a cigarette and jerk off into my towel as I listened to the cacophony of muted sex sounds that filled the air all around me, mixed with Peter Gabriel singing "Solsbury Hill" as I wallowed in my loneliness. It was the saddest song in history.

We flew to Saskatoon the next day, where I was housed in the corner turret room of the historic three-storey Senator Hotel right downtown.

Hilda arrived from Edmonton that morning, along with Jo Ann McIntyre. A local actor, Victor Sutton, would play the father. Artistic director Andy Tahn welcomed us all on behalf of 25th Street Theatre, gave us a quick tour of the minuscule facility that was housed in an old church, and we started rehearsal by reading the play.

To my ear nothing worked. Desperately I began cutting chunks of text while the actors were still reading. I excised entire scenes. Not a page remained untouched by the time the reading was complete. The cast looked at me expectantly. Layne ran his hand over his face and I could almost hear him thinking, "What the fuck am I going to do with this?" I said, "I'd like to make a few cuts" and took them through my butchering of the play over the next hour.

As cuts were made I could see some of the actors looking nervous about losing character bits, laugh lines and dramatic moments. Occasionally someone protested a cut and if they made a convincing case for why the line, scene or moment should stay I would keep it, but it took a lot to convince me. (Early in my training I'd been impressed by a piece of advice I'd read some-where, that if something doesn't contribute to character, action or atmosphere, it is unnecessary. Making those cuts to the script after hearing professional actors read the play made it clear to me why this was a wise thing to do and I have used it ever since.) As I listened to the second reading I realized that almost everything I'd excised was some voicing of the subtext that was already implicit in the play. None of it had been necessary.

After rehearsal Hilda and I were moved into the upstairs suite of one of those charmless post–WW 2 bungalows that dominate our prairie cities.

I was welcome in rehearsals, but after the first few days I was bored out of my mind. Theatre management was surprised when I asked about being paid for my attendance just like everyone else in the show. It seemed no one had considered that the play-wright should be compensated. By the end of the day it was agreed that I should indeed be paid and a cheque was issued. This became an ongoing battle in almost every production where my presence was requested. I started to understand why so many playwrights came from backgrounds of money, privilege and education. It was fucking hard to make a living.

Our first dress rehearsal was sparsely attended and the show was a dirge. There was no lift, no spark and no humour, which drove me nuts because I knew parts of the script could be very funny. When the few people had left after some desultory applause, the company looked at me expectantly. I gave them a dark, unhappy look and walked out. I stopped at the nearest Boston Pizza and ordered a beer and a pie with pepperoni, fighting not to cry. The timer had run out. There was nothing I could change at this point.

The next day I did all of the press there was to do, including an interview with the theatre critic for the *StarPhoenix* and a lunchtime interview with one of the two local television stations. When a sweet television host asked me why I wrote about such fringe topics and characters, I retorted, "Because I don't know anything about being middle-aged or middle class." When she recovered from my bluntness she asked who my major influences were, and I replied, "Tennessee Williams and Marvel Comics." She had never heard of either.

I liked being interviewed. I answered questions honestly and in complete sentences. I knowingly promoted an image that jarred with the academic white-bread people who usually represented the theatre. My cropped hair, black leather jacket with red lapels, tight jeans and Clark Gable moustache gave me an image that contrasted perfectly with the overwhelming beigeness of local media in those days. I wanted to be edgy and cool. I refused to say what I thought people wanted to hear, or were comfortable hearing, rather than what I actually thought. I wanted to be Elton John, I wanted to be Lou Reed, I wanted to be Patti Smith, but in theatre.

The opening night of *Wolfboy* was a delightful surprise. I sat with the audience and watched as the actors all did that thing actors do when they have an audience and finally come to inhabit their characters completely and discover the spine of the story even as they present it. People laughed, people gasped, people cried—there was a lot of applause at the end and many people hung around after to congratulate everyone involved.

I'd forgotten the old adage from theatre school: "Bad preview— good opening."

Kate had travelled up with a fellow drama student with heavy Sally Bowles damage and a sharp sense of humour. They slept on the floor in blankets they'd brought themselves and said they loved the show. Both were deeply affected by Angelo's truly amazing performance as David.

The next day I returned to Edmonton, hoping the show would be a huge hit, make me some money and propel me into the big-time where I deserved to be.

At that time, when Xerox machine and snail mail ruled, it took time for information to be exchanged. Having someone read you a review over the phone from a different city was about as imme-diate as it got. The best review quote from the few that came out described me as the "Wayne Gretzky of Canadian letters."

My sojourns in Toronto and Saskatoon had cost me more money than I'd made and I was working every shift possible at Boots 'n Saddle to pay my rent while trying to figure out what my next move should be.

When I finally caught up with Cam, who was moving up quickly in the world of Edmonton hairdressing, and regaled him with my travel tales, he barely acknowledged them before launching into his own "but this is what I've been doing" mono-logue. I could sense his jealousy. I have to admit I took some secret satisfaction in it. We had a few beers and then I fucked him. Later, as he was lying on my chest, I could feel the envy melt away from him along with my own sick sense of superiority.

We slept in that position for the rest of the night. Cam was one of the few people I ever slept with peacefully.

The show closed without making me any money beyond the minimal guarantee. Hilda returned home a few days later and slipped into another two-week depression. I partied enthusiastically with the guys from the bar, staved off the hands of elderly men in their forties while serving beer, and drew comic pages or experimented with my airbrush on my off-time. I still dreamed of being a comic-book artist and devoted as much time to it as I could, although I was not very good at all. Fellow PA students from two years before would drop by to smoke joints, I'd go to movies with friends, pine for someone to love me, and sometimes come home late at night to stare at my typewriter balefully.

I had nothing to give it.

*Mutants* and *Wolfboy* had been written in less than two years, with only desperate, last-minute revisions. Stylistically and in subject matter, they were connected but discrete. Both had been attempts to understand and process my complex love for men, and my strange relationship with the entire world around me, while presenting an experience that would excite audiences emotionally, intellectually and visually.

I felt like a failure.

And then Paul Thompson called again.

# PART FIVE

# RUDE NOISES (FOR A BLANK GENERATION)

PAUL WAS WORKING ON A NEW collective at Theatre Passe Muraille about street kids in Toronto, and he wanted me to be the writer. It all sounded a bit airy-fairy, but no one else was clamouring to employ me so I was more than happy to say yes and fly to Toronto for a second time.

Thompson met me at the theatre and we took the long streetcar ride through old-time Toronto in the east end, where he lived with his family. I crashed in their guest room, after going to a house party where I was introduced to many Toronto theatre people, including one of my idols, playwright Carol Bolt, who'd written the effective thriller *One Night Stand*.

The next morning I was introduced to the TPM office staff and was given a list of accommodations they could afford, which I could check out after rehearsal. I'd managed to put a couple of hundred away my last few weeks working at Boots, so I could make it to Thursday, when we were paid. The office was connected to the building that housed the theatre, but there were no rehearsal facilities. For those we had to walk a few blocks south to Bathurst and King, where the original Theatre Centre was housed in a thirties brick bank building. A number of different companies shared the space, including the brand-new Buddies in Bad Times, Canada's first gay theatre.

The rehearsal room was in a dank concrete basement with a few old couches and mismatched chairs scattered here and there. The place was crawling with spiders, roaches and centipedes, which we all studiously ignored. There was a cast of six, four men and two women. All but two of them were recent graduates of the York University acting program. They did not strike me as a group that knew much about life on the streets of Toronto.

After introductions and Paul Thompson talking about the concept behind the show—something about the courage of kids on the street and their stories that needed to be told—the cast started to improvise. Paul would watch and occasionally make a suggestion and I'd watch, take some notes, watch some more— and wait for something magical to happen. I fought the urge to get up and take part in their improv. I was there to be the writer, not another performer.

After rehearsal I consulted the list of possible accommodations, jogged back to the theatre, retrieved my bag and flagged a taxi to the Hotel Isabella, the best-sounding place on the list. I paid for a room. The elevator was broken. I had to haul my hockey bag up three flights of stairs. It had been a long day and the jet lag was catching up with me. I unlocked the door and stepped in.

The light was murky, the curtains ragged and the lower pane of a three-part window was broken, replaced with a board. Scabs of paint hung from the ceiling. On the wall above the head of the bed the words "Fuck Iran" were scrawled in red felt pen. The lumpy mattress looked exactly how a spider's nest lined with bedbug eggs would look if covered with a threadbare blanket. No stranger to squalor, I slept in my clothes, quite soundly.

I woke up feeling pretty good, showered gingerly in the squalid bathroom, checked out, caught another cab to the old YMCA on College just west of Yonge and checked in. The room was small and dingy, but if the Isabella was the best on TPM's list I knew this would be better than any of the others.

After the first couple of weeks I began to get very impatient with the scenes and ideas the actors were presenting. There was a terrible whiteness to it all, a sort of "middle-class kids exploring the streets with no real risk" thing that got on my nerves. They presented endless, meandering scenes about hookers talking to johns, strippers who couldn't dance and guys wanting to meet chicks. On breaks the actors would nervously point out that I wasn't watching them when I had my head in my hands, as I often did when they improvised. I'd smile and assure them it was because I was "listening," but I suspect they knew that they were boring me.

I made good on my promise of two years ago and contacted Paul Reynolds, who was delighted to hear from me. He took me to dinner and then back to his place for sex. He listened patiently as I moaned about the experience at TPM. He wasn't a great admirer of collective creation. Both Pauls, Thompson and Reynolds, held radically different views of the theatre. Paul Reynolds was from a large festival that was devoted to the contemporaries of George Bernard Shaw, while Paul Thompson worked at the theatre that wanted to defy everything the Shaw Festival represented. That I knew both of them so well greatly enhanced my understanding of the many things theatre can be.

After each rehearsal I'd head back to the Y, fire up my electric typewriter on the cheap, cigarette-scarred desk facing the blank wall (the window faced an air shaft) and write scenes based on that day's work. I wasn't creating a transcript of the rehearsal so much as playing with the ideas and images that stood out for me and filtering them through my own sensibility. Then I'd eat, often at the greasy short-order diner at the Y because it was cheap, and head out to the bars for the rest of the night.

My favourite was Charly's, upstairs at the St. Charles Tavern at Yonge and Alexander, one of Canada's oldest gay bars. Charly's was the first man dance bar I'd ever been to. It had a sexual energy that was connected to the music in a way even the Barn didn't have. There were no lesbians there, no drag queens, no straight people and no nervous closet cases—everyone in this bar was a fag and there to dance hard. It was a writhing mass of male flesh with only two things on its collective mind.

The DJ was playing a deadly mix of Rita Marley's "I Want to Get High" and Bonnie Tyler's "Total Eclipse of the Heart" that shook the entire building. As usual I found a corner where it was possible to observe the action from the best vantage point without being on full display. The writer side of me loved to hang back unobserved as I made mental notes about the experience and the people I watched. This bar was redolent with the sweet-and-sauerkraut rancidness of sweaty bodies, cigarette smoke, poppers and dirty drugs.

One night I met an older couple, a chunky muscular man in his forties and his "younger" (probably thirties) partner, who was lean and stylish. One was an international businessman, the other a decorator. They travelled the world and did business in all the major centres. They took me home for drinks and pot. Our first night together was a pigfest, although it quickly became clear the muscular one was most interested in fucking me while the younger one liked to watch. It was a great time, and I staggered the few blocks back to the Y with a smile on my face.

Later in the night I woke up with a piercing headache, feeling delirious and thirsty. I staggered down the hall to the bathroom to drink from the tap and then went back to bed, where I shivered despite the high fever I was running. Eventually I passed out again, only to wake a short time later feeling sick to my stomach. I puked into the wastebasket next to the desk a couple of times before passing out again. When my alarm went off a few hours later I pulled on my clothes and stumbled to the pay phone at the end of the hall. I called the theatre and asked them to let Paul Thompson and the cast know I was under the weather and wouldn't be at rehearsal. That was the only rehearsal I've missed in my life. When I woke nearly twelve hours later, whatever it was had passed. I didn't give it much thought.

Around this time more news bits began to appear reporting on the minor growth of that strange cluster of a rare cancer among gay men in New York. They were always small articles and didn't give much information. A lot of these people with the rare cancer were dying very quickly, and the doctors had no idea why. I'd shake my head and think of other things.

November turned to December and Toronto became even greyer and more Dickensian as rain fell and dirty drifts of snow turned into puddles of mud on the streets and sidewalks. This was not the bracingly cold but sunny and clear Alberta winter I grew up in. My feet were always wet. The heat in buildings was always cranked to the max, causing everyone to sweat beneath their winter coats. The streetcars smelled like goat pens.

In mid-December the collective broke for the holidays and I flew back to Edmonton. My pay from the theatre barely covered my expenses in Toronto, let alone the rent I was still paying in Edmonton. I immediately picked up waiter shifts at Boots 'n Saddle and was glad for the tip money. I used the rest of my time to work on a draft of something that could be used in the street kids collective.

The material I took back to Toronto was met with relief, and we started using these scenes as jumping-off points for more focused improvisation. After a few days it became clear to me that the actors were not going to bring in any revelatory or provocative material of their own.

At lunch one day I spoke to Paul about my frustrations. The actors were all likeable people, but the material they were bringing in wasn't matching the material I was generating. I spent my nights not just at gay clubs but at strip clubs, in alleys, at the illegal late-night boozecans that thrived all over the city because of Toronto's draconian liquor laws, interacting with junkies, hustlers, hookers and the people who orbited/loved them. I drank with them, did drugs with them, fucked with them, and not as research.

I told Paul I'd had enough. I couldn't make it work. I wanted to quit and go home.

He said, "You can't go. You're the most interesting thing in this process."

I shrugged. "This collective thing isn't working for me. I don't want to write something for some people who wouldn't really get it anyway."

"What do you want to do?"

I said, "I want to write and direct it myself with a different cast."

Paul considered my words. I could almost hear his brain clicking, weighing options, considering possibilities. Then he said, "Okay. I'll give you two weeks to write it and three weeks to direct it."

I said, "Okay."

For two weeks I holed up in an upstairs-suite sublet that belonged to an actor who owed the theatre a favour—they'd gotten tired of my Y bills—trying to pull all the ideas and influences I'd been dealing with for the last eight weeks into some kind of theatrical form. When we started auditions the script wasn't completely done and those hopeful actors only got fragments to read from. Paul suggested I bring Hilda in from Edmonton and tailor a part for her. I agreed, happy for the company.

Eventually I pulled a cast together that included Bob O, an actor I'd met years before in Edmonton when he'd roomed with friends while touring the province in a Citadel-sponsored show; Karen Woolridge from *Wolfboy*, who played the anorexic performance artist Beehive; Lawrence King Phillips, the only actor from the original cast to survive the purge; future playwright Beverley Cooper as the missing sister who spent the entire show in a store window posing as a mannequin; Matt Craven, who went on to a career as a solid Hollywood supporting player; as well as a number of apprentice actors I'd inherited from Paul, who served as a chorus.

The script told the story of Eddie, a stoned, possibly brain-damaged young man who is wandering through late-night Toronto searching for his sister, who has disappeared. He was yet another of those slightly addled characters with no filter that I've always loved so much. They allow for interesting digressions and expressions because they are not bound by the linearity of dramatized/literary thought. When the play begins he's at the end of his rope, stoned on a rooftop, considering suicide. Beehive shows up, also planning to kill herself. They strike up a conversation, and the other characters—a gay hustler, a heavy stripper named Miss Why Not (played by Hilda) and others—get pulled into the loose narrative.

This was my first time working with professional actors and encountering that odd resistance some have to doing the work required to get the show up. But I was persistent and clear in my vision, and after the first week things started to click. That was when I should've really let the actors loose and integrated their ideas into the show, but I was so arrogant about "my vision" that I only became more demanding.

I ended up doing quite a lot of press and continued to develop my public persona, always wearing my leather jacket and making a point of smoking when I could.

I was interviewed by Jon Kaplan, the theatre reviewer for the newish free weekly magazine *Now*, which was very influential in Toronto at that time. He was a charming, soft-spoken man who loved the theatre passionately. He invited me to coffee after the interview and of course I went. He made it clear he was interested in me sexually without ever being overbearing, and I let him know I wasn't interested without ever being hurtful. It was all very civilized and very clear, and by this point I was quite adept at deflecting sexual invitations without giving hurt or offence. People today might suggest there was a power imbalance. I can testify that I have never, at any point in my career, felt less powerful than a theatre reviewer.

I woke up one morning to find the glands in my neck were visibly swollen. My throat was slightly sore but I wasn't in pain. I phoned the theatre to tell the stage manager to run the play while I cooled my heels in the Toronto Western Hospital's emergency waiting room before seeing an older doctor and an intern. When I told them I had sex with men they shared a look, gave me a prescription for antibiotics and suggested I return at a later date to take a battery of tests for reasons that weren't clear to me. I assured them I would, filled the prescription, slept for the rest of the day and forgot about them and the tests after the symptoms subsided.

Shortly before the opening of *Rude Noises*, Hilda and I were drinking wine after rehearsal, going over the day's work, and in the course of the conversation she stated that her breasts were her best feature. Since she was playing a stripper who tormented the lead character with enigmatic promises of sharing information concerning his missing sister, sexually molesting him all the while, I asked her if she'd be interested in exposing her tits in the show. Her eyes slitted thoughtfully.

This was Theatre Passe Muraille. Nudity was expected. The male lead ended up revealing everything but his dick in the course of the show, so a female counterpoint was welcome. She agreed.

I told Hilda just to go ahead with the nudity whenever she was ready. A few days later she pulled them out during a scene when Eddie is splayed out on his back and she's straddling him. She swayed her breasts just over his face, her nipples nearly grazing his lips. It was a magical moment. She wept afterwards and the entire cast did that creepy, soft-shallow-clap "You're so brave" thing while also hating her a little bit, knowing she'd just stolen the show. Whatever technique Hilda lacked as an actor she made up for with courage and one of the strongest drives to perform I'd ever encountered.

The audience reaction on opening night was positive, and the actors got far more laughs than they'd expected. I attended in a brand-new pair of black leather pants I'd bought with part of the Canada Council short-term grant I'd received for a rewrite of *Wolfboy*. My short hair had grown out into a long-in-the-front-shaved-on-the-back-and-sides do. A number of people made a point of telling me how good I looked that night. I glowed from the attention.

Paul Thompson's reaction was ambivalent. I knew my style of working was the complete opposite of his and he bridled at the carefully defined physical and technical structure I gave the production. The press response was generally encouraging but hardly overwhelming. We sold quite well, and I had announced my arrival as a "promising young playwright."

Before the show closed Hilda and I decided we would seek our fortunes in Toronto. I flew home for a couple of days to return keys, pack up and say my goodbyes—there was a huge party the last night at my apartment that was so full of people it was literally shoulder to shoulder in every room. Representatives from all the groups I'd known in Edmonton were there.

Someone made a lovely speech, probably Cam, I got a bit choked up and after they left I never saw most of them again.

# PART SIX

# WOLFBOY REDUX

HILDA AND I TOOK A ONE-BEDROOM SUITE in an enormous Victorian house in the St. Clair and Dufferin area. We got the apartment only by convincing the wizened old woman who owned the place that we were married. Hilda suggested we share the bed, but I assured her I was fine sleeping on the couch.

Hilda quickly found a job, as she had clerical skills. For me it wasn't so easy. I applied for anything I was vaguely qualified for, but nothing came through for nearly a month. It became clear that my dental issues were keeping me from the more high-end jobs in retail or service. Eventually I found work as a waiter at New York Pizza at Broadview and Danforth.

Some months earlier I'd sent a revised draft of *Wolfboy* to Urjo Kareda, who had recently taken over the Tarragon Theatre after founder Bill Glasgow retired, and he tracked me down in Toronto with his response. Urjo was a former critic who'd moved into dramaturgy and play development. While he didn't love the play, overall he was very taken with the David and Bernie characters and their story. He'd also seen *Rude Noises* and thought I had promise. We arranged to meet.

Urjo was a very large man and, facially, had a Charles Laughton thing going on. His mind was brilliant. He had a terrific sense of humour with a caustic edge that was dangerous. I liked him, but he made me wary.

I'd gone into the meeting hoping I could persuade him to do a production of *Mutants* or *Wolfboy*. Urjo wasn't convinced but told me the theatre was starting a unit designed to help playwrights develop new work and he invited me to take part. It would begin in the fall. Naturally I accepted without reservation. Not only would we be meeting monthly, but there was even a small honorarium involved.

New York Pizza closed at ten thirty. The gay bars gave last call at midnight. Usually I managed to push the final tables out of the restaurant in enough time to hop on the subway and head downtown to have a beer and look for some action. Other nights I wasn't so lucky, thanks to lingering tables, and I'd have to take the extended way home.

It was a long commute, and if one connection failed to work out, the wait for the next streetcar was a half-hour. The streetcar stop was right beside a trail near the St. Clair bridge that led down into David Balfour Park. Bob O, who knew everything about furtive sex in Toronto, had informed me that there was plenty of action down there at night, so how could I resist walking down the pathway that led into the dark ravine for a late-night anonymous fuck while waiting for my ride home?

In August Hilda found out her younger sister would be moving to Toronto. Stuart Clow, who'd played Bernie in the Saskatoon production of *Wolfboy*, was also looking for a place to live, so it was decided we'd find a house we could all share. It took a few weeks, but we finally found a big place conveniently close to New York Pizza. My bed was a set of double doors laid on five milk crates, covered with a three-inch foam mattress, which led more than once to the doors opening during rigorous sex and landing me and whoever was with me on the floor.

I joined the Sherbourne Club, then Toronto's hottest gym. I'd go every morning after breakfast; a quick subway ride and a one-hour workout before heading back home to write for an hour or two before going to the restaurant. This became a routine, and my body started to show perceptible growth and change. I loved this new-found discipline, and it showed in my writing habits. For the first time in my life I inhabited both my body and my mind at the same time.

Nights off were for the bars. After a writing session I'd usually nap until eight, then eat a light supper, shower, shave, style my hair and do my bar crawl.

Usually I was happy to hang out at the sidelines, watch the crowd, listen to the music and allow my imagination to roam, influenced by the beat and whatever the atmosphere was around me. It was a strange kind of being alone while being connected to others. I often had my best ideas and most profound breakthroughs in these conditions, where the act of partying somehow aided the stimulation of my imagination. This never happened when I was out with a friend, or in a group, which was another experience entirely. And if someone should approach me, the spell would be broken.

As my body changed so did the attention that was paid to me, but that didn't necessarily lead to more sex. I'd quickly learn some people were intimidated by what they admired. I also learned some people didn't find me at all attractive no matter how much I pumped up. At first, leaving the bars on my own depressed me, but I eventually became accustomed to it. Experience taught me it was better to leave alone than with someone I'd settled for but wasn't truly attracted to. I may never have been having as much sex as I felt I deserved, but I seemed to be having more sex than a lot of people I knew.

In early September Hilda and I flew back to Edmonton to rehearse Theatre Network's production of *Wolfboy*. Hilda was staying with her mom, and I had a room in a house Kate Newby shared with a bunch of other U of A theatre students.

Kim Coates would play Bernie. Kim is now well known, not least for his amazing work in *Sons of Anarchy*. I'd met his winning girlfriend and later wife, Diana—whom I loved immediately because she raved about the play—at the *Wolfboy* opening in Saskatoon the year before, and we'd hit it off. She'd mentioned that her boyfriend, Kim, would have loved it. A year later, in Toronto, his name came up for Bernie. Theatre Network had no money to fly him in for an audition, so we met and he read for me in the living room of our commune. I hired him on the spot. Lawrence King Phillips from *Rude Noises* played David. My ardent supporter from Walterdale, Vivien Bosley, was playing the ill-fated psychiatrist part, Hilda the nurse again, and a couple of local actors were cast as the father and Annie.

As usual, after a couple of days I got impatient with the pace of rehearsals. I found Stephen Heatley's style of direction far too intellectual and talky. While I understood the necessity of understanding objective and conflict, I also knew a lot of these issues were far better realized after the staging of a scene.

But what I was really wrestling with were my own failings. Despite repeated efforts to revise the play—which I had shortened to two acts—the ending still eluded me and major parts clunked.

My relationship with Stephen became prickly. After the second week I realized my attitude wasn't helping and I withdrew until the final technical week, which now also involved a great deal of press. An appointment had been made for Stephen and me to be interviewed on the radio for a local arts program. We met the interviewer at a nearby diner for a pre-interview, and it was quickly clear to me that she and Stephen were great friends. She asked about conflict between writer and director, and I was honest and diplomatic about the need for disagreement in the creative process. I thought all was cool, but just as we were about to enter the studio the interviewer turned to me and whispered something to the effect of "Of course I'll ask you questions but, really, I don't think you have much that's interesting to say," and with a smile ushered me into the booth.

I was a mess during the interview, halting and uncertain of my answers. This was the first time I'd been intentionally sabotaged by a journalist just before being interviewed, but it wouldn't be the last. I learned early that the press wasn't always my friend. It was an important lesson and I never forgot it. I felt much less sullied a few days later when Kim and I each posed shirtless as the local right-wing newspaper's Sunshine Boys.

More articles about the mysterious disease began to appear in the gay press. The numbers weren't alarming, but the whole thing was odd and gave me a chill when the stories suggested it could be tied to using pot and poppers. I didn't use those substances as habitually as some I knew, but I wasn't exactly teetotal either.

The show opened to a full house. I paced the lobby, drinking beer and listening for laughs. My family afterwards seemed both vaguely proud and vaguely embarrassed by what they saw. When I asked her opinion my mother said, "Oh you know me, I like light theatre." Randy loved it. Kate and others of my contemporaries said good things. But the reviews were mixed. Most quite rightly balked at the script's failings, but others were clearly uncomfortable with the homoeroticism. This muted reaction was balanced a few weeks later when the Vancouver production of *Wolfboy* opened at Touchstone Theatre to some acclaim.

Quite a lot of that acclaim was directed at the actor John Moffat, who played David. I'd heard his name a few years earlier, because he'd been Bob O's lover in their acting-school days. John and I were about the same age, and he was being touted as one of Vancouver's most interesting actors. From all reports, his portrayal of David was masterful. From other reports, he was also hot. I hoped to meet him someday.

The Edmonton and Vancouver productions generated quite a lot of press but very little cash. Broker than ever, I picked up extra waiting shifts when I could and spent my nights writing various projects, few of which saw the light of day.

There were seven participants in Tarragon Theatre's Playwrights Unit in 1981/82 including future filmmaker Atom Egoyan and one or two others who would go on to have successful careers as writers.

It quickly became clear to me how different Urjo and I were in our aesthetics. While he admired the raw wit of my work, I could also tell he was threatened by it. He preferred stories made safe by a filter of nostalgia. Most of the plays I saw that he'd influenced ended with a monologue that elliptically stated what the play was all about. My reactive, pop-culture-influenced work seemed to leave everyone in the group a bit mystified, and my willingness to nosedive into bad taste both disgusted and delighted them.

This was my third experience of being one of a group of playwrights who'd been brought together to support one another's work. The conversations were wide-ranging and quite often

annoyingly academic. I suppose on some level we were all competing for Urjo's approval and the chance of a future at the
Tarragon. With four productions under my belt I was one of the
most produced playwrights in the room. At twenty-three I was
also one of the youngest.

Clarke Rogers had taken over as artistic director at Passe
Muraille when Paul Thompson left at the end of the previous
season. Clarke was a character: rusty-haired, freckled, painfully
thin, more than a little manic—often from drugs—but he was
also well-spoken and challenging. When he rolled a joint on his
desk during our first meeting in his office, lit it and passed it
across to me, I knew I'd like him. A couple of seasons earlier,
Clarke had been the youngest artistic director appointed in
Canada when he was chosen to helm Theatre Calgary. Apparently
the experience hadn't been a positive one. "I told those mother-
fucking cowboys to shove their parochial American attitudes up
their asses," he said. "I make *real* theatre." He had returned to
Toronto and directed the milestone original production of Judith
Thompson's excellent play *The Crackwalker*.

A short time later we sauntered over to the Epicure, a bistro on
Queen Street East, to consume many beers and share many laughs.
Clarke made a lot of promises in that first meeting: productions,
residencies, junior AD positions—all of which excited me no end.

None of those promises were kept. I learned on further acquaintance that Clarke ran hot and cold, sometimes your best friend,
sometimes weirdly accusatory and paranoid. I don't think his drug
problems were yet as bad as they'd become, but they were there.

Meanwhile, rejections of *Wolfboy* poured in from theatres
everywhere. I'd recently signed with Ralph Zimmerman's Great
North Artist Management, which was one of the few agencies at
the time that represented scriptwriters. I hoped this would open

doors, but all it did was reap me polite no-thank-yous. The rejections often sent me into a pit of self-hating despair where I'd wander from bar to bar until I was so drunk I'd go home with anyone who asked me and do pretty much anything they wanted to.

One of those nights I ended up at the Romans II spa, a multifloored deluxe bathhouse on Bay Street south of College. I'd been wandering the halls in a towel long enough to have sobered up somewhat when I passed an elderly gentleman speaking quietly to a Black twink. It was clear from the gentleman's tone that he was urgently begging the twink for sex.

The twink, who was obviously tempted, said, "I don't think so. There's something going around."

The gentleman said, "What's going around?"

The twink said, "A flu that causes cancer or something."

I missed the rest of their conversation as I moved past them, but again I got that chill, that sense there was something huge, unfathomable and terrible lurking on the edge of our existence.

I left without tricking that night.

The Tarragon Playwrights Unit experience culminated with readings of some of our plays. *Chainsaw Love* had a public presentation. Urjo directed it. Reaction was definitely mixed. The whole zombie/cannibal thing really flew, but my overly sexualized philosophical themes didn't. And again there was no real ending.

But when I applied to the Banff Playwrights Colony to work on the script, Urjo wrote me a letter of recommendation.

I was also finding it increasingly harder to work in a house that constantly had guests and other people circulating through it. I often came home to find food I'd bought the day before gone. I explained my predicament to Paul Reynolds and he offered me his bachelor apartment on Church Street. The unspoken agreement was that I would fuck him on those weekends he was in town from the Shaw Festival. He also gave me some cash from time to time. He wasn't keeping me; we weren't boyfriends—we were friends helping one another out with what each of us needed.

One of the rare guys I allowed to fuck me at that time gave me venereal warts. Treatment at the Hassle Free Clinic was uncomfortable and intrusive. I had to go once a week for three months, and from that point on any kind of receptive butt sex was mostly off the table as the inside of my anus was painted with a caustic wart remover.

Stories were appearing in *The Body Politic* about something called GRID—gay-related immune deficiency. Something was happening, and the community could feel it, but information was hard to come by, particularly in the mainstream press, where news about gay people tended to either belittle or condemn us. Canada banned poppers despite there being no proven connection.

I met with various artistic directors about town—and had a brief creative flirtation with Richard Rose and the Necessary Angel Theatre that ultimately went nowhere—and came away with the feeling that overtly sexual or queer material really wasn't their thing. Only Clarke expressed genuine interest in my work, but none of his promises had come to fruition. I did obtain a short-term Canada Council grant for a rewrite of *Chainsaw Love*, so felt a bit more secure knowing that money would arrive in a few weeks.

*Chainsaw Love* caused consternation and delight at Banff. There were some great actors there and a number of exciting playwrights and directors, but all of them, and whatever work I did on the play, were secondary to finally meeting John Moffat.

John was one of the most beautiful men I'd ever met. He was of medium height and build, with dark hair and dark eyes that sparkled from across the room. His nose ended in an enticing ball and his smile was like that of someone who understood all your jokes. I was disappointed to discover he was there with his lover Larry Lillo, one of Canada's most respected directors and a truly fascinating guy.

Day after day we worked and socialized together. John and I made frequent eye contact across the room, across the table. We played shuffleboard, drank, joked and got to know one another. I ached to feel his naked body next to mine.

At the end of the first week two of the older gay directors in the group announced they had to go to Calgary to see the openings of that week's new movies and invited anyone who wanted to come along. I needed a distraction from my thwarted desire and counted myself in. John and Larry were considering it before Larry announced he couldn't go. I prayed John would come anyway, but he declined.

Gloomily I got onto the bus with the directors, who sat together in front of me. As people boarded I glanced out the window and saw John standing in the line. He smiled at me. My heart fairly burst out of my chest as he came down the aisle and sat next to me.

I said, "I thought you weren't coming."

He said, "I've got to get the fuck out of here."

"Where's Larry?" I asked.

"Working with his playwright this weekend."

The two older directors in front of us shared a knowing glance. I was filled with a kind of complete gladness as John and I chatted quietly, trading intimacies from our past, our knees touching lightly.

After checking into our hotel, John and me in one room, the

directors in the other, we had dinner at a steak house and saw a forgettable movie. Later at the local gay bar, I shared two hits of acid I happened to have on me with John, and a few hours later we were flying high and sucking back beers, amusing one another no end. We didn't notice when the directors left.

After the bar closed we staggered back to the hotel room, undressed in a dim light and slipped into our respective beds a bit uncomfortably. I was praying this wouldn't be one of those situations where preamble never leads to a payoff. Then, just when I was certain that's what it was, John pushed his covers away, pulled off his underwear and jumped into bed with me.

I can still feel the silkiness of his hair, smell his skin, his breath, our tongues exploring one another's mouths, his cock pressed up against mine. Time stopped, space expanded, I eventually manoeuvred myself on top of him. He spread his legs and smiled up at me with that disarmingly open look in his eyes. "You like it on top?" I nodded. He spit into his thumb and three fingers and rubbed it on his asshole as I did the same to my dick. It was like having sex again for the first time. Everything was revelatory, important and pleasurable beyond understanding. We never really slept, we never really woke, and we never really separated that night. I lost count of the number of times we came.

The remainder of my stay was heightened by intense desire and frustration. I craved him every moment of every day but barely got to see him alone. We snatched an afternoon quickie one day when he was supposed to have been at the gym, so brief it was frustrating.

The final night there was a huge party at the house a bunch of people were staying in, and John and I got stupid drunk, necking and carrying on in the kitchen, scandalizing everyone present as Larry was drinking with friends in the next room. The entire thing culminated with me fucking him standing up in the middle of Tunnel Mountain Road under a black sky full of powdered stars.

I returned to Toronto broke and "deeply" in love with John, certain our lives would bring us together soon.

The fiscal situation was a nightmare. My old waiting job was no longer open. I hit the streets, dropping off resumés and filling out applications after trudging around downtown Toronto in punishing heat and humidity. I applied at all the gay bars and the better restaurants and got nothing. In Toronto, there were plenty of people with nicer teeth for these positions.

Money was rationed for food and transit. I had nothing for the bars or beer. I spent my time drawing an audition story for Marvel Comics, further developing *Chainsaw Love* and making notes and doing research for a play that combined Arthurian legend with video game conventions and eventually became *Young Art*. I was always at my most productive when I was broke. I made phone calls to Clarke, Urjo and everyone else I knew looking for ways to make money. Paul Reynolds, who was usually good for a loan, was at his busiest at the festival and unavailable. I hocked my prized Smith-Corona electric typewriter for fifteen dollars, which got me through another week. When I called the Canada Council to see what had happened to my grant I was informed there'd been an administrative snafu and it would be arriving in a few more weeks.

Through all of this I'd been cleaving desperately to my dream of a life with John Moffat. Everything I wrote somehow related to him. I sent him mix tapes with me speaking between songs and called him long-distance late at night when I was drunk. He was amused, then civil, then leaving town for a while and wouldn't be available.

A few weeks later Paul Reynolds came to town and took me to

dinner. He seemed oddly subdued. As we got into bed he said, "I met your John Moffat."

I was instantly wary, and I could tell Paul wanted me to be. As he turned his back on me, something he never did, he said, "At the Stratford opening. He's very friendly."

In that moment he made it clear that he'd fucked John and that I must understand he was not telling me from any kind of malice. He knew I'd been running my mouth about my and John's great love and he wanted me to know the truth. Although I hated him intensely for a long moment I knew he was right. My heart was shattered. I was grateful Paul didn't try to touch me that night.

He was very gentle with me in the morning and left me enough money for food and smokes before leaving for Niagara-on-the-Lake.

When the misdirected Canada Council money finally arrived, I already owed half of it to people who'd helped me out. But at least now a couple of beers and some music in a bar were within my reach.

In late August, Clarke called me to say Passe Muraille had managed to get a residency grant for me for the upcoming six months and that they'd be doing *Wolfboy* in the spring. It was amazing news—the residency money wouldn't entirely support me but it would really help, and there was a small guarantee for the production as well. I found a waiter job that was a step up from the pizza place. My friend Leslie, whom I'd known since PA and who'd moved to Toronto around the same time, decided we should be roommates and we were looking at apartments. Paul Reynolds had found himself a boyfriend so I knew my time was limited at his place. Things were looking up.

New Year's Eve I went to a party. It was a total theatre crowd and decidedly unsexy, so I had a couple of drinks then ghosted, arriving at Chaps, which was the hot new bar, shortly before midnight.

As the countdown to midnight started I ducked into the bathroom to avoid being grabbed, groped and kissed by people I didn't know, which always happened at midnight on New Year's Eve in gay bars. The count hit one; there was a loud horn and the sound of strangers kissing one another. As I looked at my reflection in the mirror one of the stall doors behind me opened and a vision walked out.

Uncharacteristically, I smiled at him. He smiled back. I said, "Were you hiding from the countdown?"

He nodded, his smile growing wider, revealing slightly irregular but gleaming white teeth. He had determinedly moussed brown hair, a heavy brow, a prominent jaw and beard line. He was a good six inches shorter than me but immensely muscular, with shoulders and a chest that seemed to fill the room. He said, "I don't like strangers grabbing me."

I nodded in recognition and offered to buy him a beer. He accepted. We introduced ourselves. His name was Daniel. I had seen him around before and never for a moment thought he'd be attracted to me. Turns out I was wrong. 1984 was beginning in a very promising manner.

After five dates over two weeks we were in love.

Daniel was hot. He was also weird. He had thick, curly hair that he hated—and would spend hours slicking it down with a ton of product until it was as stiff as cardboard—but was reluctant to have it cut. He told me he was estranged from his wealthy Jewish parents (not an unusual scenario in the queer world), and he lived with a roommate I never met, even though

I'd been to the one-bedroom apartment they shared (also not unusual). Daniel slept on a pullout couch in the living room.

Daniel was vague about what he did and didn't seem to work much, and when we went out I always paid—which he got away with for about a month before I finally got tired of it and demanded to know what was going on. He had a part-time job helping out some designer friends, but not a lot of money. He claimed he'd be just as happy if we stayed home and spent no money, and so we started to do a lot of that.

Meanwhile, we were auditioning actors for the upcoming *Wolfboy* production. Clarke had hired John Palmer, who had once been something of an early bad boy on the scene; gay, out, tortured, John had written a number of interesting plays and talked a good talk but seemed indecisive to me.

Every hot up-and-coming actor in Toronto was vying to play Bernie or David. They included Scott Thompson, who would go on to fame with the brilliant sketch-comedy troupe *The Kids in the Hall*, and Kiefer Sutherland, whose reading I barely remember but whose mother, Shirley Douglas (daughter of the father of Canadian universal healthcare, Tommy Douglas), played Dr. Sherrot in the character's final appearance, as she would be excised in the published version.

I hung around to express my opinion on the auditions but in the end left the decisions to John. It was his production, and I felt it was important for me to stay as far away as possible so I didn't start trying to take control. The play was going on as written; there'd be no revisions.

In the end Keanu Reeves and Carl Marotte were cast as Bernie and David respectively. Joanne Vannicola, an intense young actress whose audition had blown both Clarke and me away, was cast as Annie; Beverley Cooper, who'd been in *Rude Noises*, was cast as Cherry; and Bob Collins, from the very first reading two years earlier, returned as the father.

With the new boyfriend, the waitering shifts and the press I was doing for the show, I had plenty to keep me busy. Leslie and I found a tiny two-bedroom condo in a high-rise on Homewood Avenue.

I was growing disturbed by Daniel's controlling and manipulative behaviour. Although he rarely slept over, we were together nearly every night and he was constantly questioning me about what was going on in rehearsal, even though he knew nothing about the process. "You know this could make you famous, right?" he'd say. "What if someone wants to make it into a movie? That could mean a lot of money." I'd shake my head and tell him it didn't really work like that. He wanted to know how much I'd made in tips each night, and berated me for the money I spent on cigarettes, comic books and beer. I came to feel that he resented the attention I was getting on the rare nights we went out, now that my picture was appearing in the papers here and there. I wasn't stupid enough to give him any of my money, and I'd grown up with two controlling, manipulative personalities working me so I wasn't unaware of that either, but he was so fucking hot and I so wanted the relationship to work that I let these things slide, blinded by his continent-sized chest and distracted by everything I was juggling.

In addition to all of this I was writing a story for *The Body Politic* about the history of gays in comics. This meant trips to the main reference library, which yielded very little, as most people at that time could barely summon a glimmer of interest for either gays or comics, and working my way through my own collection, which I'd dedicatedly carried around with me. Gerald Hannon, the gay writer, historian, rebel, curator, archivist, teacher and sex worker who has been an inspiration to me for forty years now, was my editor and patiently worked his way through my overwritten draft.

Writing this story was important to me. Growing up, I'd felt like the only gay comic fan in the world. I'd been picking up issues of *Gay Comix*, an anthology of queer work that was published sporadically in those days, and through it learned there were many other gay fans out there. The story I wrote for *TBP* was my reaching out to them.

Two days before Leslie and I were to move into our new apartment, Daniel announced he would like to move in with us. I was torn, as I had no idea how Leslie would react, and a bit thrilled because I'd never lived with a boyfriend before. Daniel said his relationship with his roommate had become unbearable, that they'd had a huge fight and he had been given his walking papers. I said we could do it if he found a job. He promised he would. Leslie balked, but I bullied her into agreeing, and two days later we were picking up Daniel's things in a van and adding them to ours before we all moved into our new home.

The move had been long and exhausting. Leslie and I were surprised and frankly a bit thrilled by the quality of the furnishings and decorations that had come with Daniel. They were all far better than the stuff we could afford.

The last of the boxes had been dragged up to the apartment and we'd just ordered pizza when the intercom rang from the lobby. The voice on the other end announced that it was the Toronto police and they were looking for a Daniel Grable and demanded to be let in. Moments later two cops, one male, one female, arrived at the door with a "friend" of Daniel's I'd met briefly a couple of times.

"What's going on?" I asked.

The male cop said, "We have a complaint that Daniel has stolen a number of items from his partner." I stared at Daniel in shock.

Daniel said, "I only took what was mine."

The briefly-met friend said, "Blaine sent me to get his stuff."

The female cop said, "We can return the disputed items to the last apartment or we can charge you with theft. You choose."

Daniel's face turned red and he looked like he could kill. Then he said, "I'll take everything down to the truck and return it to the apartment." Leslie and I helped him carry most of what he'd brought back to the elevator, but we didn't descend with him to transfer it back to the rental truck. We were both freaked out. What had we just been party to?

Daniel was apologetic and charming the next morning. Unfortunately the tale he spun about a misunderstanding between him and his "roommate" about the furniture they'd bought together was unconvincing. I let it drop, though, because he'd finally gotten a job, as a busboy at Katrina's, and promised me he was trying to change his life, and because I was thinking with my dick and wanted a committed, monogamous relationship.

We had recently learned that the mysterious killer of gay men was a virus that spread through sexual contact. It was now called AIDS, for acquired immune deficiency syndrome, and authorities were unsure how many of those who contracted the virus would survive. What was being discussed, this sexually transmitted death sentence, was too immense to be truly comprehended. The entire gay community went into an intense period of shock and fear.

To the straight world it was a novelty news story. To the budding gay community, just coming into their civic and social power, it was a bombshell that would lead to even greater disagreement and discord within the community than had existed among the various factions before. All of the recommendations to stop the spread of the virus seemed to tie directly into the sex-shaming we'd always gotten from the het majority. There was something mean and manipulative in the way the disease was reported. There was no test, no way to find out who might get it until someone was afflicted.

The signs and symptoms were maddeningly common: fevers, night sweats, swollen lymph glands—I recalled with panic my mysterious illness during rehearsal over a year ago. All of us were vigilant in checking our bodies for telltale lesions.

People from New York, the epicentre of the disease, were shunned in Toronto. Everyone seemed to be drinking more and everyone going to the tubs seemed to be drunk or high. A lot of guys, myself included, stopped fucking entirely. Even oral was suspect. There was a lot of frottage and jerking off together. Daniel and I fucked each other but swore to be true. I was, but with his late-night bar job I suspected he was not living up to his end of the bargain.

That spring, one of the major TV networks ran an hour-long prime-time documentary on AIDS, and every gay person in North America was talking about it the next day. The information and images were beyond horrific. The profiles of once beautiful men now stricken, skeletal like the survivors of concentration camps, their skin riddled with lesions and sores, were chilling. Many different treatments were being tried, some of them as horrifying as the disease, but with little effect.

Suddenly we were all Schrödinger's fags, both alive and dead at the same time—until some doctor diagnosed us.

I'd finally gone to a *Wolfboy* rehearsal and found things were very strange. Privately a couple of the actors admitted they were adrift and the director, John Palmer, wasn't helping them focus. At their urging I spoke to John, asking if he was all right or needed anything. He assured me he was fine and seemed to resent my concern, so I backed off.

A few days later I got a letter at the theatre. It was from Daniel's "roommate," who, just as I'd suspected, turned out to be his ex-lover. It was clearly a revenge letter, pointing out that Daniel was a grifter and not to be trusted. I learned that basically everything Daniel had told me about his background was false. He wasn't estranged from a wealthy Jewish family but had been turned out by his middle-class Christian parents after a number of shocking events. He'd had affairs with closeted men whom he'd later tried to blackmail. The ex ended his letter by saying he'd been reading about my career and was sure Daniel had attached himself to me in hopes of making it rich.

That night I gave Daniel the letter. He read it, then set the letter down, not looking at me. After a long moment tears began to roll down his cheeks. He admitted everything was true. He'd been living this way for a couple of years, wanted a way out, and was hoping being with me would help him to change. He was so sincere my heart melted and five minutes later we were in bed.

As the show was about to move from the rehearsal hall to the theatre, John Palmer called me and asked if I'd drop in for their first few days on the stage. I promised I would, happily.

But after witnessing a run-through of the play, I was far from happy. The actors knew where to move and what to say, but there was no indication they had any idea what it all meant. Everything they were doing was surface; there was no underlying tension to the performances. It was as if they'd rehearsed without ever having really discussed what the play was about.

As they ran through again, I began to stop them after particular sections and ask simple questions about objectives, for which they had no answers. This was particularly true of Keanu, who had a lot of charisma even then but no technique. Even worse, the relationship between David and Bernie, which was written to be so hot and consuming, came across as tepid and unconvincing. I began making suggestions, asking more questions—in short, doing the director's job—and everyone appeared relieved by it, including the director. At one point Keanu said, "Wow, now we're doing the work we've been avoiding for the last three weeks"—which pretty much summed it all up. When I left that rehearsal I hoped I'd helped the cast, but I had my reservations. With good reason, as opening night would prove.

The only word I can use to describe that production is "listless." The actors had come a long way in the last few days of rehearsal, but their work couldn't hide the director's deficiencies, or mine. Perhaps under a stronger directorial hand some of the script's failings might have been downplayed or glossed over; perhaps if the script had been stronger, John's flaws wouldn't have stood out. But those things hadn't happened.

After the opening, people congratulated me in the hearty way they do when they've disliked something. I felt like shit and did some mushrooms one of the technicians shared with me. After leaving the theatre with Daniel, I angrily hurled my beer bottle at the window of a warehouse across the street, thankfully missing so it smashed against the brick wall.

"What's wrong with you?" Daniel asked.

"I'm high and it's not going very well."

"You're high?"

"Yeah. I did some mushrooms."

He hit me in the face.

Not the best thing to do. I flashed back to my father hitting me as a child and my fist shot out, hitting him in the nose hard enough to release a spurt of blood. Within seconds we were at one another's throats, all of the frustrations of our relationship finding physical expression as we pummelled one another, roaring in rage until the owner of the restaurant whose parking lot we were fighting in came out screaming, sending us on our way.

After that Daniel and I avoided one another as much as two people sharing a bed could. Our times together were sullen and silent. The relationship was over; all that was left was the extricating. It had only been five months since we'd met.

The play bombed. The reviews were mixed, with the more right-wing writers uncomfortable with the homoeroticism and the more left-wing commentators leery of the misogyny of the characters, which they also attributed to the author. I'd assumed most people would realize that two young male characters on the cusp of manhood who were both brought up by fucked-up moms and weird dads would have issues with gender hatred but, as would be so often the case throughout my career, the points reviewers hated most were the ones I was most intent on making. All the press I'd been doing dried up and box office reports were miserable.

If anyone ever tells you they saw the production of *Wolfboy* in Toronto in 1984 starring Keanu Reeves, there's a strong possibility they're lying. I made no money.

And then I lost my waiting job when a dispute over the hated tip pool resulted in everyone being fired.

That was enough. With borrowed money I bought a Greyhound ticket back to Edmonton, packed up what I needed, stored the rest, apologized to Leslie, told Daniel he had to be out at the end of the month and went home in defeat and shame.

And, although I would never verbalize it to anyone, I was also running away from the rabid three-headed dog called AIDS. I prayed I wasn't infected but I suspected I was.

# PART SEVEN

# CHAINSAW LOVE

AFTER SEVENTY-TWO HOURS of traversing endless prairie I arrived in Edmonton, tired, sore and missing one contact lens, which had disappeared from my eye while I was sleeping. It would take me a month to make enough money to replace it.

Randy picked me up at the bus station and drove me to my mom's place, where I'd arranged to stay until I figured things out.

I felt like an absolute loser.

Alberta was in the throes of the first big oil bust. Prices were dropping and speculators were running scared. People's houses were suddenly worth less than their mortgages. Edmonton was in rough shape, and the downtown core in particular was suffering.

I found a job in an art supplies shop, supplemented by a waiting job at a new gay bar, gradually got in touch with old friends and ended up taking the second bedroom at Cam's new apartment. I was sick of the theatre and felt I would never be allowed to fit in.

Given the gay press I was getting, I thought it might be best to finally speak to my mother about my sexuality. In the interviews I'd done no one had ever asked me if I was gay, although I often sensed some of them wanted to. Most just assumed I was straight. I never did anything that publicly said "Hey, I'm gay" except make these appearances and speak candidly in Canada's few gay periodicals, which most straight people were completely unaware of anyway.

Sharon and I met at the Kresge's lunch counter, taking a chrome booth with a colourful Formica table, and ordered dishes composed of grease, starch and meat. After a bit of small talk I said, "Because of these interviews and things that've come out I thought I should probably tell you I'm gay."

She stared at me for a moment, then said, "I have breast cancer."

I recognized this as one of her "whatever you just said I have to outdo" moments and was not fooled. "Breast cancer?"

From her expression I could tell she knew this wasn't working, so she quickly added, "Benign cysts. Don't ever tell your father what you are."

I said, "Why?"

She said, "He'll kill you."

I shrugged and ate my clubhouse. That she claimed to care about the opinion of a man she hated was another feint. She sipped her Coke, then checked her lipstick with the makeup mirror in her purse. She was confused. For the first time in either of our lives she didn't know how to make this about her.

Months later my mother would tell me that her prayer group had spent weeks beseeching god to turn me straight. To this day their prayers have gone unanswered.

As for the press, one day an arts writer referred to me in an article with the descriptor "Fraser, who has never made a secret about the fact he is gay," and I was publicly out without ever having announced it.

One day, after we'd been roommates for a few months, Cam told me he'd like me to move out at the end of the month. I looked at him, shocked.

"Seriously?"

He nodded casually as he got something from the fridge. "Yeah. My friend Dwayne broke up with his boyfriend and needs a place. He's got a lot of nice stuff."

"I thought we were going to be roommates."

"No. You were just staying here until you found another place."

I was weirded out. "That's not what we said."

"Brad, that's what I understood."

"Have I done something wrong?"

"Oh no, not at all. We've always gotten along. But you—I want Dwayne to move in."

I was speechless for a moment before saying, "Okay, if that's what you want."

He smiled and nodded and went into his room. That was that.

I moved into a house in the downtown Oliver area shared by an older gay couple in their late thirties. They had the downstairs of the house, we shared a kitchen and a large bathroom, and I had an immense loft-style room to myself on the second floor. The arrangement was temporary from the start, but it would get me through the winter.

It became clear that my friendship with Randy had changed. We still shared our best-friend intimacy and trust, but our social interests had taken divergent paths. After I'd gone to Toronto he spent less time at Flashback and more time with his straight friends. We saw one another a couple times a week, and frequently spoke on the phone, but our earlier, intense codependency was gone.

In fact, since AIDS had been discovered, the entire free-love/ hedonism/experimentation of the late seventies had collapsed.

A great many of the openly bi or sexually fluid people I'd known on the scene had fled back to their former hetero lives. The move toward a sexually democratic society had been halted.

While working at the new gay bar, I clicked with two other waiters: a muscular, lean graphic artist named Richard, who was too observant and funny to ever be truly butch, and a hot Italian-looking guy named Tad, who was strangely deferential around me. Later he would tell me it was because the mohawk Cam had given me had intimidated him.

Tad was a flight attendant experiencing one of the lengthy layoffs that were common in that business at the time. The three of us hung around together in different iterations depending on who was working. By the end of the summer the bar was waning and we were all let go for lack of business.

By that time I had dumped the art shop for a job serving lunches at Walden's, one of Edmonton's best restaurants. Money was good and so was morale. I made friends at this job who are still friends today.

One night after Tad and I had been out, struck out, and had too much to drink, he staggered home with me and I fucked him. We had a great time, but the partner thing wasn't flying. Instead we became great friends who would still fuck from time to time.

Kate Newby, who'd just completed her MFA in acting, and I decided to rent a two-bedroom together. The hunt for a place proved pretty frustrating, not because there weren't vacancies—apartments were plentiful—but because of our busy schedules. She was working at the Crêperie, a restaurant owned by the same people who ran Walden's, to pay off her student debt. Fed up with our prevaricating, one day she looked at an apartment by herself and called me at work. After a quick description, I told her to take it.

The apartment was in an Edwardian building called the Westminster. It was a charming, low-slung, three-storey building faced with brown brick and sandstone. Our suite was in the basement and the rent was cheap. It had large rooms, except for the kitchen, which was so small the fridge was in the dining room, and an old claw-foot bathtub with no shower. Large pipes running across the ceiling of each room carried steam and water to the rest of the building. They were wrapped in something that looked like asbestos tape. We cleaned the place like crazy, spiffed it up with bright, cheap furniture, and lived there in relative security for the next few years.

One night I ran into Benny at the Roost. He was as beefy and handsome as ever. We hugged and he filled me in on what was going on in his life. His younger brother had gotten into some trouble doing recreational cocaine in South America, and Benny was working to bail him out. The night as usual ended with us back at wherever he was staying and I would thank my lucky stars for this amazing guy who bottomed like a porn star. We would run into one another frequently over the next couple of years and end up in sexual situations, occasionally with another party or two.

In Toronto I'd grown used to going out on my own. If one was hunting, a pack could be a detriment, and anyway I didn't have a lot of gay friends there. With Richard and Tad, I had a couple of buddies in arms. We all worked out, wore identical white wifebeaters and 501s, and had moustaches and similar haircuts. We even got our nipples pierced together, by Richard's friend, a bisexual female nurse with a taste for S&M and a wicked sense of humour. Pierced nipples were a novelty then, and mine would freak people out for the next ten years. In the mid-nineties, when everyone was getting everything pierced, I took my ring out and let the hole close up. You know a trend's been ruined when white straight people take it up.

That autumn Kate left town to do a show, and Tad sublet his place and moved in with me. One autumn night after leaving the club with Richard, the three of us went for a bite at a nearby restaurant. Afterwards we took a shortcut through the alley that ran next to the Odeon Theatre. By the time we were partway up the alley we realized we were being followed by four men about our age. We shared a quick look and quickened our step. Our pursuers did the same, saying they were going to take Tad's fleece-lined leather coat off him.

Tad said to them, "Come on, guys. We don't need any trouble."

They laughed. We could hear them whispering, ". . . faggots . . . cocksuckers . . . why you walking so fast . . . scared?"

We were terrified. We were also three guys who worked out and they didn't look all that big. Just as we emerged from the alley across the street from the Hudson's Bay store they rushed us. I could feel adrenaline flushing through my system. My father didn't teach me much in my childhood but he did teach me how to put up a guard and throw a punch, and I started roaring insults at them in my most demonic voice. I blocked a couple of punches and slapped my attacker away just as I heard Tad call my name. Two of them were moving in on him. Richard was holding his own with his attacker, landing a few decent blows, so I punched one of Tad's assailants in the side of the head. He made a pained noise and amazingly they all took off.

As we walked up Jasper Avenue we were sky-high with our victory, giddy and shaky. We dropped Richard off at his place and continued on to mine. As we passed under the dark shadow of the old train overpass that used to cross Jasper just west of 109th

Street, we became aware of footsteps behind us. Our hearts sank. The whispering started again. The quartet was back, and now we were just two.

Tad and I began to run. The hoods were hot on our heels. The only place open at that time of night was the Mac's store up the block. We sprinted toward its bright lights.

We flew into the store and straight to the counter where Tad asked the clerk, a gay guy we slightly knew from the bars, to call the cops just as our pursuers entered. The store was moderately busy, mostly with gay guys we'd just seen an hour earlier at the club. As soon as it became obvious what was going down, they all cleared out.

I shared a look with Tad. He nodded and turned, grabbing the guy who was right behind him and pushing him to the back of the store. The guy and his friends were so surprised they didn't know what to do as Tad shoved their buddy into a tall Coke display that toppled, exploding sticky soda all over the floor. Tad's target slipped and fell.

I grabbed the guy next to me and ran him to the door, smashing him into it so hard it opened. I'd meant to throw him out, but his buddy came up from behind and pushed me out the door as well. Tad and the third guy followed us and it became a free-for-all of hurled insults, punches and kicks. We were holding our own, but trying to fend four off was getting difficult.

The likely bloodbath in which I'd be crippled for life was curtailed by the appearance of the diminutive store clerk brandishing a baseball bat with a couple of nails in the end screaming at the bashers to get the hell out of there because the cops were on the way. The sound of a siren convinced them, and they took off.

Tad came to me and we sagged into one another's arms. All of the adrenaline vanished and we could barely stand. We leaned against the building, pulled out cigarettes and sucked on them desperately, thanking the clerk as a cop car with flashing lights pulled up.

Tad had a split lip and a bruise on his cheek. I had no idea what I looked like but I could feel the blood running from my nose over my lips and chin before splashing onto the front of my coat. We finished our smokes and the cops put us in the back of the squad car where we recounted everything that had taken place after leaving the restaurant. They were a male and female cop, early thirties I'd guess. The male cop said, "Where were you before the restaurant?"

Tad and I shared a look. This is the point every queer person had to deal with when reporting a bashing, the point where the cops will either turn out to be assholes (usual) or allies (rare). After all, these were the people who hung around in the shadows of the Flashback parking lot targeting and busting gays in a way they never would at a straight club.

I said, "Flashback."

The look they exchanged let us know these two would not be allies.

The female cop said, "So you got into a fight."

I said, "There were four of them."

The male cop said, "Who won?"

I couldn't help but sneer at his shit attitude as I said, "Apparently you did."

Tad snickered, but the cops didn't get it.

The male cop asked us if we wanted a ride home. In my mind I said, "No, we want to walk just in case those assholes are still hanging around waiting for us again, you patronizing breeder fuck!" Instead I just nodded and gave them the address and they drove us there silently.

In my apartment we were suddenly terrified and paranoid. The basement suite didn't have blinds on all the windows, so we hung towels over them.

We examined our wounds in the bathroom mirror. In addition to my traumatized nose I had a shiner under one eye, an abrasion on my forehead and a couple of large bruises on my torso from body blows I hadn't even been aware of taking. Tad with his split lip and bruised cheek was in slightly better shape. We drank a few beers, smoked more cigarettes and relived the entire experience moment by moment, unable to let it go.

Eventually we slipped into my bed. Neither of us wanted to sleep alone that night. He curled his back against my chest, snuggling his ass against my crotch, and even though the energy was slipping out of us I got a hard-on. He whispered, "Go ahead." I did. It seemed appropriate.

On my way to work the next day, having used Kate's makeup to conceal the worst of my wounds, I passed the alley where we'd encountered our bashers. My heart was pounding in my ears. I couldn't seem to get a breath. I glanced around, panicked, sure they were waiting for me.

I would feel this way every time I passed that alley for the next few weeks. This feeling gradually lessened, but it never really disappeared. Eventually the attack became an amusing anecdote to relate at parties. After all, what was a minor gay bashing compared to the horror show of disease and death that was going on around me?

The gay community was in a state of barely controlled hysteria. A test had been developed that could tell if people were infected with HIV. We were told that having the virus didn't necessarily mean you had AIDS. There were still a lot of questions to be answered, but we were assured that condoms were the best defence. For many queer people this felt like a direct attempt to continue the heterosexual obsession with controlling our desires and sex lives.

We lived all of this while the rest of the world looked away, in some cases with disgust, but in most cases with indifference. The press loved to report, with obvious disapproval, salacious details of our sexual acts. That demented neo-con cunt Ronald Reagan, who started his presidential term by demonizing people of colour, the poor, the mentally ill and anyone else who didn't fit into the straight white Christian paradigm, was president for nearly five years before he even uttered the word AIDS. Canada's Conservative government and their border agents responded by making all mentions of anal sex illegal, making it that much more difficult to educate the community about the spread of the disease.

Thankfully the community mobilized at the grassroots level. The gay press printed everything they could about AIDS and about the benefits of using condoms and restricting anal sex. While dying patients were being abandoned in hospital rooms by medical staff too frightened to care for them, gay men, lesbians and straight women, and likely a few straight men, everywhere were working to alleviate the suffering as best they could.

Of course not everyone in the community was a paragon of virtue. Anyone growing up in a society that overwhelmingly rejects and judges you, that actively hates you and calls you sick, is inevitably going to absorb a certain amount of self-hatred. I don't know a single queer person of any generation who hasn't struggled with feelings of worthlessness because of their differences. I have often marvelled that any of us are able to lead productive lives, and yet we do. Lives that are often made better for the adversity we've learned to face. The AIDS crisis galvanized and changed queer communities worldwide.

Walden's had recently offered their employees a dental plan. I met a dentist who was sympathetic to my many problems and he devised an overlay denture that fit over my real teeth while making them more conventionally even. I still had the overbite but at least I wasn't constantly trying to pull my upper lip down whenever I laughed or smiled in order to hide my teeth. Thus started a dental journey that has lasted to this day.

Despite my resolve to stay away from the theatre, I'd been tinkering with *Chainsaw Love* and decided to send it to Gerry Potter, whose Workshop West Playwrights' Theatre had developed an audience in town.

Gerry called me and we met at the theatre offices in the beautiful late-deco McLeod Building across from the Westin Hotel. It was clear from Gerry's reaction that he didn't quite know what to make of *Chainsaw Love*. It certainly wasn't the kind of show his theatre usually did. As we threw around ideas for possible ways to workshop the show, he asked me if I'd like to direct it for the Fringe. The Edmonton Fringe Festival, based on the Edinburgh Fringe Festival, had started two years before and was presented in the nearly deserted Old Strathcona area on the south side.

I didn't hesitate for a second—of course I wanted to direct it for the Fringe. Doing the show for free while working full-time would be challenging, but I had unending energy at the time and made the commitment.

I cast Kate as Donna the Dead, the brain-damaged daughter who was a bit of a send-up of Judith Thompson's Theresa in *The Crackwalker*, as well as my go-to mystical character along with a mixed bag of performers with varying degrees of experience.

We rehearsed in one of the vacant offices at the McLeod Building, and people from nearby offices would knock on the door to complain when the screaming got too loud.

My direction at that time consisted of blocking the show, discussing motivation with the actors and then running them through it physically until the rhythm of the text and the drive of the production took hold on a deeper level. As soon as they started talking and moving, I started taking notes for every moment that didn't work. After a few rehearsals of this sort Kate broke from character, walked over to me, snatched my notebook out of my hand and said, "Don't write. Just watch what the fuck we're doing."

I put my pen down and did just that. I stopped being so detail-obsessed and talked to the actors about the films that had influenced what we were doing. Everyone got better after that.

Sadly, the play did not. *Chainsaw Love* was a great idea, it had some amazing conceits, but in the end my ambition exceeded my skills by more than a bit.

Randy had come up with the title a few years earlier. We'd been afternoon drinking in one of Edmonton's coozier bars, the Drake or maybe the York, and I'd given him a rundown on an early version of the script. I wanted to merge Tennessee Williams, George Romero and Tobe Hooper into a play. As I spoke, Soft Cell's "Tainted Love" was playing over the sound system. Randy said, "Call it *Chainsaw Love*."

The first act was great fun. Donna the Dead is one of the best characters I've ever written, and the others in the play had great potential. The vampire/cannibal/zombie themes—second nature to me—were fresh meat in the theatre. The incest storyline was played for comedy and a send-up of all of the revelatory "I was abused as a child" theatre going on at the time.

The end of act one, when Donna thinks she has escaped the clutches of her evil father and the muscle guy in the leather mask bursts through a door and jams a meat hook into the base of her spine, is one of my favourite writer/director moments ever. Donna screams for him to take it out because it's too big as he lifts her off her feet and drags her into the darkened basement. Her screams were broadcast through the holding area for the audience (there was no lobby) during intermission. It was both hilarious and horrifying—just as I'd intended.

The second act had little of the charm or anarchy of the first. It became a series of dialogues and monologues explaining the play's themes and deconstructing horror-movie tropes in a way I once thought would seduce Urjo into producing the show. I couldn't find a way to make the promise of the concept support the weight of a full-length narrative, though that was hardly a fatal issue for a Fringe show.

Things picked up in the final scenes, with its disco zombie apocalypse in which the muscle guy has his guts spilled on the stage (prosthetic stomach cover with the contents of a full can of Alphagetti behind it) and the father has his brains bashed out with a hammer (blood bag explodes on contact with soft hammer). There were many other low-rent Grand Guignol effects that made the show a Fringe must-see, even if criticism of the script was fierce.

For better or worse, I was back in the theatre.

## PART EIGHT

## YOUNG ART

*YOUNG ART* WAS SOMETHING I'd started chipping away at during my summer of poverty in Toronto. I'd always loved the Arthurian legends and had read Malory, White, Renaud and many other versions of the story. But I wanted to play with it in a contemporary fashion, so I decided I would pattern it after video games—which I'd become obsessed with, as they were a great way to while away time in a bar while waiting for the beer to kick in—with the quick set-up, the chase for particular goals, the twist and the resolution. I wanted to write something that reflected the Arthur/Guinevere/Lancelot triangle without repro-ducing it. It was full of diverse, time-travelling characters, magic effects, a dragon, a devil and a mind switch that led to some gender/sex role-playing that was subversive and hilarious.

When I sent the play out, people had no idea what to make of it, as it was so different from *Mutants* and *Wolfboy*, which was totally my intention. I had done the gritty, reality-based script twice and both plays were highly derivative of other theatrical works. With *Young Art* I took a necessary step away from theatre influences and let my background of comic books, fantasy and video games inform what I was writing. The fact that each of the young leads spoke in an argot particular to their time made reading the play more difficult than people were accustomed to with my scripts. Some people felt it was a children's play; someone else thought it would work better as a musical. Urjo was not impressed.

When I returned to Edmonton I entered it in the 1985 Alberta Culture Playwriting Competition, and when it failed to win even second or third place, I was devastated for a day, as I always was. But I took all of the notes and kept rewriting, eventually streamlining it into a much sleeker play. When I sent this to Paul Thompson, he took it to Clarke at Passe Muraille because he wanted to direct it. To our surprise Clarke said yes. The show would rehearse over November/December and open in January as the inaugural show of 1986.

After obtaining a leave of absence from Walden's, I flew back to Toronto for the first time since my humiliating retreat. The theatre had found me a basement suite in a local agent's Victorian house. Paul Thompson had assembled an exciting cast, and an amazing design team had created an enormous cave with multiple entrances and fabulous effects.

Having learned from experience, I'd decided on a balance between being in rehearsals and giving feedback and staying away to allow director and cast to work without having to consider the playwright. During these away-from-rehearsal periods I reacquainted myself with "two years later" Toronto.

In the time I'd been gone, the AIDS crisis had made itself apparent. While none of my immediate friends seemed to be infected, they all knew people who were sick or dying. Nevertheless, the clubs were busier than ever. Most of the bathhouses had been closed—although, unlike in most American cities, this would prove temporary.

I also noticed a new openness (for Toronto) at the bars. People were more approachable, a little more human, a little less hostile—but there was also an edge of hysteria to a lot of the partying, an end-of-the-world freedom that some people gave themselves over to entirely. Instead of being barred, drag queens were now a mainstay in all the clubs, often hosting AIDS fundraisers. Safe-sex pamphlets, condoms and directories of community services were everywhere, even if a lot of people just ignored them.

*Young Art* opened on a cold January night to a full house. I watched the first ten minutes of the show from the second floor seating area, then slipped out to the Epicure Café for a drink. Linda Griffiths was there and motioned for me to join her, even though we'd only met once or twice casually. She was there for moral support for Paul and had seen the preview the night before. I ordered a beer. She saw my hand shake when I took it from the waiter, but instead of asking me if I was nervous she started talking about something completely unrelated that took my mind off my show. We spent the rest of the evening talking. I was so engrossed by her charm that I completely lost track of time, and it was Linda who pointed out the show had come down.

We raced back to the theatre just as it was getting out and headed upstairs to the bar. Many people had hung around after, which was always a good sign, and the responses I got were far more genuine than anything anyone had said to me after the *Wolfboy* opening.

The reviews for *Young Art* were more positive than they'd been for *Wolfboy*. Most of them carped that the "environmental concerns" that preoccupy the sixties drug-addicted character's narrative were dated. That was the eighties corporate press for you. Even while pollution was growing exponentially, they all found concerns about it dated.

I loved the show. I felt Paul had really stretched himself beyond the collective template and acquitted himself nicely. The cast, design, everything really, was superb. There had been quite a lot of press. But the show didn't make any money. Toronto was hit with one of its biggest-ever blizzards at the time, but whatever people said I knew that wasn't the real issue. The real issue was this play was directed at young people—not children—young people in their late teens and early twenties—and they hadn't found it.

That would be the last time I worked with Paul Thompson. However, he has continued to be a source of inspiration and support to me. He is a brilliant man, and I owe him a great deal for his belief in me when many had none.

When I got home to Edmonton, Tad and I decided we would get tested for AIDS. The test had been around for a while, but we were hesitant to take it, as were many men we knew. Almost everyone in our circle who had been tested came back positive. We had watched them spiral into depression and blind panic and we had asked ourselves if we wanted to know. We both assumed we were positive. Many of our lovers had already been told they were, and we'd both had sex with them long before condoms were ever a consideration. Since there was no known treatment for the disease, there was limited advantage in knowing our status. Eventually, when we found out people stood a better chance if treated earlier, we changed our minds, and went to our respective gay doctors and got the test.

We had to wait an agonizing three weeks for our results. Every possible scenario went through my head. What would I do when

I found out I was positive? How would I react? How would my friends and family react? How long would I live?

We'd all watched Rock Hudson die horribly and publicly the year before. Even this rich, once beautiful movie star—the male sex symbol of my parents' generation—couldn't defeat the scourge. He was the first major celebrity to go, and even the straight world was stunned for a moment. If Rock Hudson could be stricken, what chance did any of us have? Why prolong the painful, humiliating, horrifying end?

When my doctor told me the result I couldn't understand what he said. His lips moved. Some sounds came out. But I had no idea what they'd meant.

He leaned across his desk slightly and said again, "You're negative, Brad."

I refused to believe it. "That can't be right."

He shrugged with a sigh. "None of it's absolute. We don't know if it requires multiple exposures or if the strain of the virus has a more potent period. We don't know much at the moment. Be happy. I'm giving you good news. "

For the first time in what seemed like years a certain tension left my body. I was floating, flying, feeling sooooo relieved—and horny as fuck.

The thing I most wanted to do as I air-walked my way out of the doctor's office was fuck someone's raw ass and dump my load deep in their guts and have the same thing done to me.

That was the weird thing about a negative test at that time— the sense of triumph and dangerous invincibility that came along with it.

# UNIDENTIFIED HUMAN REMAINS

## (MURDER)

# CADAVRE NON IDENTIFIÉ

## (MEURTRE)

THE ABOVE PHOTOGRAPHS ARE A FACIAL RECONSTRUCTION OF THE BODY FOUND IN APRIL, 1977

LES PHOTOGRAPHIES CI-DESSUS SONT UNE RECONSTITUTION DU VISAGE DU CADAVRE RETROUVÉ EN AVRIL 1977

THE R.C.M.P., GIS, EDMONTON, ALBERTA IS ENDEAVOURING TO IDENTIFY A BADLY DECOMPOSED MALE BODY THAT WAS LOCATED APRIL 13, 1977 ON A ABANDONED FARM 35 MILES EAST OF EDMONTON NEAR TOFIELD, ALTA.

THE BODY WAS LOCATED IN A SEPTIC TANK, WRAPPED IN A BED SHEET AND TIED WITH NYLON ROPE. LIME WAS PLACED ON THE BODY. EXAMINATION REVEALED THAT PARTS OF THE BODY WERE MUTILATED AND THAT THE VICTIM HAD BEEN SHOT.

THE FOLLOWING IS THE ONLY DESCRIPTION AVAILABLE OF THE BODY:

| | |
|---|---|
| SEX: | MALE |
| AGE: | 26 TO 40 YEARS |
| HEIGHT: | 5'3" TO 5'9" |
| WEIGHT: | 145 TO 165 LBS. |
| HAIR: | DARK |
| TEETH: | ALL NATURAL TEETH PRESENT, WITH SOME FILLINGS. DENTAL CHARTS AVAILABLE. |
| CLOTHING: | BLUE JEANS, BLUE WORK SHIRT: T-SHIRT, GREY WOOL SOCKS, AND IMITATION WALLABEE SHOES. |

ANYONE HAVING INFORMATION REGARDING THE IDENTITY OF THIS MAN SHOULD IMMEDIATELY CONTACT THE NEAREST POLICE AUTHORITY OR THE **RCMP, GIS, HOMICIDE SECTION, EDMONTON, ALTA (TEL: (403) 425-7743** OR CPIC AB15002) WITH ADVICE TO THE **COMMISSIONER, RCMP, OTTAWA, ONT.**

AMENDMENT TO:
SPECIAL WANTED CIRCULAR
NO. 255 — 77-05-17

## RCMP IDENTIFICATION SERVICES
80-04-16

CONTACT CPL. GRAHAM - 479-9500
SOURCES WILL BE KEPT EXTREMELY CONFIDENTIAL

LA SECTION DES ENQUÊTES GÉNÉRALES DE LA G.R.C. À EDMONTON, TENTE D'IDENTIFIER UN CADAVRE DANS UN ÉTAT DE DÉCOMPOSITION AVANCÉE DÉCOUVERT, LE 13 AVRIL 1977, SUR UNE FERME ABANDONNÉE, À 35 MILLES À L'EST D'EDMONTON, PRÈS DE TOFIELD, ALB.

L'HOMME, TROUVÉ DANS UNE FOSSE SEPTIQUE, ÉTAIT ENVELOPPÉ D'UN DRAP DE LIT ET ATTACHÉ AVEC DE LA CORDE DE NYLON. DE LA CHAUX AVAIT ÉTÉ RÉPANDUE SUR LUI. L'EXAMEN RÉVÉLA QUE LE CORPS AVAIT ÉTÉ MUTILÉ PAR ENDROITS ET QUE LA VICTIME AVAIT ÉTÉ TIRÉE.

LE SEUL SIGNALEMENT DISPONIBLE EST LE SUIVANT:

| | |
|---|---|
| SEXE: | MASCULIN |
| ÂGE: | 26 — 40 ANS |
| TAILLE: | 5'3" — 5'9" |
| POIDS: | 145 — 165 LIV. |
| CHEVEUX: | FONCÉS |
| DENTS: | DENTITION NATURELLE COMPLÈTE. QUELQUES OBTURATIONS. ODONTOGRAMME DISPONIBLE. |
| VÊTEMENTS: | BLUE-JEAN, CHEMISE BLEUE DE TRAVAIL, TEE-SHIRT, CHAUSSETTES DE LAINE GRISES, CHAUSSURES IMITATION "WALLABEES". |

QUICONQUE A DES RENSEIGNEMENTS CONCERNANT L'IDENTITÉ DE CET INDIVIDU EST PRIÉ DE COMMUNIQUER IMMÉDIATEMENT AVEC LE SERVICE DE POLICE LE PLUS PRÈS OU AVEC LA **SECTION DES HOMICIDES,** A LA S.E.G. DE LA **GRC À EDMONTON, ALB. (TEL.:(403) 425-7743** OU C.I.P.C. **AB15002)** ET D'EN INFORMER LE **COMMISSAIRE, GRC, OTTAWA, ONT.**

MODIFICATION CSPR 77-05-17
CIRCULAIRE SPÉCIALE DE PERSONNES
RECHERCHÉES NO 255, LE 15 AVRIL 1977

## SERVICES DE L'IDENTITÉ DE LA G.R.C.

# PART NINE

# REMAINS: GENESIS

DURING THE PREVIOUS YEAR, through a series of small grants from Alberta Culture and the support of Workshop West, where actress/director Dorothy-Ann Haug had taken over as AD for a year while Gerry Potter took a sabbatical, I'd started work on what would eventually become known as *Unidentified Human Remains and the True Nature of Love* and later *Love and Human Remains*.

My frustration with most of the theatre I was seeing was the slavish dedication to the form of the "well-made" play. At that time the term meant a play that was, generally speaking, in two acts, used one set and had a cast of fewer than five actors. People talked a lot but very little happened. For me even the best of these experiences felt more like television than theatre. I found them predictable and tedious, and I usually left at the end of the first act because I already knew what was going to happen by the end of the second.

I was also aware of my literary Beat influences—Kerouac, Ginsberg, Burroughs, etc.—and trying my best to make my life interesting enough to write about. I'd always experienced life both inside and outside of myself—that strange ability to watch one's actions as they unfold despite being involved in them that many writers talk about. I wanted to decode why people said the things they said when they often meant something quite different.

I'd learned to listen carefully from a young age, in the way that kids of emotionally and physically volatile parents do, discerning which tones and body or facial expressions indicated threat or reward. One learns to listen with the eyes as well as the ears.

In adolescence, like all boys who are shorter, fatter, uglier, somehow different, I learned to listen for the telltale murmur of a word—"faggot," in my case—to pick it out of a cacophony of boisterous boy sounds the same way an antelope might recognize the susurration of the belly of a lioness in the grass and be ready for instant flight or fight. The difference for the shorter, fatter, uglier straight kids is they always had the queer kid to subject to the same treatment they received from their own tormenters.

I wanted to capture all those nuances in authentic language, not the stilted literary dialogue that so many older plays had, nor the stylized poetry of Shepard, Rabe and Mamet, which still tipped toward the literary. I knew it wasn't just about words and images. What I was aiming for was jagged, irregular dialogue that felt closer to the way people actually communicate.

There were a few other things I knew I wanted to do. The first was to create a gay lead character who wasn't wrestling with coming out, begging for acceptance or waiting to die from AIDS—someone who was just living his life like everyone else. The second was to create a female lead who was terrible at following society's rules for how a woman should act, someone with an elastic sexuality that got her into trouble. The third was to challenge the usual binary gay/straight notion of sexuality.

I knocked out a sprawling collection of scenes and monologues that were read at Workshop West one afternoon.

Responses were mixed but generally encouraging. I started another version, more honed down and focused. I had the tone and the characters, but I still didn't have a plot.

Then one morning I opened the *Edmonton Journal* and read that the body of a young woman had been found in the North Saskatchewan River. She'd disappeared from a club a few days earlier and no suspects had been identified at that point. And there was this other weird connection: the place where her body had been found was the launching spot of the only canoe trip I'd ever taken in my life.

Months earlier, on my twenty-sixth birthday, Randy had invited me on a weekend canoe trip with two of his friends. He assured me the stretch of river we'd be travelling was safe for beginners, and he was right. It was mostly twenty-four hours of rather tedious exercise on a muddy, slow-moving river with excellent company.

In one of those unforgettable moments when my experience, my imagination and some outside stimuli collide, an idea was born. I asked myself, "What if Randy did it?" That thought led to the question "What if you found out your best friend was a serial killer?," which led to a million other questions and possibilities and the central plot of the play.

Serial killers were not yet the hoary plot devices they would shortly become, and after reading *Hunting Humans* and a few other early books featuring fictional and actual serial killers, I became obsessed with them. The idea of people, mostly straight white men, who lived among us while actively hunting and killing other humans for complex psychological and emotional reasons was a horrifying reality, and its cultural resonances captured my imagination.

Serial killers were the AIDS virus given flesh. Communities of minorities were often their most common victims. Ultimately the attack/infection was both random and somehow expected, which hinted at the idea of "deserved." The murder and disappearance of sex workers, hitchhikers and queers was given none of the press coverage of the murders and disappearances of white college girls.

The play was never meant to be a whodunit, and the productions that try to present it that way almost always come across as twee. Rather, it's about the devastation of learning that someone you love is not the person they claim to be. Most people can relate to that.

After a year of work I finally completed the last scene of the first draft. The feeling was hugely cathartic. I sat in the stiff kitchen chair I had to use in those days, rocked, wept and hugged myself— genuinely moved by what I'd just finished. I pulled myself together, laid my hand on the considerable pile of papers that gave testament to my accomplishment and realized I didn't have a title.

Years earlier, when I was working at Boots 'n Saddle, a police poster for a missing person had been put up on the wall of the bar. The poster was headed "Unidentified Human Remains" and featured the facial reconstruction of a man who'd been horribly murdered and dumped in a septic tank just outside Edmonton years earlier. His identity, let alone who killed him, has not been discovered to this day. A story about the mystery appears in newspapers every decade or so.

The poster fascinated me so much that I eventually took it from the wall and put it on the bulletin board I've always maintained in my work area, filled with ideas, notes and pertinent or inspiring newspaper clippings. I found it chilling that someone could disappear and be so little missed that no one contacted the authorities. The high-cheekboned, dead-eyed face reconstructed over the victim's skull could have been almost anyone—including me.

However, as a title, the phrase "unidentified human remains" wasn't quite enough. There needed to be a twist that gave some indication that this was much more than a murder mystery. That's when the phrase "and the true nature of love" came to my mind. The two ideas seemed ridiculous together, which was perfect.

The title may have been perverse, but given that the play broke with every other tradition, it fit. As I typed it onto the title page for the first time I actually giggled, knowing I'd just made a script that was already a hard sell even harder to sell. I sent it out to every theatre in Canada.

From most of them I got the terse "this play isn't right for us" response, with a few disapproving comments about the play's darkness and nihilism. Urjo, who responded to every script he received and should be anointed for doing so, was, again, not impressed. He felt the serial killer plotline was melodramatic and unnecessary and suggested my multiple settings, quick action and physical requirements showed a shocking lack of knowledge about how the theatre worked.

I sent him a letter addressing his musings and signed off with "Thank you for your comments on the play—and fuck you." So much of *Remains* was written as a reaction against precisely what Urjo preached; ending our relationship with a "fuck you" felt not only right but obligatory. When I saw him again years later, he laughed at the memory in good humour.

One night I got a call from John Moffat. We'd stayed in touch over the years, evolving a friendship mostly by phone that was surprisingly intimate despite the distances involved. When he said, after some uncomfortable preamble, "I have AIDS," I wasn't surprised, but I was heartbroken. He revealed that he and Larry had both been diagnosed and were already manifesting symptoms, thankfully of conditions that could be treated. He thought

I should know in case I hadn't been tested. I told him I was negative. He was relieved, but I could tell he was also feeling that "Why me and not you?" thing every intimate partner whose sexual partners weren't infected felt. We cried as if we were together and continued to hang on the phone long after every possible cliché about strength and hope could be exploited, saying nothing, listening to one another breathe, contemplating death.

That moment with John is just a snapshot of what was going on in most gay people's lives at that time. The community was quickly dividing into those who were negative and those who were positive. I knew there were guys who'd tested positive and weren't sharing the news with anyone, and I didn't blame them a bit. The ignorance about the disease and the demonization of the gay community were worse than ever. It was a time of great paranoia. People with AIDS were being fired from their jobs and evicted from their apartments.

Feeling stultified and in need of a change, I moved to Calgary.

None of the theatres in Edmonton had shown the slightest interest in producing *Remains* or anything else I'd written. I had no real relationship with the theatre community there beyond Workshop West.

Earlier in the year, when Dorothy-Ann Haug had invited me to accompany her to Calgary for the inaugural Blitz Weekend of Alberta Theatre Projects' playRites Festival, dedicated entirely to new Canadian plays, I jumped at the chance. I saw all three of the produced plays that weekend, including a Sky Gilbert play. I remember thinking, "If they've produced Sky's play they might produce mine," which is what put the idea of Calgary into my head.

This decision was further reinforced by the knowledge that Calgary would host the Winter Olympics the following year, 1988. This was the talk of the Alberta service industry because Calgary was going to need us, and lots of us.

Walden's was dying a slow death in the faltering economy. It was time to go.

Kate greeted my notice on the apartment with a nod that made it clear we both knew this was coming. That our friendship would ultimately survive our cohabitation says a great deal about our genuine love for one another.

A few days before moving I had everything packed up; twelve boxes, mostly filled with comic books and early versions of my plays, and a few sticks of furniture were my worldly possessions. The phone rang. It was Cam; he was at his drug dealer's place across the street and wanted me to meet him at the front door. He apologized for being a horrible friend.

Which he had been: almost entirely absent from my life, despite my occasional messages suggesting we meet up, since kicking me out of his apartment. I went out and asked him what was going on. He gestured to his car, which had a U-Haul trailer on the back, and said, "I'm moving back to Vancouver." I told him I was about to move to Calgary and we both laughed, then he kissed me on the lips and said, "I love you." We hugged. We both got a bit weepy. I let him go.

## PART TEN


# REMAINS: CALGARY


A FEW DAYS LATER MY FRIEND Kerrie and I made our move. Kerrie, who I'd worked with at Walden's, was escaping a bad marriage. She was at the wheel of a big-ass moving van and I was riding shotgun for the three-and-a-half hour drive to downtown Calgary. This is where an ex-boyfriend, Stephen (there had been a string of boyfriends in Edmonton, three of them named Stephen), had a one-bedroom apartment he was willing to share with us until we found a place of our own. But first we had to get jobs, as we had only a few hundred dollars each—enough to live on for a month as long as we were frugal, which we never were.

After the great oil crash, central Calgary was worse than downtown Edmonton—street after dusty street filled with For Sale and For Rent signs and half-completed skyscrapers standing out like post-apocalyptic ruins on the skyline. And yet the heart of the city, the financial district and the surrounding area that serviced it, still buzzed during the day in a way Edmonton didn't. Calgary was aggressive and merciless. It reminded me of Toronto.

Kerrie and I both found waiter jobs in short order and, within a few weeks, a large two-bedroom in a thirties walkup near the Stampede grounds. We were working at competing pasta restaurants. Chianti, the one that employed me, was the more successful.

I haunted the three gay clubs after work and on my nights off. I found it hard to meet guys. Most of the sex I had was with Stephen, who, like me, was quite happy to revert to ex-boyfriend sex after a few drinks and a night of no luck.

Allen MacInnis, who'd been so amazing in a Waterdale production of *Boys in the Band* nearly ten years earlier, was working at Alberta Theatre Projects, or ATP. I called him up and he invited me to meet him for a tour of the new theatre complex and confab. He'd read *Remains* and felt it was excessively bleak and that the ending didn't work. I assured him I was working on both, and I was.

Allen said, "I think it's right for the new play festival, but we'll have to convince Dobbin." He meant Michael Dobbin, who was the artistic director at ATP.

That summer I received a Canada Council short-term grant for a rewrite of *Remains*, which was a bit of encouragement in a sea of ongoing rejection. I used some of the money to take the train to Vancouver and hang out with Cam.

Cam, who could be a selfish asshole with an amazing lack of self-awareness, was at his best. He was one of the city's top stylists and was winning awards. He could get us into any bar or club with a smile. He also knew the best drug dealers. We did a lot of blow and cruised the seawall. We also spent a magical day sunbathing nude on Wreck Beach while high on mushrooms. My final night we cuddled in bed and I playfully rubbed my dick against his ass. He pushed me away, muttered something about not feeling like it, and we fell asleep. It was the first time he'd ever rejected me.

Shortly after I returned home, I had my first meeting with Michael Dobbin. When he asked me why I'd moved to Calgary, I said, "So you'd do my fucking play."

He'd read the play and found it dark and disturbing, perhaps too dark and disturbing. Nonetheless, he was considering it for a staged reading during the next playRites Festival, which would be part of the Olympic Arts Festival scheduled to run concurrently with the Games. He also mentioned the possibility of a residency.

Four months earlier I had learned of a new film training program being launched in Edmonton called DramaLab, sponsored by the National Screen Institute. The six-week program was designed to bring emerging writers, directors and producers together in hopes of promoting and advancing Canadian filmmaking. I'd sent off my application, enclosing my resumé, the latest draft of *Remains* and a copy of *Wolfboy*. Somehow they'd tracked me down in Calgary—I was terrible at leaving forwarding addresses—and told me that I had been accepted to the program, which happened to cost a lot of money I didn't have.

As luck would have it, the guy who'd gotten me the job at Chianti was opening a second restaurant in Edmonton just before the Fringe. Since the DramaLab program offered housing, and part-time shifts at the new restaurant would cover most of the tuition and living expenses, I sublet my room in the apartment with Kerrie's blessing and found myself back in Edmonton.

On the first day, in the improvised offices in the old bus barns building behind the Walterdale Theatre, all participants were asked to briefly introduce themselves. I was succinct to a fault, as I tended to be in those days, stating, "I'm here because most Canadian TV and movies are shit and I want to change that"—as usual, endearing myself to my peers. We continued around the room.

Finally came the turn of a short, wizened woman of advanced age. Her name was Ulla Ryghe. She had a thick northern European accent and spoke for nearly an hour about her life and her career as the film editor for a number of Ingmar Bergman films. It was absolute torture. Not only was she hard to understand, she was also boring. By the time she was finished, all existing energy had been sucked out of the room.

Naturally she was the person hired to lead the writers' unit of the program.

The writers were a brainy, combative lot and not at all afraid to voice their opinions. Ulla seemed to think her Bergman connection gave her some sort of screenwriting genius by proxy, allowing her to be prescriptive and absolute in her opinions. Many of us bridled at this, but instead of listening to our concerns and addressing them, she got defensive and often made the sessions feel like a power struggle, rather than a venue where everyone could learn something.

One night she screened *Persona*, and while it didn't necessarily make us respect her more, it did give us some context for her accomplishments. During the next session, just as things were reaching their usual impasse, I said, "Hey, Ulla, why don't you teach us about editing?" She and everyone else in the class were dazzled by my brilliance.

Ulla arranged for an old-style Steenbeck film-editing machine and actual takes from *The French Lieutenant's Woman* to be brought in. We watched all the takes, she took us through her editing decisions, then she cut the film with a razor, spliced it together with tape, hung the excess film on the rack beside the Steenbeck and moved on to the next cut. I think we all developed a new respect for Ulla when we saw her doing something she actually knew how to do.

It was all elementary but I found something in film editing similar to what I'd been exploring in my writing with *Remains*: the idea of creating material as the first part of the process, and cutting and reassembling that material as the next part of the process. I learned quite a few important things during that program despite its being a very rocky experience at times. My fascination with film editing started there and would inform my work for the rest of my life.

Also, I fell in love. More importantly, someone fell in love with me.

Participants in the program were separated into producer/director/writer teams for a number of projects. For one of these I was put together with the program's other bad-boy director, David Wellington (who went on to direct *I Love a Man in Uniform* and other notable film and TV projects). For that assignment I'd written a short scene about a gay male couple waiting for something with great trepidation that turned out to be the HIV results for one of them, which were expected with the morning mail. Two actors were hired for the scene. I'm afraid I have no memory of who the other actor was because Peter Stockton was performing opposite him.

Pete was on the compact side, with a solid body and a face that was the best of Brad Davis in *Midnight Express* and the young Bill Murray. He was sympathetic to the material and listened eagerly to everything I had to say. There was an immediate connection between us, not exactly sexual but somehow physical. We joked around between takes as if we were friends already. Later on, when I was editing the material together, I'd linger over his takes, filled with the most complex set of desires I'd experienced. I had to see him again.

So, for our next assignment, I wrote a scene that required an actor a lot like Pete, requested him specifically and directed the scene myself. We spent a full day in a men's room, where the scene was set, with a small cast and crew. I learned he was also a writer and had had a hit at the Fringe the previous summer. By the end of the day we'd exchanged numbers and made plans to get together.

After a couple of long telephone conversations filled with laughter and a genuine interest in one another, we had some drinks and exchanged scripts—I gave him the most recent draft of *Remains*, he gave me his Fringe script—and we made plans to get together again soon.

I loved his script, and he loved *Remains*. We drank and talked about our lives. He told me about the girlfriend he'd recently broken up with. I listened sympathetically and said, "You know I'm gay, right?" He nodded, smiling. That was that. We talked more and drank more. Eventually it got too late for him to leave and we slept together, spooning in the hotel bed. There was no sex but there was a connection we both craved, even if we couldn't understand it.

When the program ended and we had to say goodbye, we both acknowledged to the other that we shared something special. We hugged for a long time before I pulled myself away and caught the bus back to Calgary.

While I was gone, Kerrie and Stephen had found a three-bedroom house that was cheaper for us to share than the apartment had been. They'd moved in while I was gone and stuffed all my shit into my bedroom. I sorted through it, set myself up quickly and returned to Chianti while continuing my association with ATP.

CBC Radio had recently sponsored a contest for Alberta writers in which two winners would write a topical comedy sketch to be broadcast live each morning at one of the Olympic venues. The series was called "Hip Check Harry's" and featured the hoariest of Canadian clichés—lumberjacks, a native guy, hockey players and a tomboyish female who was completely incidental to everything. Never being one to overlook an opportunity, however questionable, I'd gamely dashed off a comic scene based on recent headlines, as the entry rules had stipulated, and sent it off without much thought.

A couple of weeks after returning to Calgary and settling into the house, Pete phoned me. Though we'd spoken nearly every night since my return, I could tell there was something different about his voice this time. He told me there was this CBC Radio writing contest he'd entered that was to take place during the Olympics and he'd won. My heart sank, but I congratulated him heartily. Then he said, "There was a second winner as well." My heart skipped a beat. I asked, "Did they say who it was?" He whooped: "You!"

It was official. Pete and I were going to be employed by the CBC for the duration of the Olympic Games. The competition prize had been the contract, but there was nothing in Pete's winnings to cover housing. We decided he'd stay with me. I had only one bed, but he assured me he was fine with it. Of course this led to sex.

The morning after the first time it happened I looked at him across the table as we ate our breakfast and said, "Do you still want to stay here?"

He met my eyes over his toast. "Why wouldn't I?"

His response was so opposite to what I'd expected that I was confused. "Well, usually when this happens with straight guys— they run away."

He smiled. "I'm not like those straight guys," he said, and we shared my bed quite comfortably from that point on.

Pete made me want to be a better person. I'd been actively working to be less of an asshole since my walk of shame from

Toronto back to Edmonton. I'd learned that, while I was very talented, I wasn't nearly as good as I'd once believed, and this extended into my personal life. I was always honest with Pete about how I was feeling, and he reciprocated.

In the mornings we'd get up early, after always having drunk too much beer the night before, read and discuss the morning's headlines in the *Calgary Herald*, and then take a cab across the river to the CBC building, where we'd meet with the producers, discuss the ideas for the sketch and then retire to a room to write.

Pete would sit across the desk from me and I'd type while we talked because I was the faster typist. The director and producer would read the sketch, make comments, and we'd retire back to our featureless writers' room to polish it. That afternoon it would be taped before a live audience in the lobby of a downtown office building. It gave us a steady and healthy paycheque for a month and a privilege pass into the arts segment of the Olympic celebrations.

The playRites Festival produced a number of interesting plays that year, but the talk of the community was the reading of *Remains* that happened in the lobby of the Martha Cohen Theatre one afternoon for a rather large group of people who had no idea what they were getting into.

The reading was galvanizing for both participants and audience. The actors had never read anything quite like it and the audience had never heard anything quite like it. Allen MacInnis, who directed, refused to judge the material, treating it as he would any other play, which gave the actors a much-needed stability.

Pete and I listened in wonder, both agreeing that it was far funnier onstage than it was on the page, which is what I'd hoped for. Audience feedback forms proved people were shocked, some offended, but many were intrigued. Word around the theatre was mixed. Some liked the play and some said they found it gratuitously shocking. Artistic director Michael Dobbin was still hedging on whether it would be programmed for the 1989 festival. Allen MacInnis was clear in his support for the play opening at the festival. I resolved to rewrite it yet again.

Pete and I got to know a great many Canadian theatre artists at that time, particularly Blake Brooker, Denise Clarke, Michael Green, Andy Curtis and the other members of the One Yellow Rabbit troupe that were doing such amazing work on the stage.

Ronnie Burkett, who'd already won an Emmy for his amazing puppet work, was very much on the scene, as he was also trying to get work as an actor in those days. Michael Dobbin hired him for a number of the ancillary events at the festival. Ronnie and I shared a cynical, dry humour that started a friendship that has grown immensely and complexly over the decades.

Daniel MacIvor also came through town with his bravura one-man show *House*. Pete and I loved the show, and arrangements had been made for the three of us to meet at a nearby bar after seeing it. Years later Daniel would say, "That image of you and Pete walking into the bar was so beautiful I wanted to know you both." He, Ronnie and I would form a sort of queer triumvirate of our generation that would lead to all sorts of comparisons, collaborations and rivalries. To this day they remain my brothers in envelope-pushing and artisan excellence.

The night of the closing ceremonies of the Games, people gathered in immense crowds all over the city, many of them heading to Olympic Plaza directly in front of the Calgary Centre for the Performing Arts. Above us fireworks exploded in a glassy sky as Pete and I slipped our arms around one another, smiling.

---

Immediately after the Games ended the city was plunged into a period of dark depression. The influx of so much money and so much attention ended so abruptly, it was like the worst coke crash ever. As citizens recovered and opportunists counted their money and beat it out of town, a pall fell over the city—most of which I was spared because the second portion of the DramaLab program kicked in and I flew off to Montreal to write a short episode of a series being made for the National Film Board of Canada.

I was put up in the elegant but then crumbling Queen Elizabeth Hotel, which had a modernist exterior and a dated late-fifties interior. I'd heard great things about Montreal gay life over the years, and on a sleety January weeknight I set out to find the Gay Village dressed the same way I would have for a commensurate temperature in Edmonton or Calgary. This meant I wore a winter coat and runners, because on the prairies winters are generally dry enough that insulated footwear is optional. After two blocks of trudging through ankle-deep slush I was chilled to the bone and shaking so much I could barely register the garish sights of Ste-Catherine Street.

I can't remember the details of my NFB episode, but I do remember endless meetings with the producer and director about whatever it was I'd written—which always required endless rewrites based on notes they'd given me, most of which indicated they hadn't actually read what I'd written at all. It was not a happy time. I spent a lot of money commiserating with Pete on the phone.

When we were apart he was dating women and I'd sometimes see other men. We'd talked about this early in our relationship. We both felt monogamy was an unrealistic expectation for most people and, given our divergent sexual tastes, found it made little sense to swear to fuck only one another. We were both candid with one another about these encounters and swore that if any of these experiences threatened our relationship we would share that with the other immediately. Although we would have our codependency/jealousy issues, they would never be sexual.

It was a relief to finally fly back to Calgary. Pete was doing a school tour with a children's theatre troupe in Edmonton, and I had decided it was time to find new living arrangements. Living with Stephen and Kerrie was like living with two rowdy teenagers, and as a mature man of twenty-eight, I'd had my fill.

Doug, a friend I'd made in Edmonton the previous year, was a straight guy who loved poetry and working with his hands, a hard-living/drinking/loving former frat boy with an amazing design sense and a dreamy manner. When he told me about an apartment next to his above a corner store, I jumped at the chance to check it out. The apartment was a long, narrow boxcar-style suite. Doug had renovated his own suite so there was a spacious living area in the front, a kitchen and bathroom in the centre, and a work area at the back. The one I was looking at, though, had been a flophouse for years and was a nightmare of wood panelling, greasy cupboards and liquefied foodstuffs in the filthy fridge. But the rent was unbelievably low, and Doug assured me the owner of the building would pay for all the materials for a reno and give me a cut in the rent while it was happening. What's more, Doug would walk me through everything that needed to be done. I took the place and we started the renovation.

Tomoko Sato was a precocious and talented Calgary high school student who had submitted her play to the ATP student playwriting unit, and everyone had been impressed by it. *Josh's Plane* was about a high school jock who gets AIDS from a blood transfusion. While it showed the writer's inexperience, it still packed a punch, and Dobbin decided it should be produced at Tomoko's school. The school board agreed, and I was asked to direct, which, given my affinity for the subject matter, I was more than happy to do.

This was my first time directing students, and I was an authoritarian control freak. But I allowed the large cast to share their voices and ideas, and the AIDS education that accompanied the show was profound for everyone involved. The play ran to capacity houses and created quite a stir in Calgary, although most of the potential controversy was neutralized by the fact the only mention of anything homosexual in the play was the straight main character's passing concern that others would think he was gay.

Later that spring I flew back to Montreal for the last phase of the DramaLab program, which was the final realization of our short films for the NFB. I spent hours in my hotel room desperately rewriting scenes for some pointless project I no longer remember for anything other than the consternation it caused me. In fact, this was where my indifference to film and television took root. Eventually I just said "Fuck it," signed off emotionally and wrote whatever the director or producers asked me to, even though I knew it was complete bullshit.

One night, after a particularly stressful day, I was standing at the window gazing out at the Montreal skyline that sparkled with skyscraper windows lit by fluorescents, when suddenly the city disappeared. This was the great Montreal blackout of 1988.

I was trapped on the eighteenth floor. Thankfully the phones were still working, and I had at least four beers in the minibar that now had to be drunk, so I spent the next couple of hours talking to Pete on the phone.

Word of our relationship had started to get out. Pete's friends were particularly baffled, as they'd only known him as not only resolutely heterosexual but a bit of a hound as well. My friends, who were all well aware of my wide-ranging tastes and inconsistent sexual history, were less confused. By the end of the conversation we decided Pete should come to Montreal.

He arrived a few days later. We fell into one another's arms and moved onto the bed. He stretched his smaller frame out on top of my larger one. We breathed together until our hearts were in sync. He curled his face into the side of my neck. We both admitted nothing felt as right as our being together.

While swilling beer and snorting coke one evening, we decided it was time to move in together. We would be a domestic team as well as a writing team.

Reactions to us going public with our relationship were mixed. Sexual ambiguity and experimentation is hardly rare in the arts, with one encountering "alternative" relationships more frequently than in the non-arts disciplines. As the old joke goes, there is straight and then there is actor straight. Given that an actor's job is to understand and convey the experiences of other people, at their best they tend to be people who aren't afraid of new experiences. On the other hand, homophobia, sexism and racism are hardly unknown in any of the arts.

Michael Dobbin called. He and Allen MacInnis wanted to see me at the theatre. My anus was clenched. I needed this production. *Wolfboy* was four years in my past, *Young Art* two. If I had any hope of a credible career in the theatre, it had to happen with this play.

Dobbin still wasn't sure whether to put the show into the playRites Festival. He had no idea how the audience or the sponsors, most of them oil corporations, would respond. Allen reminded him that the festival had been created to take risks. Dobbin conceded. *Remains* would be done.

It wasn't all good news. They informed me that Allen would soon leave Alberta Theatre Projects to move on to his new role as AD of Prairie Theatre Exchange in Winnipeg. Allen would be replaced by Bob White, the former AD at Factory Theatre in Toronto who, along with Passe Muraille and the Tarragon, had been one of the earliest producers of exclusively new Canadian work. Allen had been my first choice for director.

When I received my contract for *Remains* I read it thoroughly, then asked for a meeting with the general manager at ATP. I told him the only clause I had an issue with was the one stating that the theatre would get a certain percentage of my royalties for a period of time. This was a common clause then, and may still be now. Producers have always bilked creators for an inordinate share of their usually limited profits. If they had commissioned the script, I might have considered the clause for a limited time after production——but considering this was a festival with a limited number of performances and limited possibilities for financial remuneration, the clause struck me as very one-sided, and I would not sign off on it.

The general manager, who had already given his notice to leave the company for another job, said, "You're right. We've never had a show go on to a second production anyway, so just strike that paragraph out of the contract and initial it."

I did. Quickly. And I never regretted it, even though it caused the former GM and theatre management some grief after the fact.

This taught me an important lesson about subsidiary rights for intellectual properties, and I've been judicious in granting them throughout my career. Does the producing theatre have a right to future profits for producing the play for the first time? I've always acknowledged the risk in producing any new play, and it's my opinion that a first-rate production should share in future rights for five years if—and only if—it is a demonstrably first-rate production that has turned enough of a profit for the play-wright to earn specific royalty amounts. A play's failure to draw an audience is rarely the script's fault alone. A bad actor, an inept director or a useless publicity department can ruin the best of plays. Why should the playwright be forced to give the theatre subsequent royalty splits if the theatre didn't do its job?

Michael Dobbin and Bob White called me in for a meeting to get my thoughts on who I'd like to direct the play. My first choice was Peter Hinton, a brilliant, uncompromising director in Toronto. They both immediately rejected him because "he's never worked at the festival or the theatre." My counter-argument, that their argument was idiotic since the festival was only in its third year and hardly anyone had worked in it, fell on deaf ears. When I asked for Bob himself I found out he'd already committed to another play. When I suggested Paul Thompson I finally understood what the phrase "they visibly blanched" meant. Then I said, "I can do it," but Bob and Michael shot that down immediately, saying they didn't want to set any kind of precedent with writers direct-ing their own shows. It was clear they had already decided who they wanted, so I suggested they just fucking tell me.

The director they suggested was someone I'd met, and a close friend of Michael's, Susan Ferley. I protested that I'd never seen Susan's work.

Michael said, "You have to appreciate what a great risk we're taking—"

I cut him off. "Yeah. The risk of actually making some money."

Bob laughed, but Michael continued seriously. "This is a new festival in Calgary—not always the most open-minded place on the planet. I need someone I know in charge. This is the only play in the festival we haven't found a corporate sponsor for . . ."

He let the sentence dangle, implying I'd somehow let the festival down by not attracting a corporate sponsor. I knew from their expressions I wasn't going to win this one, and I shrugged. Susan Ferley would direct *Remains*.

Having lost at choosing the director, when it came to casting I was uncompromising. I wanted John Moffat to play David. Again there were objections. Both of them had heard dodgy things about John's health and were unsure he'd be up to the challenge. I'd already spoken to John; he'd assured me that he was strong enough to do the job.

I also wanted Kate Newby to play Benita, the psychic hooker, and Pete to play Kane, the sexually uncertain busboy, and they were fine with these choices. Luckily the rest of the company that had already been chosen were almost perfect actors for the parts: hulking Peter Smith as Bernie, Ellen-Ray Hennessy as Candy, Wendy Noel as Jerri and David LeReaney as Robert.

The day of the first reading of the script, when everyone who worked at the theatre in any capacity was present, there was a tension in the air—a cold front of disapproval meeting a warm front of acceptance that resulted in odd bursts of supportive laughter and barely concealed sighs and snorts of derision. Many uncertain looks were exchanged, particularly when the words "fuck" and "cunt" were used and there was talk of gay sex. I looked at the director smiling nervously and got a terrible feeling in the pit of my stomach.

Because I'd been working on the script for so long, I had little rewriting to do, so I wished everyone good luck and went home. I'd learned that a playwright who'd done a decent job had no real reason to hang around rehearsals making everyone nervous. But I'd also learned that I'd be an idiot not to check in regularly.

In the early days it was all bonhomie and drinks at the bar after rehearsal as everyone got to know one another. John looked to be in good health. I smiled secretly to myself as I saw him working his charm on various members of the company, seducing his next on-the-road lover. It was generally known that John had AIDS, but he was still so attractive and magnetic that it made little difference even in the days when the stigma and fear were at their height.

Pete knew the whole story of my history with John and was nervous. I took him through the AIDS educational material I'd been compiling since the beginning of the plague: books, articles and essays by reputable experts who made it clear that passing on the virus through casual contact was unknown, and through mouth-to-mouth contact, very rare. Pete and John exchanged a kiss, but it was a stage kiss, their lips didn't touch.

After two weeks of working on other stuff I dropped in to see how rehearsals were going. The actors were wandering around listlessly, speaking in monotones. There was a torpid passive-aggressive tension in the air, a sense of wheels being spun and no work being done. Finally Kate said to Susan—with that certain ring in her voice that said "I've had just about enough of this shit" which I knew so well—"I have no idea where I'm supposed to go."

Everyone stopped. Everyone looked to Susan. Susan said something about following the journey and gestured for them to continue. They did. I watched an hour of their work before we broke for lunch.

As they all wandered off I approached Susan. With any production, my most important alliance is always with the director. I asked her if everything was all right. She said it was just one of those days. I wasn't persuaded and talked to her about how uncommitted some of the acting had been, suggesting it seemed to result from people not knowing where to go. She told me she liked to let the actors claim the space and the story before formalizing the movement.

Susan mentioned she was finding John resistant to her way of working, which always varies according to director, and that seemed to be affecting the rest of the cast. I asked her if she wanted me to sound him out to make sure everything was all right. She thought that would be a good idea.

John was at lunch with Ellen-Ray and Kate, but the ladies, sensing something was up, excused themselves as I was diplomatic about it, but I let him know I was very confused by what he was doing in the rehearsal hall and asked him if everything was all right.

Everything was not all right. John said he had worked with Susan before and he hadn't enjoyed the experience. When I asked him why he hadn't told me this at the outset, he replied that he thought he could deal with it because he loved the script so much. He had major issues with some of Susan's directorial techniques, and he complained about her unwillingness to commit to any kind of physical life for the play.

I talked to him about honouring each other's process and trying to make them mesh and, if he couldn't do that, being candid with Susan about his own needs. I said, "In the end, it's your performance. You can do what you want to. Don't be resistant." He assured me he wouldn't and I left, hoping that I had at least opened the door to some sort of connection between the director and the lead actor.

On my way out I ran into Bob White and gave him a rundown of my experience in and after rehearsal. He told me to relax, it was early days. I reminded him we were two weeks in and no blocking had been done. He waved my concerns away with a laugh and hurried off to his own rehearsal.

Unless you've worked in a major undertaking with a multitude of creative personalities under intense pressure, you have no idea how bad things can get when just a few personalities within a theatre company grow destructive. Fear and fatigue are a dangerous combo with actors, and the bitterly cold Calgary winter that kept everyone indoors wasn't helping.

In the beginning Pete would come home from rehearsal bubbling with stories about the day, but as time went by he became quieter. We'd talk of other things while sharing a joint and enjoying a beer, but I knew something was wrong. The cold sores he suffered from when under stress were beginning to show just above his lip. I demanded to know what was going on.

Pete's eyes filled with tears. "It's horrible."

I was stunned. "Horrible?"

Pete said, "We're doing it all wrong. It's all this lovey-dovey, touchy-feely shit. The pace is all wrong. No one knows what to do and we're starting to hate the play."

Now it was my turn to cry tears of rage and frustration. After the years of being turned down and criticized, to have this play fucked up by forces beyond my control was too much to consider. I vented, he listened. He vented, I listened. Then I spoke with each of the cast members privately, telling them what Pete had told me and asking them to be completely candid in their responses. Five of the seven actors felt Susan was negatively judging the characters and their actions and causing the actors to do the same thing. As Ellen-Ray so eloquently put it, "I feel like I'm in fucking *Long Day's Journey into Night*."

The next morning I slipped into rehearsal and watched a run of the first act. It was even worse than Pete had led me to believe. I listened to the final scene with my head in my hands and slipped out while Susan was giving the company notes.

I demanded an emergency meeting with Bob White and Michael Dobbin. I briskly brought them up to date on what the actors had said to me and my own concerns for the show, considering how close to opening we were. Again my concerns were brushed off. "It'll be fine by opening" was their attitude as they both headed back to their own rehearsals.

I returned to the rehearsal hall and asked for a quick meeting before they started. Susan looked at me curiously. Some of the actors were looking nervous. I took a seat on a set piece in the centre of the rehearsal hall and calmly told Susan everything that had been said to me, then followed up with my own concerns after watching the run-through.

She looked completely stunned. Turning to the actors, she asked if this was true.

The actors were all suddenly interested in the state of their nails or the tips of their shoes.

I stared at them in shock, realizing they were about to sell me out.

Pete said tentatively, "I'm not sure we've got the pace right."

The rest shrugged and nodded, making vaguely reassuring noises. Susan looked at me, confused. I shook my head in disgust and walked out of the rehearsal hall.

When Pete got home from rehearsal he said, "Sorry that didn't go better."

I gave him a wounded look, grabbed my coat and left the apartment. I wandered the streets for a while, feeling exactly like I remembered feeling in Saskatoon and then Toronto when watching *Wolfboy* fall apart—powerless.

Eventually I ended up at the gay bar. I checked my parka and sidled up to the bar. There were more staff than patrons, but I wasn't here for company. As I ordered my usual Labatt's Blue I caught the eye of an emaciated older man in an expensive leather jacket staring at me from the other side of the square bar. Something about him was familiar. He smiled.

It was Benny. My old fuck bud, Benny the beautiful muscle man with the fat, uncut cock, melon-like ass-cheeks and girlishly smooth skin. It was obvious he was in the late stages of AIDS.

As I moved around the bar to greet him I tried to hide my shock behind a surprised smile, but he saw right through it. As we hugged he said, "It's okay," and that was the extent of our conversation about his health.

I took the stool next to his as he looked me over with a smile, saying, "You're all right?"

I nodded.

"Good," he said. "Some of the guys I fucked with—they're not all right."

Having no idea how to respond, I said, "It's good to see you."

"You too. When I first got sick I was laid up for a while—but I read about you when I started travelling again."

Something hit me. "What happened to your accent?" Benny always had that sexy Texan twang. I remembered what he'd told me about himself in our first few meetings: born in Texas, a couple of brothers, worked at something to do with the steel industry— sales, maybe—had a life partner who was much younger and a brother who'd got into drug trouble in South America.

Benny said, "Everything I told you about myself is a lie." He went on to explain to me that he wasn't from Texas, he was from some- place in the Maritimes, and he didn't work in the steel industry, he worked for a major coke cartel that had been smuggling blow into the country. I was so gobsmacked. Most people have an alter ego, but queer people in those days often had many identities, mostly forged out of necessity. We did what we had to in order to survive. Nonetheless, when he was done, all I could do was gape at him.

I said, "Everything?"

He said, "Except the stuff about my partner. That was real."

I had no idea what to say.

Benny said, "All of those condos and apartments we fucked in were safe houses. You have no idea the danger I put you and other people in. I had some pretty nasty people after my ass."

I shook my head in shock. He put his hand over mine. It was cool, already slightly dead. "So what's happening with you?"

Benny ordered us two more beers and I brought him up to date with my life, Pete and the play. When I was done I could tell he was tired. I offered to see him back to his hotel, but he said he was fine. He got off his stool to hug me, and I could feel his bones move loosely beneath his skin like the last few pretzel sticks in a nearly empty bag.

Benny said, "Don't waste a minute." I kissed him quickly.

I walked home in a teary daze. Pete was in bed but wide awake. I told him about meeting Benny. He held me while I cried. After a joint we went back to the subject of the play.

Pete said, "What are we gonna do?"

I said, "I'll think about that tomorrow."

As I dropped off into sleep I realized Benny hadn't mentioned why he was in Calgary. I would never find out.

After Pete left for rehearsal the next morning I got a phone call from Ellen-Ray, who wasn't called for that day. She apologized for not being able to say anything during rehearsal and admitted she was at her wits' end. She had no idea what the play was about or what she was doing with her character.

I made a crucial decision in that moment. This was my play. I knew what it was about and I knew how it would work. Although it defied everything I'd learned about professionalism and never contradicting the director, I felt I had no other choice. So I told Ellen-Ray that everything she was doing was wrong. Candy wasn't a weepy, sensitive woman hopelessly in love with David, as it was being played. She was hard, cynical and outspoken. She wasn't a victim; she was a predator who was out to get what she wanted. She was caustic and witty. "Put the joy and fun back into it," I told her before hanging up.

I began to get calls from other cast members, more than half, who'd obviously spoken to Ellen-Ray. I said basically the same thing to each of them and reminded them my influences were rock videos, comic books and sitcoms. I told each of them to quit worrying about what Susan was asking for and to do what their instincts told them to do.

The next morning, a couple hours after rehearsal started, the phone rang. "You'd better get down here," Pete said. I asked him what was happening, and he said Susan had been upset by Elly's reinterpretation of Candy and, when she'd questioned her about it, Elly had said she was doing what I'd told her to do. Susan had walked out of rehearsal.

I raced to the theatre expecting to find the cast and crew fretting over things, but, thankfully, the stage manager was putting them through a run of the show. I watched a bit of it, pleased to see some of the actors shrugging off the funereal energy they'd been dealing with and starting to play. Then I headed to Dobbin's office, Michael and Bob were waiting for me. Susan wasn't there.

I'd expected fireworks and accusations of unprofessional sabotage, but got neither. They informed me that Susan had decided to leave the show and take her name off it because she didn't feel she had the support of the playwright. I said that was probably for the best and asked what they planned to do now. Bob acknowledged that the basic blocking and analysis were pretty much done and, since his show was opening shortly, he'd take over for the technical rehearsals that were to come.

We then went down and informed the cast, who were, of course, unnerved by the director's departure. Bob reminded them that we were all professionals, we still had a show to open, and these things sometimes happened.

I sat with Bob as he worked to shift the energy of the show in a new direction. The actors grew more confident and took more chances. Bob encouraged them to go further, to work for a snappier pace. The play began to show signs of life.

The cast was now galvanized. Things with the director had gone much more wrong than most of them had imagined, and I think a few of them were questioning their own culpability in what had played out. Now they became consummate professionals and were doing everything they could to support one another.

Susan was a popular figure in the Calgary theatre community, and many people had enjoyed working with her over the years. They couldn't imagine what it might take to cause her to quit a show and cast me as the villain. I was snubbed by many and told off by some. This is what I'd expected, and I'd prepared myself emotionally for the chilling disapproval that I knew was going to follow—nice people in the Canadian theatre didn't upset other nice people even if it meant producing mediocrity. Of course my indifference to their animosity only made it worse.

As the opening approached I grew more nervous. I felt like the play was already cursed. I had no idea how people would react. Had the actors and Susan been justified in the terror they'd seemed to feel? Was *Remains* really that offensive?

Our first preview was a fundraiser for the local AIDS network and was packed to the rafters with a queer and queer-friendly audience. I sat on the top balcony in the worst seat of the house, where few could see me, my palms sweating, heart pounding.

There was applause as Michael Dobbin took the stage for the traditional pre-show chat (which I always found unbearable whoever was doing it), but his turned out to be far different than the usual patter. The original 1931 *Frankenstein* film opens with a scene of a stern gentleman coming out from behind the curtain to warn the audience, on behalf of the producer, that they are about to witness images that might horrify them and now was their chance to leave. That's basically what Dobbin did. He warned the audience that what they were about to see would not be to everyone's taste and, if anyone wanted to change their mind now, the box office would happily refund their money.

Had this been done as a marketing ploy it would've been brilliant, but he was sincere. If Susan's apologetic production couldn't make it to the stage, he'd come out and apologize for the play before it even began.

No one took him up on his offer.

The house lights dimmed and the stage lights rose on the cast doing their chorus bit. Then Kate as Benita, in a Louise Brooks wig and S&M gear, standing at the top of the two-storey metal-and-leather set, started the urban-legend monologue that opens the play. I could feel an electricity in the house. Everyone was in a state of intense collective listening. There were a few titters at the end of her speech, but when the next scene started, with David arriving at the apartment and calling out, "Honey, I'm homo," the theatre exploded with laughter and the ride began.

Initially the cast was thrown off by the laughter. They'd had bleakness drilled into them for so long they were completely unprepared for the blinding flashes of light the humour brought to the show. They adjusted quickly, and after a couple of scenes they, like the audience, like the playwright, were riding the roller coaster that was *Unidentified Human Remains and the True Nature of Love* experiencing its first audience.

Every actor in the show rose to the occasion, and, as I knew he would be, John was the perfect David McMillan. He managed to be defiant and broken, horrible and lovable. He caught all of the character's nuances, turning in a masterful performance.

After that preview, the opening seemed incidental, but it went equally well, despite another huge blizzard that made me late for my own premiere.

At the start of every show Dobbin came out and offered the buyers their money back if they wanted to leave. No one ever left then, but Pete reported to me that there had been a number of walk-outs at the midway point in act one where Candy kisses her lesbian friend Jerri. This delighted me. I've always felt that theatre the right people walk out of is theatre that matters.

Reviews were mostly positive. The reviewer at the *Calgary Herald* was particularly taken with it and gave it a rave. Some were troubled by the nudity. Some dismissed my obvious pop-culture influences. The *Globe and Mail*, as would become tradition, was sniffy, including a homophobic comment about "homosexual wish fulfilment" that straight white male reviewers were still getting away with in those days. Most of them refused to acknowledge that a physical love could exist between straight and gay men. My experience exposed their lies, but, worse, they never called their straight counterparts out for the endless plays by het men that involve a lovely young woman falling in love with a middle-aged man who has no redeeming characteristics at all.

A few days later, the folksy, much-loved, Peter Gzowski interviewed me for *As It Happens* on CBC Radio and asked, with a snide tone, "And what about the critics who have called it 'homosexual wish-fulfilment'?" I replied, "I'm writing about the interesting straight men, not guys who write reviews. Sexuality is far more contextual and varied than the boring straight people like to believe." For the first time in the interview he looked down at his notes to find the next question.

There were also those who denounced the show. This was Alberta, after all, and some in the Bible belt didn't appreciate this dark faggot shit in their local theatre. This chorus of protesters who felt it necessary to denounce the "lifestyle" of my characters—"lifestyle" being code for gay—would become a constant refrain anywhere the play was produced, and continues in some places today.

The other thing that became clear during this limited run of the play, and with my later plays, is that the people coming to see the show in large numbers were not the usual demographic that goes to the theatre. Most were younger, hipper and willing to spend their money on something that spoke to them.

Reactions to the play among those working in the theatre were varied. A lot of the old guard were flummoxed by the show's popularity. There was something about it that threatened them, which probably had to do with every character in the play being under thirty, but also had to do with a traditional sense of class decorum within the theatre which I'd just roughly butt-fucked with my play.

I have never for a moment regretted anything I did in that situation and never again had a premiere production where I didn't have approval of the director.

The final show was on the last day of the festival, a cold Sunday afternoon. Pete had gone ahead to prep before the show. I walked to the theatre.

As I approached the Centre for the Performing Arts, I noticed a long lineup outside the building. It was people who'd come hoping for a ticket to *Remains*. As I passed by, some of them called out to me to get them a ticket. I shrugged apologetically. I'd just smoked a joint and was high as a kite. This was not what I'd expected.

The theatre was a madhouse as people roiled in the lobby waiting to get into the theatre. A Sold Out sign hung in the ticket window. I gave my seat up to someone in line and climbed to the third balcony, hoping for a place to hide in the shadows and see my show.

There was no hiding. The house was literally standing-room-only, so I was forced to stand at the railing with numerous other people as the house lights came down and the stage lights came up on the last Calgary performance of the play that was about to change my life.

# ACT TWO

## Fin de Siècle

# REMAINS: EDMONTON/
# TORONTO/MONTREAL

AS FUN, ROMANTIC AND NARRATIVELY satisfying as tales of overnight success are, they have been non-existent in my life. In the case of *Remains* it was a particularly slow burn. Despite the flurry of controversy and press that had accompanied the opening, things were decidedly not spiralling beyond my control.

Most of the theatres known for producing Canadian work were less than supportive of the script. Many of the artistic directors expressed discomfort with the play's lack of adherence to the constantly shifting, frequently classist neo-con/lib hegemony that had only recently been established in academia and was worming its way into the theatre.

This school of thought, which essentially tries to dictate a series of social rules for the populace rooted in a perceived hierarchy of privilege based on race, gender, sexuality—anything but class, which those who can afford to attend university like to steer clear of—while also ignoring context and nuance, was relatively new at the time but had already infected most liberal arts programs and government-funded theatres. Their excuses for rejecting the play were that it was too (if they were a feminist theatre) male, too (if they were run by a straight person, male or female) queer, too (if they were run by a "survivor" of something) violent, too (if run by a gay person) homophobic and so on.

To my greatest surprise even Theatre Passe Muraille passed on the play. Decades later, someone who'd been in on the decision admitted it was because some found the play too gay.

I was less surprised when Urjo Kareda also passed on it for the Tarragon, because I'd already seen his reaction to the show in Calgary. It had been at a matinee performance; I'd just dropped something off to Pete in his dressing room, hung around to watch curtain call, and walked out into the theatre after I thought the audience had left. Because of his bad knees that required him to use double canes, Urjo usually sat on an aisle in the front row and remained seated until everyone else had gone. I nearly bumped into him as I was leaving. We greeted one another.

"Well," he said, "you're hot in the west," lips pursing slightly with disapproval.

I extended my arm. "Do you need any help getting out of the theatre?"

He laughed at my bitchiness and winked at me.

I jerked my thumb to indicate the stage and said, "This play's gonna be hot everywhere. You should do it."

He laughed derisively as I exited.

I'd met Jim Millan in Calgary the year before. He was connected to the One Yellow Rabbit group and we'd all spent many nights after the shows laughing and swilling beer until the proprietor threw us out of the bar. Jim had been a supporter from the first public reading of *Remains*, and after its success he began to propose a production at Crow's Theatre, which he had founded in Toronto. Jim's confident self-promotion made my judgmental

Scottish side nervous, although I also found him charming and quite fun. However, I remained noncommittal.

Knowing my residence at Alberta Theatre Projects was at an end and unlikely to be renewed after everything that had gone on with *Remains*, Pete and I had both been seeking employment in Edmonton, and we scored.

Not only was I to direct the script he'd written for the Citadel's Teen Festival, but Northern Light Theatre had commissioned us to adapt *The Revenger's Tragedy*, a seventeenth-century blood-and-gore genre script. I called my buddy at Chianti and secured a couple of waiter shifts a week, and we sublet the Calgary apartment and moved into Pete's very junior one-bedroom apartment near the university in Edmonton.

We were in that apartment when Pete found out he'd been invited to be part of the acting company at the Stratford Festival the next summer. He was elated. So was I. But there was this thing we both had when the other got something we weren't part of that was tinged with competitive professional jealousy. Although we always sold ourselves as a team of writers, we'd both had other irons in the fire before our merger, and a number of those came to fruition during this period.

Between waiting shifts and partying, Pete and I put the finishing touches on his script for the Teen Festival. *Blood Buddies* was written by Pete with significant input by me. The exact plot now eludes me—something about gangs in schools on which we hung a number of issues we wanted to talk about, including being a gay teen, sexual assault and bullying. There were over twenty characters, ranging through all shapes, sizes and races. The climactic moment was the gang rape of one of our female protagonists and her bloody revenge on the boy who's led the attack. There was also a gay bashing and an overweight lesbian-ish character who terrorized all the men.

Because we'd been offered the large Shoctor Theatre, a space I'd dreamed of working in since my first trip in high school, I encouraged Pete to make the script as wide-ranging and theatrical as possible. This was my first chance to direct something with such scope, and I wanted to learn as much as I possibly could.

The designer, David Skelton, my most frequent collaborator throughout my career, came up with an amazing two-level set surrounded by backstop wire. The "furniture pieces" on the floor were rusted metal drums and boxes. His model had a bleak, dystopian feel that fit the show perfectly. He's a brilliant designer, and working with him is always challenging and rewarding.

We had an endless week of casting, enduring hours of painful auditions each day to discover some amazing talent here and there. I tended to cast the quirky kids and anyone who was any sort of minority, visible or not. I knew the good-looking ones generally got the parts even if they weren't as skilled. I always wanted to give the underdogs a chance.

Pete left for Stratford a few days before rehearsals started. The night before he left we discussed everything that had to be done with the play while he was gone.

My directing approach, reinforced after my experience with the vagaries of teenage commitment with Tomoko Sato's *Josh's Plane* in Calgary, can best be described as somewhere between Bob Fosse as depicted in *All That Jazz* and Erich von Stroheim. I laid out all the rules at the beginning of the process, and I mercilessly fired latecomers and those who didn't do their homework to make it clear to the cast that I wasn't dicking around.

The thing I love about working with new actors is teaching them my theatrical vocabulary, which is both technical and intuitive. I was learning to combine my high school teacher Billy Bob's physical staging with Paul Thompson's process of making the artists responsible for their own choices rather than always looking to the director to tell them what to do. It wasn't easy, and it took a lot of reinforcement, but I'd learned that if you give the performers a strong physical structure for the show, and also keep working with them to get inside their characters, they almost always get it enough to serve their function within the production.

When Pete had negotiated his contract with Stratford he'd insisted on an allowance to come home for the opening of his show. I was eager to show him what I'd done, and after sitting through a dress rehearsal he was very excited about the opening.

That first high school audience of eight hundred were shocked by what they were seeing. The cast was shocked to discover they were shocking their peers. There was some inappropriate laughter and commentary from the spectators, which disturbed the actors. When, during the gang rape at the end, certain male members of the audience were yelling "Do the bitch!" I knew we were in trouble.

After the show Pete looked at me in shock. I assured him the next show would be the one. Then I went back to the dressing rooms to assemble the cast and remind them that they were the ones who were supposed to control the show whereas tonight they had let the audience control them.

For the second show, the cast was entirely in control. The rhythm of the piece, the pauses, the syncopating of characters' voices and objectives were all clear, and when the lights came up many in the audience were openly weeping. The failure in the first show had galvanized us for the second.

Pete was ecstatic. That was the show he'd hoped to see. Before he returned to Stratford we made arrangements to sublet his place so I could travel out to stay with him for the last six weeks of his contract. This time in Stratford would allow us to do the requisite research and analysis of *The Revenger's Tragedy* so we could adapt it before we returned home.

I turned thirty that summer and threw a huge party for myself called the Black Cotillion, at the home of one of the cooks from Chianti. A great many people came and it was legendary; family members, Beverly friends, folks from PA, endless restaurant workers, the gays, the straights, drag queens, people from Calgary and Toronto, it was a microcosm of my life to that point.

The next morning I was hungover and depressed. I had always told myself that if I hadn't made some kind of mark in the theatre world by thirty, I'd go back to school and take something that would give me a real job to take me into the future. Was it time to sacrifice myself to something I could make a secure living at?

That's what I was considering when Gerry Potter from Workshop West called to tell me he had decided to program *Remains* for the following winter and wanted me to direct. I accepted and thanked him emphatically. I'd genuinely been thinking the play, like most Canadian plays, wouldn't have a second production.

Shortly after that Jim Millan called. He also wanted to commit to producing the play the following winter in Toronto. After speaking with Gerry, we decided Jim could premiere the show and our production would open a month later in Edmonton. I received small advances from both theatres when the contracts were sent, which, not having spoken to my agent in a few years, I ran past the Playwrights Guild of Canada before signing. It was an embarrassingly small amount of money, but it would offset the time in Stratford, where I wouldn't be earning anything.

Although our reunion was tender, Pete's gruelling schedule of rehearsals, performances, classes and workshops meant we'd do little more than sleep together for the first couple of weeks. I played the dutiful Stratford wife, ensuring dinner was on the table when he got home so we could have a few hours to chat and watch TV before retiring. I went to all the shows Pete was in as well as a couple of others we got discounted tickets for.

One of those shows was director Kelly Handerek's production of *The Changeling*, which, just like the show we were adapting, was a Jacobean revenge tragedy. Since I was already steeping myself in the period and the style, I decided I would let those influences inform my next play. For my follow-up to *Remains* I stepped as far away from its influences as I possibly could and adapted *The Changeling* for a contemporary audience.

One of the main criticisms of *Remains* within the theatre community was that the characters weren't "likeable" enough. I had no idea what this meant, because for me characters, like people, were often likeable and unlikeable simultaneously. I never looked at characters in my shows through the lens of likeability, but rather in terms of complexity and nuance. Who's likeable in *Hamlet*? Who's likeable in *Oedipus Rex*? Memorable characters are rarely remembered for their likeability. The Canadian theatre's obsession back then with likeability drove me crazy, so I decided I would challenge it with a play driven almost exclusively by plot. All the characters would serve the storyline and none of them would be "likeable."

*The Ugly Man* is one of those titles that came to me along with the idea for the play. I originally subtitled the script "A Gothic Horror Melodrama," as it was meant to be a stylized satire with pop-culture references in a framework of Jacobean structure.

I'd created characters that were more or less analogous to certain characters from *The Changeling*. Villain/anti-hero De Flores was replaced with Forest, the mysterious stranger with the terribly scarred face, and the patriarch was replaced with complex Barbara Stanwyck–style anti-heroine Sabina. The young suitors from the original became doomed, likeable Acker, his shy half-brother with the cleft palate, Leslie, and their sexual mercenary boyhood friend Cole. True to the source material, there was a comic maid named Lottie.

From there I followed the plot where I wanted to and deviated where I wanted to. The ranch setting spoke to me of my rural youth, and the creepily sexy and bloody original plot gave me plenty to play with. My only rules were no nudity and no profanity, to disprove those critics who'd said my main appeal was easy shock effects.

I took the train into Toronto to stay with Bob O for a weekend, who would then drive me back to Stratford and see a few shows. He was always a gracious and patient host when I was in TO.

I did some partying that weekend and ended up at the tubs one night. An edgy, desperate air had replaced the collegial energy I remembered from my first visits. A couple of guys approached me, but when they revealed they wanted to be fucked without a condom, I demurred. As usual I ended up beating off into my towel before heading back to Bob O's.

Monday morning, while driving back to Stratford, Bob broke off whatever inanity we'd been nattering about to say, "Now look, things have changed a bit since the last time I saw you."

I knew from his tone of voice and my growing familiarity with these sorts of conversations what was to come. I said, "When did you find out?"

His eyes filmed over. "A few months ago."

"Are you okay? We can pull over."

He shook his head. "I'm good."

"You're not tempted to drive headlong into traffic and take me with you?"

He laughed, wiping at each eye with a quick finger. "No."

I put my hand on his arm. "Good."

We drove on for a while saying nothing, then from him: "I had this sore throat and my neck glands were swollen—we know what that means, right? So I got the test."

I nodded, lighting us both cigarettes and handing one to him.

"Full-out breakdown. *Why me?*" he said, making loud, comical crying sounds. "It's so weird what your body can do. I felt something different inside me, something that didn't belong there and I just—just—curled into myself."

"Any other symptoms?"

He stubbed out his cigarette in the ashtray. "Nothing so far, but we know how these things work."

I nodded.

"Look, this is just between us, right? I haven't told many people and if they found out at work . . ." He was teaching at a Catholic school.

"I'll have to tell Pete."

"Will he be okay with it?"

Pete, who'd just done an intimate show with John Moffat, was fine with it.

The highlight of the trip for Bob and me was seeing Susan Wright in a wistful but compelling production of O'Neill's *Ah Wilderness!* After he left I pounded out a rough first draft of *The Ugly Man* while Pete finished up his obligations to the festival. I was dying to get home, where we had to find a new place to live that could contain both of us.

We looked at a number of apartments before deciding on a compact two-bedroom at the Arlington, one of Edmonton's few remaining historical buildings.

We turned in our draft of *The Revenger's Tragedy*, met with the director a couple of times to refine and polish, and left her to it. Having to mine a classic text so thoroughly had been an amazing exercise and, although the production is quite rightly lost to history, working on it informed my redrafting of *The Ugly Man* significantly.

We got our first computer that fall. The next six months was a vortex of misuse, ignorance, lost files and screaming frustration, but even with all the bullshit I could see the advantages it had over the typewriter. The second draft of *The Ugly Man* was the first thing I wrote entirely on a computer. I never used my typewriter again.

We decorated the apartment for Christmas. I gave Pete an expensive camera. He gave me a vintage Batmobile he knew I wanted for my growing comic-merchandise collection. We had a quiet New Year's Eve. We watched movies and cried unashamedly at the sad parts. We wrote some comedy bits for radio stations across the country. We partied with friends, playing cards and Risk while drinking beer and smoking endless joints on those cold Edmonton nights. We got a kitten from a friend whose parents' farm cat had had a litter. We named him Spooz and spoiled him rotten in that anthropomorphically chauvinistic way many couples without children have with their pets.

That same Christmas, Randy got married. He'd been dating a hairdresser with dark sparkling hair and eyes for a couple of years, and he asked us to spend Christmas Day at his folks' place for a small wedding. As they said their "I dos" I looked at Pete. His expression was thoughtful and a bit sad.

I knew Pete was being razzed by the straight guys he worked with about our relationship, and their disapproval was just as strong as that of my gay friends whose "this guy has got to be gay or you've got to be deluded" subtext was written in neon.

A couple times a week Pete would be very late returning home. I didn't ask him about it and he never offered anything. We frequently told one another how much we loved each other. We cuddled, but we rarely sucked each other's cocks anymore.

Early in the new year, 1990, Crow's Theatre found the money to fly me to Toronto for the premiere of *Remains*. Pete was doing a show and wouldn't be able to accompany me.

I was nervous as hell. My track record in Toronto wasn't great and I had no idea what Jim Millan would do with the show. Bob O put me up, and I had a couple to days to catch up with old friends and burn through the bars before the opening.

The Poor Alex Theatre was just around the corner from Bob O's apartment in the Annex neighbourhood, and I made a point of dropping by and introducing myself to Mackenzie Gray, the producer, and the rest of the theatre staff. I was invited to the preview that night but declined for fear of how I might react if I didn't like what I saw. But later I returned to the theatre and listened to the last fifteen minutes through the crack in the door leading into the cramped auditorium. It was only a small audience, but what I heard and saw plunged me into a pit of despair. It all sounded so stagey and fake.

When I got back to Bob O's he said, "Well?"

I shook my head sadly. "I'll give you your money back if you insist." I knew he'd already purchased tickets for later in the run.

He laughed. "Oh, it can't be that bad."

"It totally could," I replied, then shut myself in the guest room and cried over the phone to Pete about how the show was sure to bomb in uptight old Toronto.

I'd invited Paul Reynolds to be my date for the opening. I'd learned he was HIV-positive and having health issues. But he'd finally found love and was genuinely happy with a man his own age. As we approached the theatre I cautioned him that I'd had no control over what we were about to see. He laughed and squeezed my hand, saying, "Darling, I never know what you're going to give us. That's why I love you." We hugged spontaneously and went into the theatre.

Jim Millan had found a truly remarkable company for his production. Brent Carver, who was a bona fide Canadian star and whom I'd seen in *Romeo and Juliet* at the Citadel when I was in high school, played David. Lenore Zann, whom I'd also seen at the Citadel, in *Hey, Marilyn!*, a rather tepid musical version of the life of Marilyn Monroe that Lenore had shone in, was engaged as Candy. Daniel Kash played Bernie; Duncan Ollerenshaw played Kane; Arlene Mazerolle played Jerri; Joe-Norman Shaw was Robert; and Kristina Nicoll played Benita. The dreary performance I'd witnessed through the crack between doors the night before was nowhere in evidence on opening. The cast was loud, hard and strong. When the laughs started in the first scene I knew we'd be okay. Everyone hung around the after-show party until very late.

This was the first time I met Susan Wright, an esteemed actress I had admired in a number of productions over the years. She, along with her sisters Janet and Anne and brother John, who lived in Edmonton, were the first Canadian family of the stage. She was Brent Carver's best friend of many years and had shown up to support him. When Brent introduced us, she was halfway through a twenty-sixer of vodka but still managed to sound sober as she complimented me on the play. At some point Brent and I staggered back to his place and crashed in his bed. When we got up the next morning the door to Susan's bedroom was open and she greeted us blearily from her rumpled bed. I felt like I'd woken up in the Canadian theatre version of Buckingham Palace.

Brent and I encountered one another frequently throughout the coming decade, and many of those encounters would culminate with us drunk and stumbling into bed. He was one of the most gifted performers I've ever known, and his interpretation of David McMillan had been, like John Moffat's, a revelation.

When I got home Pete was dying to know what I'd thought of the show. I'd been diplomatic on the phone, always telling Pete how great the performances were, because I had some serious reservations about the direction. Jim's production had ignored the play's only stage direction: "None of the actors should leave the stage unless absolutely necessary." I had stipulated this specifically because of the problems I'd encountered with the episodic structure of *Wolfboy* and its maddening blackouts.

I'd learned there are many ways to convey the passage of time and the dislocation of space on the stage without having to resort to blackouts so actors can hurry offstage and rush through frequent and pointless costume changes. In most cases the most minor of costume alterations—a sweater, a scarf, a blazer—will suffice and the audience won't be the least disturbed. In truth, the only thing the actor really has to change to indicate a shift in time or space is their attitude. I wrote *Remains* to challenge the ways we usually created theatre, and whenever someone resorted to blackouts between the staccato scenes I let my disappointment be known. But the one thing I will never deny is that Jim Millan is a brilliant producer.

For the next few days we went about our lives in the usual fashion. I picked up shifts at Chianti when we needed money and otherwise reworked *Young Art*, which I was prepping for the next Teen Fest.

I was also casting *Remains* for Workshop West. Pete was reconfirmed as Kane, Kate had agreed to play Candy—brave, considering the character was loosely based on her—and the rest of the cast was filled with Edmonton's best actors.

Five days after the show opened in Toronto, an envelope arrived from Crow's Theatre containing a photocopy of the review in the *Toronto Star*. To my surprise, the review was an unqualified rave. I read it out to Pete, emphasizing the passages that praised the originality of the script. Other reviews trickled in over the next few days and ranged from raves to raves with slight reservations.

A few mornings later the phone rang at an unusually early hour when we were still asleep. Pete answered, listened for a moment, then said "He's right here" and handed me the phone.

I squinted at him, reached for my glasses and whispered, "Who is it?"

He said, "Your agent."

I stared at him for a moment. I'd completely forgotten I had an agent.

It wasn't Ralph Zimmerman, who I'd initially signed with. It was Shain Jaffe, former stage manager, now the second member of Great North Artists Management, who handled the writers. The first thing he said to me was, "Are we still representing you?"

I shot Pete an impressed look. "Well, no one else seems to be representing me."

"What kind of contract did you sign with Crow's?"

"The standard Playwrights Guild contract."

He said, "Great. The show's a huge hit here."

I sat up in bed. "It is?"

"The whole town's talking about it. We saw it the other night. Ralph thought it would be a good idea to give you a call just to remind you that you do have an agent."

"Do you think I'll need an agent?"

"I do. Give me a call when you're more awake and we'll get to know each other better."

I hung up. Pete gave me a questioning look.

"Apparently the show's a hit."

Pete said, "What does that mean?"

I said, "I have no idea," and pulled him close, huddling back under the covers for another hour's sleep before we both had to get to our waitering jobs. Neither of us slept, though. Neither of us spoke. We both knew things were going to change.

When I spoke with Shain later it was clear he thought *Remains* could have a strong commercial life. He was smart and aggressive. I liked that. He told me he'd fly out to Edmonton to see my production of the show and we'd speak further then.

David Skelton, who always pushed me away from the representational toward the more abstract or expressionistic, came up with a set that was a sort of exploding star with plenty of triangular platforms that had to be negotiated carefully given the complex physical life of the play. There were no doors or walls, but there were areas where people could be hidden for surprise entrances and exits as needed. There were no offstage costume changes and no blackouts. Following my own dictates, none of the actors left the stage unless they absolutely had to.

This was the first production I directed that had nudity in it. All the actors knew this was something they were going to have to do when they were hired for the play. Honestly, I felt uncomfortable directing actors when they were naked, but hid it by being as clinical as possible while always keeping my eyes focused on their faces.

Shows like *Oh! Calcutta!*, a series of smutty sex sketches that ran endlessly in the seventies, and *I Love, You Baby Blue* had used nudity to force the audience to deal with the comic potential of the naked body. But I wanted to create an erotic atmosphere where the audience could believe sex was actually taking place between the characters to the point where the audience might actually become aroused. I'd always felt the stage had this potential for raw eroticism and it was rarely explored.

In the end, what made the nudity erotic was what I *didn't* allow the audience to see. Strategic lighting, carefully placed set and costume pieces and the actors' intensity made everything going on seem much more graphic than it was. One might have caught a glimpse of shaft, ass or vulva, but only very quickly. Critics have often carped that male actors shouldn't do nude sex scenes because it's so obvious they aren't hard—and getting a hard-on on cue from people who can rarely get a fake slap right is almost impossible—so I ensured the shadowy mime made people think they were seeing a lot more than they actually were.

There was a great deal of press in Edmonton before the show opened based on the reactions in Calgary and Toronto. I was on the cover page of everything.

Opening night, as I arrived fifteen minutes before curtain looking as suave as someone who looks like me can look, I felt every eye turn to me as I came down the stairs into the lobby. I had always dreamed of this moment, but now that it was happening the only thing I felt was self-conscious and pudgy.

I was tremendously proud of that production. It had a strong sense of visual and physical rhythm and the scenes were all exact and highly charged. Certain lines that were specific to Edmonton literally stopped the show. The audience stood as one at the end, and the party afterwards was full of energy and optimism. I was so busy being congratulated and fussed over that I hardly saw Pete until we left.

In the cab home I took his hand across the seat and said, "I think this is going to happen. I really do."

He smiled and squeezed my hand, saying nothing.

The reviews were laudatory, but they didn't really matter. Word of mouth from the previews had the box office phones ringing off the hook. There was no time for my usual crash after opening, as I was appearing on at least one of the local radio or television stations every day. In both Toronto and Edmonton, a secondary wave of press was starting to happen. People were now writing about the play's success as well as airing the views of those who objected to the play—and they were many. Thankfully the show also had many passionate fans and defenders who filled houses every night. For me, the most important thing was ticket sales, which were over 100 percent thanks to overflow seating.

Shain was on the phone to me every few days. The show in Toronto had been successful enough for Jim Millan to already be plotting an extension. Théâtre de Quat'Sous in Montreal had inquired about the rights in Quebec, which was quite a coup, as very few English-Canadian playwrights were produced in French.

Pete hung with the cast a lot after the show. Things between us weren't exactly strained, but I knew he was feeling like I had in Stratford the previous summer—all but invisible. Local gossip columnists were running items about something I'd said to another theatre artist, or about a prominent politician. I was already well known at most of the city's best restaurants because of my years as a waiter, but now there would be a palpable stir among the patrons in the room when Pete and I entered for a bite to eat. People said hello to me on the street. I began to get invitations to all sorts of social functions I'd been overlooked for previously. Actors and directors who were coming through town would make a point of calling up and inviting me for drinks.

I also began to make a bit of money. I splurged on a new TV, VCR and stereo. I bought Pete an expensive lens for the expensive camera I'd given him for Christmas. We no longer had to scrounge and save to have money for beer or pot. We'd do cocaine at least one night on the weekend. I went from cheap T-shirts to expensive T-shirts. It was all a lot of fun, but I could feel Pete bridling because we were spending my money, not our money.

At a party one night I met a middle-aged newly out lesbian named Peni Christopher. Peni was an assistant-editor at the *Edmonton Bullet*, the weekly alternative-press giveaway of the time. I was already quite well known for my caustic letters to the editor at various publications, and Peni felt I should have a regular column. I loved the idea and threw myself into it as much as my time would permit, doing my best to keep local columnists and critics honest by pointing out their deficiencies and hypocrisies. I was green, but I trusted my ability to turn a phrase, and Peni helped make my work more coherent than it was in first-draft form. The tone and observations of my column occasionally sent the city, and particularly the theatre community, into howls of outrage. I loved finding ways to press their buttons.

Pete was hired to do a show at the Phoenix Theatre just as I was casting *Young Art*. The dynamic of our relationship had changed radically since we'd left Calgary. Earlier we'd been a writing team who worked together, but that had evolved to his mostly working as an actor and my being hired for writing projects on my own. We still got along well, but that creative thing that we had enjoyed so much and done so well together barely existed anymore. He was becoming more withdrawn. These silences weren't sullen. They were sad. I kept waiting for him to say something.

We also remounted our production of *Remains* in my old workplace, the Roxy Theatre on 124th, which had recently been purchased by Theatre Network. I found it literarily unlikely that the place where I wrote in high school, dreaming of being a well-known writer, was about to house a production that would help make me exactly that—and yet there we were.

The theatre had barely been altered from its cinema days; basically there was now a stage where the torn screen used to be. It still had the same worn hardwood floors and the greyed, frayed seats still smelled of decades of cigarette smoke, bodily secretions and the decaying horsehair that filled them. There was no sink or dressing room backstage, but we got the show up and squeezed another well-sold month out of it.

One night after Pete got home I opened each of us a beer, switched the TV off and sat in the chair across from him—a sure sign something serious was going to happen, as we usually sat side by side on the couch. I said, "I know something's wrong."

He nodded, looking miserable.

I said, "Just say it."

He said, "I love you. I've never loved anyone the way I love you. But living together like this—I don't know if I can do it."

"Are you seeing a woman?"

He shook his head. "No. It's not that. It's—" He took a deep breath. "People are saying I'm only with you because you're doing so well."

"We're suddenly concerned about what people say?"

He laughed. Then he began to cry. Then I began to cry. I moved to the couch, took my place beside him, and we held each other and wept. Then we climbed into bed and clung together, pretending to be sleeping as we considered the future.

The next morning we were extremely careful with one another. We went for breakfast at the greasy spoon at the Ambassador Hotel down the block. As we tucked into our bacon and eggs I said, "I want the cat."

He nodded. "It'll take me a while to find a place."

"Will it bother you if we live together until then?"

"Will it bother you?"

"We don't have much choice."

"Are we going to tell people?"

I said, "Why don't we save that until you've moved out?"

He nodded and we finished our breakfast, sharing different sections of the paper as the other finished with it as we always had.

My heart was fragmenting.

# PLAYBILL

ORPHEUM THEATRE

UNIDENTIFIED HUMAN REMAINS AND THE TRUE NATURE OF LOVE

# REMAINS:
## CHICAGO/NEW YORK

FOR THE NEXT FEW MONTHS Pete and I got on with our careers while renegotiating our relationship. Luckily we were both busy. He slept on the futon in the office. The only time we saw one another was when one of us stumbled in late after rehearsal and drinks, accidentally waking the other to briefly apologize.

Young Art was the opposite of *Blood Buddies* in that it had a much smaller cast and more obviously relatable themes. A number of the kids I cast in the show were performers who'd distinguished themselves in the previous years, and the seven of them became a cohesive team despite their varying levels of experience and expectation. The three juvenile leads worked beautifully together.

The Rice Theatre at the Citadel was an intimate, malleable space that could be configured any number of ways. We made most of the audience feel like they were sitting in Merlin's lair, implements and items from different time periods and realities heaped all around them. The kids ate it up, screaming with laughter and horror when the characters' minds were transferred to the wrong bodies and Art and Lance almost kiss. The reviews were enthusiastic and it was a hit.

That spring, our adaptation of *The Revenger's Tragedy* opened and we did a bit of press together. The phone rang one afternoon; it was an arts reporter from the CBC who wanted to interview me. I reminded him the show had been adapted by both Pete and me. He said, "Yeah, but we have limited time and, frankly, Pete's not news. You are." I protested, but the reporter doubled down: it was me they wanted to talk to.

Pete was looking at me when I hung up. "What're you gonna do?" he asked.

I grabbed my jacket and said, "I'm going to do my job," and headed out to do the interview.

When a trendy downtown publicist put together a bohemian tour to New York relatively inexpensively, I leaped at the chance to go, and Randy joined me. This was pre-neo-liberalism/Disney NY, and we were just a few blocks from Times Square where Broadway and squalid danger lived side by side. The entire city smelled like someone had pissed in a cup of sugar and then set it on fire.

The first thing we did was visit the Empire State Building, which was something of a square thing to do in those days so there were no lineups. I marvelled at the beauty of the deco design and was inspecting every nook and cranny for a long time before we even took the elevator to the top. In my childhood dreams I'd always imagined myself to be the illegitimate love child of Wonder Woman and the Empire State Building. From the observation deck we could see the stunning Chrysler Building, the Flatiron, every landmark in the city. I had an architecture-inspired chubby for most of the trip.

We saw a number of Broadway shows after lining up at half-price TKTS in the morning, the best being Tyne Daly starring in

*Gypsy*—a musical even a straight guy like Randy could love because it had strippers—and the worst being *The Phantom of the Opera*, which I'd insisted on seeing to look at the tech and design. We snickered all the way through it.

In the afternoons we saw the sights or visited museums and art galleries. MoMA had a Francis Bacon retrospective I wanted to see. At night we cruised the clubs and bars, straight and gay. Randy was particularly impressed when I took him to the Stonewall Inn and told him about the riots that had started the gay rights movement. We drank to excess but were surprisingly well-behaved. He had a wife at home and I was terrified of AIDS, signs of which were everywhere. This was the most time we'd spent together in a couple of years, and we got along well.

I arrived back to find Pete had moved out and that I'd been accepted to an apprentice director program at Stratford. Pete would take care of Spooz while I was there. The Stratford experience was a bit baffling because everyone we were supposed to work with was much too busy to actually do work with us. Still, I took advantage of the classes and workshops and learned as much as I could.

The one bright spot to the entire experience was Susan Wright, who was starring in a number of shows while living in Brent Carver's house right along the river. I saw all the shows she was in, and few stage actresses have given me the kind of immense pleasure Susan did. David William, who was running the Stratford Festival at the time, once referred to her and her sister Janet as "acting continents," and I knew exactly what he meant. Often I'd go over for a late bite to eat and a lot to drink. As with so many alcoholics I've known, Susan's drunkenness went through stages. The early stage was bright and fun, the medium stage was heavier but often brilliant with observations and insights, and the late stage was either bitterness and bile or maudlin self-pity. I'd go through all of them with her as she finished a bottle of vodka and I put back a few beers.

When I got back to Edmonton I had to pick Spooz up from Pete's apartment. We parted with a stiff hug. I went into a deep depression that would eventually worry my friends. I started going back to the gay bars, which were dire. Most of the guys I'd worked with nearly a decade earlier at Boots 'n Saddle and Steppin' Out were sick, dying or dead. Old friends, old tricks, old nemeses, the beautiful, the plain, the loud, the quiet—the virus didn't discriminate.

A number of people would come out to me about testing positive, casually, over a beer at the club, almost throwing it away as if to say "now you know but we don't need to discuss it." Sometimes we'd discuss it anyway; sometimes I'd give them a reassuring sympathetic nod and we'd change the subject. A few of the guys became quite emotional and I'd give them a hug because I knew some of them had no one else to talk to. If it felt inappropriate considering the setting and the general casualness of our acquaintance, I never let it show.

Getting laid in Edmonton hadn't been easy when I was young, and now that I was over thirty it was even harder. In my time with Pete the gym had slipped away. I had put on weight and was not really dealing with my thinning hair. Sam, a baton-twirling drag queen buddy of yesteryear, had become a popular stylist, and I went to him whenever I could afford it. As he tucked the cape around me and snipped his scissors together playfully he said, "So what are you doing this time?"

I said, "My hair's really thinning. What do you suggest?"

Sam leaned over to whisper into my ear, "Start working out again and develop a better personality."

I would take his advice to heart.

Getting my body back into shape took a lot longer than the haircut. Pete and I had shared a lot of bacon, waffle and whipped cream breakfasts and even more bottles of beer during our time together. I was tipping the scales at nearly 240 pounds when we broke up and was carrying most of it in my belly and under my chin. Also I was a terrible cook and quite happy to order pizza four nights a week rather than shop for groceries. I did manage to cut the calorie count down, though, and getting back to the gym really helped.

I was on the phone with Shain a lot. Already inquiries were coming in about the movie rights for *Remains*, since the Crow's Theatre revival had been running at Theatre Passe Muraille and was selling nicely. Brent Carver eventually left that show and was replaced by John Moffat, who was happy to step into the part. Sadly, I was never in Toronto when he was doing the show, although he kept me apprised of the experience through our frequent phone calls.

That production would run for months before touring to Winnipeg, Ottawa and Mexico City where it garnered the usual love it/hate it response. A lot of well-known actors cycled through the cast, including Henry Czerny and MuchMusic VJ of the day Erica Ehm.

When *Remains* opened in Montreal, it was a big hit and things got even zanier. I never saw the Théâtre de Quat'Sous production. It was translated and directed by André Brassard, who had worked extensively with Michel Tremblay, a long-time idol of mine. Being a Western Canadian English writer with a hit show at a Montreal theatre was a real feather in my cap, and questions about other possible translations started to roll in.

I got a nice royalty cheque from that production and celebrated by buying myself a beautiful Avirex distressed-leather biker jacket for the ungodly sum of $1,000 at a trendy store. This jacket would become my signature for the next decade.

One afternoon I was writing when the phone rang.

"Hi, Brad, it's [Well-fed female gossip columnist/arts writer for the local right-wing tabloid]. How are you?"

"Great, [Well-fed female gossip columnist/arts writer for the local right-wing tabloid]. What's going on?"

"I hear you're single."

"That's old news."

"I hear he left you for a woman."

"Who do you think you are, fucking Hedda Hopper?"

"So is that a no or you don't know?"

"If you run a 'straight actor leaves gay playwright for woman' item I will write the meanest thing about you in the *Bullet* I can think of. And you know how mean I can be."

She giggled nervously. "So, any word on a New York production?"

I said, grudgingly, "Let's just say there might be something happening in Chicago."

"Chicago?" Her interest was real.

"I can't say anything else but when we've signed something you'll be the first to know."

"I'd appreciate that."

We exchanged a few neutral pleasantries and hung up. In her column the next day there was an item about rumours of a Chicago production of *Remains*, but nothing about Pete. And when the time came and the contract was signed, I did call her first and give her the scoop.

Alberta Theatre Projects did a staged reading of *The Ugly Man* as part of its new play festival that was good enough to get Michael Dobbin to commit to it for the following year's playRites Festival.

Life in the Arlington sans Pete was getting scary. The building had been set on fire three times since we'd moved in, and the antiquated steam heat would often go out on the coldest winter nights. Also I couldn't live with the carpet in the bathroom anymore. So I rented a tiny bungalow on the north side of town and impulsively bought a kitten dubbed Sushi to keep Spooz company as I was away so much. They eventually became inseperable and Sushi was always Spooz's cat, rather than mine.

Shain finally nailed down the New York deal, and the details of the Chicago tryout were taking shape. Derek Goldby, whose stunning production of *Cyrano de Bergerac* I'd seen at the Shaw Festival a few years earlier, was hired to direct. The main producer, Michael Frazier, and one of his three other producing partners called me to express their admiration for the play and their belief it could have a life in New York. At one point Michael said to me, "Don't be offended but I have to ask, are you gay?"

I said, "Have you read the play?"

We all laughed. As it turned out, they were all gay as well.

A lot of names were bandied around for casting, with Brad Davis and Tom Hulce being the top contenders for David. I would have been happy with either. Davis was sexy as fuck and read as very sexually ambiguous. I hadn't thought much of *Querelle* as a film, but I had loved Davis in it. Hulce had been brilliant in his Oscar-nominated role in *Amadeus*. Someone suggested Madonna for Benita, but that was in the days when someone suggested Madonna for pretty much anything. John Moffat's intermittent health issues kept him out of the running. I suggested Brent, but the producers said they could only bring one Canadian in for the show and they all loved Lenore Zann (as Candy) and were going with her. I told them I thought they were making a mistake not hiring Brent. In the end Scott Renderer, who worked a lot with the experimental Wooster Group at the time, got the part.

A few months later it was announced in the press that Brad Davis was sick with AIDS. He died a short time later.

Paul Reynolds, who I had not spoken to in months because he'd sounded so weak the last time I'd called, also died around that time. Pete was working in Toronto and called to tell me as soon as he heard. Pete, more than any of the straight people I knew, saw the effects of the plague close up and was always empathetic and supportive. Eventually I thanked him and said, "I love you." He said, "I love you too."

In Chicago we out-of-towners were housed in the historic Roosevelt Hotel, an enormous wedding-cake-shaped late nineteenth-century marvel with huge suites that were still in original condition and mostly filled with elderly people who lived there permanently. It was a short and scenic walk to the Halsted Theatre Centre where the show would open in four weeks.

The morning I arrived, which was also the morning the Gulf War was started by the first Bush in the White House—a subject Derek had gotten into a bitter argument about with our cab driver in from the airport—we were whisked off to a press conference at the theatre. I was kind of blown away. We were sitting at a table with quite a number of press people lobbing questions at us about the play. Once I calmed down I managed to be witty and irreverent to counteract how stuffy Derek and some of the producers sounded. I also sensed a certain holding back from the reporters, a slight edge of disapproval. When I asked Michael Frazier about it later he said, "We're in shit because we don't have any Chicago actors in the show." I smiled and nodded but inside I was rolling my eyes. Opening a show in a major city without the support of the local community can be a problem.

After the press conference we were taken to the rehearsal hall for our introductory meeting with all creative and administrative personnel gathered together for the first time. This was completely unlike the play's Canadian first-day counterpart because the sales, advertising and promotion teams got as much time to present their contribution as the design and directorial teams did. Meetings were set up for me to talk to the sales team about my ideas for customer outreach.

After finding food and drink, we reconvened in the rehearsal hall around the long table where the reading would take place. At the assigned time everyone who was required to be there was seated and ready to go, except for Lenore and Michelle Kronin, who had been cast as Jerri. Five minutes past the assigned time we were all wondering what the holdup was. Then Lenore and Michelle entered wearing nothing but high heels. The women took their seats primly and the reading began. I loved them both for doing that because they set a tone of "anything goes" for the production from the outset and made things easier for everyone, especially the nudity.

Chicago had a chip-on-its-shoulder prairie attitude I recognized. I did my usual architecture tours and neighbourhood walkabouts. I went to the Chicago Art Institute and fought back tears of some undefined emotion that made my chest tight as I toured its exhaustive collection of impressionist masterpieces.

Late one night while I was lying in bed listening to music, I became aware of another, discordant sound. I pulled off my headphones and realized the fire alarm was ringing. I leaped out of bed and pulled on my clothes. I could hear approaching sirens. I opened the door and peered into the hall. There was a thin haze of smoke in the air. I grabbed my jacket and key and left my room.

As I moved into the hall I saw there were probably fifteen to twenty elderly people wandering around in confusion while making quietly alarmed sounds. My impulse was to run to the stairwell, but my comic-book-imposed morality said, "Brad, you have to help these senior citizens." After all, that was what Superman, Wonder Woman or Batman would do.

I clapped my hands to get their attention. I knew there were emergency stairwells on each side of the building. I arbitrarily chose the exit to the right and called for everyone in the vicinity to follow me. The smoke was getting thicker. It was clear the seniors had been looking for someone to take control, and they fell into line quickly as I led them to the stairs and ushered them down the seven stories to the lobby. All around us we could hear people shouting in confusion. The lights in the stairwell flickered. The reek of smoke was everywhere.

I finally got them to the door to the lobby and pushed the handle only to discover the emergency exit was locked. I banged on the door, but there was no response from the other side. I yelled for the seniors to turn around, we had to go back up one floor. There were cries of frustration and confusion. I herded them through the door and down the hall to the stairs on the other side. I felt like I was in the fucking *Poseidon Adventure*.

This time the door opened onto the lobby and the seniors all pushed past me and streamed out of the hotel without an acknowledgement of any kind.

I went up to a nearby doorman, pointed to the emergency exit door and yelled, "That fucking door is locked!"

He looked panicked. "What?"

"If the fire had been worse we'd all be dead."

He paled and nodded to indicate the head of security, who was speaking to the head fireman. "I'll let him know," he said. I joined the other hotel guests on the street. Eventually we were given an all-clear and sent back to our rooms.

Although I was there for early previews, I never saw the opening. They still had two weeks to go when I had to fly back to Edmonton to direct another Teen Fest show, a musical I'd been working on called *Prom Night of the Living Dead*.

*Remains* opened to what could be called, at best, grudgingly acceptable reviews by most of the local critics. No one was full of praise for the show. The producers were disappointed because they'd wanted raves to carry them into New York. Optimistic publicists kept reminding us we had "excellent pull quotes" (out-of-context quotes from mixed reviews that made the critic's opinion sound better).

On the phone Shain said to me, "Let's wait and see."

I was the reigning Edmonton media star when Robin Phillips took over as the artistic director of the Citadel Theatre while we were rehearsing for the Teen Fest.

Canadian arts institutions had to that point invariably been placed in the hands of usually mediocre English or American talents with a moderate resumé, because anyone Canadian would've seemed unqualified to them. While some, like Tyrone Guthrie in establishing the Stratford Festival, John Neville in his leadership of various regionals, or Christopher Newton and the opportunities he'd give to the Canadian actors and directors at the Vancouver Playhouse and the Shaw Festival, actually contributed something to the cultural fabric of this country, far too many of them were men of dubious talent whose privileged birthrights had elevated them in a new country to a level they would not have been afforded in their own. For most of its history these sorts of losers set policy for the Canadian arts. It was only near the end of the twentieth century that Canadians finally started taking control of their own national arts organizations, although our sad national inferiority complex is still too evident today.

Robin Phillips had a spotty history in Britain for direction and had made a wan impression as an actor in the 1972 Joan Collins vehicle *Tales from the Crypt*. After some time as the AD of the Chichester Festival in England, he had arrived in Stratford and taken over the festival, where he'd achieve great acclaim from the critics, who, it must be said, tended to be a rather provincial and fawning lot of Caucasians. Whether the questionable Canadian press contingent were accurate in their reviews of his work at Stratford, I don't know. I do know that by the time Robin arrived at the Citadel, his career was winding down or he wouldn't've been in Edmonton.

Everyone working at the theatre was summoned to individual meetings with La Phillips. I was hoping we'd like one another a lot and he'd hire me to direct in the season, and went in with my charm button turned up high. Robin greeted me from the other side of his desk with a sweet smile. We chatted brightly. I asked how he was finding Edmonton. He congratulated me on the success of my *Remains*. I could feel something—a barely concealed vibe of resentment and condescension. Finally he said, "The thing is, Brad, we have a bit of a problem."

This took me off guard. "Problem?"

He leaned across the desk with a slow, thin-lipped smile. "Yes. You see, *The Mousetrap*"—the perennial Agatha Christie production that was currently running in the Shoctor Theatre where we were scheduled to perform—"has been doing awfully well at the box office. So well, in fact, we have to cancel both your technical and dress rehearsal to add two extra shows which will make us a lot of money. I'm sure you understand."

I said, "You realize we're opening a musical featuring fifty young, amateur actors with four trucks"—large moveable set pieces—"and five traps"—trap doors in the floor for exits, entrances and effects—"as well as numerous microphones and both live and synthesized orchestrations that will require hours of practice?"

Robin tented his fingertips and gave me another iguana smile. "It's only a teen festival, darling. No one really cares."

I gave him an equally reptilian smile as I said, "I care. The creative team cares. Those kids care. We've been working on it for months. You're not going to take our tech time away."

Robin said, "If you're not happy with that we can always fire you."

From the look in his eyes I knew he was used to people who capitulated. I said, "I'm going to get the cast and we're going to leave now. We'll come back when you've got a better offer." I gave him a friendly smile, returned to the rehearsal hall and told the cast and crew exactly what had happened. Then we walked out of the theatre together.

I knew the pre-sales for the show were high and that the cast wouldn't go on without my consent. In the long run the theatre stood to lose more money from cancelled shows at the teen festival than they did by losing an extended performance of *The Mousetrap*.

After three days the Citadel's producer sent me a diplomatic letter suggesting my meeting with Robin had been a misunderstanding and that we should speak as soon as possible. I wrote back that if that fat has-been was willing to apologize, I could probably convince the cast and crew to return. No apology was forthcoming, but we came to a compromise that lost none of our technical time because it was moved and they got one extra show. This could've been solved in the original meeting if Phillips hadn't wanted a dickdown. I'm not sure why he chose to approach me that way, but I had made a mildly powerful enemy in Robin Phillips.

To occupy my mind while waiting for word on the possible New York production, I waged a war with him in the Edmonton media. The entire local arts-writer clique had basically bowed down to him as he made abundantly clear what he would tolerate (flattery) and what he would not (valid criticism). While they were almost all guilty of this, the main reviewer for the *Edmonton Journal* basically crawled up his ass and stayed there for the duration of Robin's time at the Citadel. At one point he had me banned from attending the theatre. I ignored his ban gleefully.

A couple of days after *Prom Night of the Living Dead* closed, I got a phone call from Shain, and two days later there was a story in the papers saying that the producers of *Remains* had secured more backers in New York and the play would open off-Broadway at the Orpheum Theatre in September. It was huge news across the country.

I spent the intervening months polishing *The Ugly Man*, being a local celebrity and having the occasional dalliance with homosexuals travelling through town. The annual arrival of the Ice Capades tour was highly anticipated by local tops in the same way grizzlies anticipate the spawning of salmon.

Randy and his wife had, by sheer happenstance, rented a bungalow just like mine a few blocks away. I called him the night before I left for New York and asked him to come over. We drank beer and I poured out my fear of failure, of being made fun of.

He put his arm around my shoulders and said, "Birdley"— which he only called me when he was drinking and wanted to be affectionate—"you've been working for this from the day I met you. You can do it."

"I'm scared."

He pulled me closer, ran his hand over my nearly shaved head, tapped my chest with two fingers and said, quoting my own words from *Wolfboy* back at me, "If it's not scary it's not worth doing."

I arrived in New York in mid-August 1991, when the entire city was wilting beneath a heat wave that made everyone bitchy. The producers had found me a hideous one-bedroom sublet in Hell's Kitchen, a festival of shag carpeting, dusty bookshelves and furtive cockroaches lingering just always on the edge of your vision, with a small bedroom that led to a smaller bathroom.

We rehearsed in a thirties building on Broadway about halfway to the theatre, which was in the East Village. There was no air conditioning, and the giant fans that had been set up did little to alleviate the fetid humidity that permeated the city. Most of the actors couldn't wait to take their clothes off. Derek sat shirtless, sweating like an angry cave troll, smoking and waving his hand, calling out to the frustrated actors in his dry English accent, "No. No. For fuck's sake, no. Stop talking. Think about what you're saying."

We took our breaks on the wide stone ledge of the gigantic windows that overlooked the avenue, fearlessly ignoring the thirty-storey drop. I get retro-vertigo thinking about it now.

There had been changes to the cast since Chicago. The cast we finally opened with in New York had Scott Renderer as David, Lenore Zann as Candy, Kimberley Pistone as Benita, Clark Gregg (Marvel's Agent Coulson) as Bernie, Sam Rockwell (later Oscar winner for *Three Billboards Outside Ebbing, Missouri*) as Robert, Michael Connor as Kane, and Michelle Kronin as Jerri.

I had done a number of small but significant rewrites between Chicago and New York and they were integrated into the new production.

Stage Manager George Boyd was a rangy Texan with a grizzled beard and beautiful laugh lines that ringed his face. He was a showbiz veteran as well as a rare survivor of his generation of New York theatrical gays. He was also my pot connection, and we'd usually get high together after rehearsal. He was an old friend of, and staying with, Marge Champion, wife and dance partner of Gower Champion. Marge and Gower had been stars of stage and screen as one of America's most accomplished dance couples for decades in the early to mid-twentieth century.

Some of my fondest memories of this time are of the evenings George and I would meet in Marge's mid-town condo—on the fiftieth floor of a seventies building that was beautifully appointed in that "gilt and mirror" way New Yorkers love so much—getting high while George regaled me with stories of New York during its pig-slut years in the seventies and early eighties, before AIDS.

One night I asked him, "How many did you lose?"

George said, "All of them."

I tried to hand him the joint but he waved it away and stared out the window.

The publicist had me doing interviews all over town. I finally appeared in *Blueboy* magazine, the gay equivalent of *Playboy*, achieving a seventies gay dream just before the mag failed, wearing torn jean cut-offs, heavy socks and high-tops, a green T-shirt and bad hair—perfectly exemplifying the beginning of the 1990s.

The rest of the time I had to myself, but I didn't have much money. Thankfully, Tad showed up.

When a Canadian gay dude gets a gig in New York that includes an apartment, you can be sure his erratically seen flight attendant friend will make an appearance. Tad had relocated to Toronto just before I moved back to Edmonton, and though we spoke on the phone quite often we hadn't spent any real time together in a couple of years. He had fallen in love with a former model, and nursed the model as he slowly died of AIDS. I had not seen him at all through that period.

I was happy to have a friend to explore the bars and sex scene with. At that time, the only scene was basically J's Hangout near the West Side Highway, a dark, unlicensed (you could bring your own beer) check-your-clothes-and-suck-cock-all-night-long kinda place. I went once but it wasn't really my scene. Tad was there every night.

When *Remains* finally went into three weeks of previews at the Orpheum, Tad saw the first public presentation of the play in New York. Like a great many of my truest friends, Tad had no connection to the theatre at all. The only theatre he'd ever seen or been interested in was mine, because I forced him to go. People like Tad were the ones whose opinions I valued the most, because I knew they would give me their unvarnished truth.

Of *Remains* he said, "Wow, Brad, you made me feel like we were back in Edmonton again."

Previews were not without their tensions, and the producers were a bit spooked by how the early audiences were reacting. Were there meant to be that many laughs? I assured them there were, that the play was constructed to constantly challenge the line between comedy and tragedy, between commentary and exploitation. Derek knew what he was doing, but most of the cast were slow to catch on. A number of the actors were playing with radically different acting styles and, in doing so, were sacrificing the rhythm and precision of the lines and exchanges to their own "method" acting styles, which doesn't work with my stuff. It was driving me crazy, although Derek kept telling me not to worry; he'd get them all on the same page before opening.

The night before Tad was to leave we did a bar crawl and ended up trolling a couple of the gay porn theatres on Eighth Avenue. On the way back to the apartment, Tad insisted on stopping at a twenty-four-hour deli for something to eat. He took his turkey sandwich back to the apartment and ate it as we had a final beer. "Want some?" he asked, brandishing the half-eaten sandwich dripping mayo. I waved it away. We finished our drinks and staggered to bed.

I'd only been asleep for a few hours when there was an urgent knock at the bedroom door. "What?" I said.

Tad raced through the bedroom to the bathroom and slammed the door. I heard him groan like a woman going into labour, followed by the firehose gush of his bowels. When he was finally done, the apartment smelled like an outhouse filled with florid corpses, making my eyes water..

"You okay?"

Tad moaned, "I think I've got food poisoning."

He was meant to leave later that day, but called in sick. Because he needed constant access to the bathroom, I moved him into the bedroom and slept on the hide-a-bed in the living room. We were both hoping it would clear up in a day or two.

No such luck. After five days the apartment was becoming a depressing place to hang out in. I tried to tempt him with soup, crackers, fruit and other light snacks to keep his strength up, but he could only handle water. He seemed to be losing pounds a day. One night I was wakened by his voice. I sat up in bed listening as he had an unconscious, garbled discussion with his recently dead partner. Eventually he slept, but I didn't.

One night I went to a party promoting the show at the

Limelight, the legendary nightclub in a historic Catholic church, notoriously run by Canadian Peter Gatien, who would get into all kinds of legal trouble a short time later. I was obligated to attend this event regardless of how Tad was feeling. I didn't have money for big-time nightclubbing, so I was primed for a good time, as the party was on the house.

The entire cast came, the DJ made some announcement, tickets were given away, and I was introduced to a great many people who were impressed to know my play was opening off-Broadway. In those days we smoked weed in New York bars and on the streets unabashedly, and I was pretty lit after a few hours.

The reporter who'd interviewed me for *Blueboy* was there, commiserating as I told him about Tad wasting away in my sublet. He took my hand, said, "Come with me," and led me across the dance floor, through a doorway and up a series of stairwells that led to the top of the steeple. When we got to the door at the top of the stairs, he smiled and motioned for me to go through as he left.

I walked into a long, narrow passage that followed the apex of the roofline. It was dim but not dark, and I could make out rooms on either side of me, open to the passageway, in which groupings of people were lounging, drinking, shooting drugs and generally being as New York as fuck. Gay, straight, male, female, trans, all ages, all races, everyone was represented. As I moved down the corridor the activities in the rooms became more sexual. In one room a man had a woman over his lap. Her pants were pulled down and he was lightly smacking her ass while she sucked the cock of a guy sitting right next to them and staring into space indifferently. On the other side a tall drag queen was ass-to-crotch grind dancing with a butch woman with pierced nipples. An open doorway was ahead of me and a dark room beyond it. I stepped through.

This was a larger room with absolutely no light, although as my eyes adjusted I could make out dim forms. The air was oily with the smells of cock, cunt, ass, sperm and various other bodily secretions. Every imaginable kind of coupling was going on around me without regard to labels like "straight" or "gay."

Leaning against the wall next to me was a tall, muscular man with his pants pushed down to his thighs stroking an enormous cock. I was so hard I ached, but this was AIDS central. I couldn't tell in this light if condoms were being used, and that turned me on even more. The tall man with the giant dong lightly touched my thigh. I gathered up my last bit of self-control and hurried back to the party downstairs.

Cam arrived the next afternoon. I brought him up to date with what was happening with Tad, and they shared a quick hello through the bedroom door. Oddly, they'd never met before, although both had heard plenty about the other. Cam came with money to spend and was very generous, taking me out for meals and to clubs he'd always wanted to check out. I got him into my show the night he arrived. He was genuinely blown away by the experience.

At this time neither of us was the willowy boy we'd each been when we'd met. I was still packing an extra ten pounds at 210, and Cam had been working out and taking steroids and so was just as big. The double hide-a-bed wasn't big enough, but we'd slept together many times over the years so it wasn't a big deal.

Both of us were pretty drunk after a crawl through the Village and a late-night meal when we stripped to our underwear and climbed into bed. We turned our backs to one another. After a while I could tell he wasn't sleeping.

Finally Cam said, "How does it feel?"

I rolled onto my back, got a cigarette from the coffee table and set the ashtray on the arm of the couch. "It's a lot less glamorous than I expected—as you can tell."

As if on cue, Tad moaned quietly in his sleep from the bedroom.

"But you're opening a show in New York!"

I nodded.

"I can't help being jealous."

I nodded.

"You know—thinking what if I hadn't become a hairdresser? What if I'd followed my dream? Maybe it'd be me here."

"You make amazing money. You have lots of friends and a boyfriend."

"I know," Cam said. "But everyone's talking about you in Canada. You're in the news all the time."

"And I'm living in a squalid Times Square apartment sharing a hide-a-bed with a girlfriend while another one croaks in the bedroom."

He took the cigarette from me and inhaled deeply. I gaped. He'd quit smoking years ago. He waved my concern off casually and handed the smoke back to me. "I just needed a drag."

"Why?"

"I have AIDS."

I'd known what he was going to say before he said it but it still made my eyes sting.

"It's why I left Edmonton."

I sat up in the bed. "You've known that long?"

"Oh yeah. I was one of the first guys diagnosed. But I never told anyone.

"Why not?"

"Because I didn't want it to be what I'm about. I planned to tell people if I got sick and they had to know, but I didn't get sick so . . ."

I put my arm around him and he leaned back into my shoulder. "Are you getting sick now?"

"I had a lung problem a few months ago and my viral count is high. I'm going on some new meds when I get home." There was a moment of silence, and then Cam said, "I'm pretty sure I got it from Benny."

I wondered how many people had been infected by the well-travelled Benny and, again, why I hadn't.

After a few minutes he pulled away. I could tell he was crying, so I put one hand on his shoulder and just left it there. I took a long, angry drag on my cigarette and listened to the sibilant sizzle of the tobacco and paper burning.

In the bedroom, delirious Tad called out for his lover and whimpered.

Tad recovered and they both left two days later. I did my best to launder everything and air out the apartment, grateful to be on my own again.

As we got closer to opening, the show started to come together. Derek was very good with notes on the actors' performances and speaking to them in a way that was always challenging but enlightening. There was a buzz around town about the show, but it wasn't all positive. Even before opening there were whispers that the show was homophobic, misogynist and unnecessarily brutal.

My schedule had amped up considerably, with meetings, interviews and photo shoots occupying most days. A number of agents had seen the show and wanted to meet with me, as well as a few film producers. Everyone was interested to see the response when it opened. I did my best to be authentic and charming in every meeting and interview. I'd learned something about handling the press, and I didn't want to antagonize anyone needlessly. I bit my tongue whenever I wanted to make a smart-ass, glib quip. The image I projected was urbane and edgy, even if inside I might've felt like a hick kid from the country.

As I was leaving a preview one day, Michael Frazier, the main producer, called me over. He was standing with two handsome, rich-looking middle-aged gay men. Michael said, "Brad, I want you to meet my friend Michael—"

"Michael Cristofer," I said, taking the hand of the man he indicated and shaking it vigorously. I knew exactly who he was. "Author of *The Shadow Box*. I'm so pleased to meet you."

Michael Cristofer introduced me to his partner. They both said encouraging things about the play. I said, "I can't tell you how much that means to me. Your play was a huge stylistic influence on this one."

He gave me a sardonic smile and said archly, "It certainly was."

I was horrified that he might think I'd plagiarized something from his show. He laughed to let me know he was joking and said, "You took it much further than I did. Congratulations."

He was charming and supportive and I was glad I had met him. All playwrights echo within one another.

Every few days I'd call Shain. He was getting production inquiries from Britain, Japan, Italy and other countries.

A number of friends from Edmonton came to the opening, although there was no Canadian press at the show. Randy wasn't able to come, although he did send flowers. Everyone was keyed up and excited to be at an actual opening in NYC and wore their very best. I wore a black T-shirt, jeans, boots and my leather jacket, as it was now September and the city had cooled considerably. I was glad my Edmo homies had made it and took great pride in introducing them to the cast and crew.

There was a poncy after-party at an East Village restaurant, and the publicist took me around the room and introduced me to everybody. The real standouts for me were famed drag queen Hedda Lettuce; Michael Musto, who was a long-time writer for the *Village Voice*; and playwright/actor/drag performer/national gift Charles Busch, whose subversive off-Broadway cult hits I'd been reading about for years.

The crowning meeting of the night, though, was being introduced to Quentin Crisp, author of *The Naked Civil Servant* and queer icon. I truly was meeting a legend. He held his hand out and I wasn't sure whether to shake it or kiss it so I just kinda touched it with my hand and asked the one question I *never* ask anyone at an opening party: "Did you like the show?"

Mr. Crisp said, "Oh no. No, not at all. Far too scary for me. All that blood and sex. No. No."

I said, "O-kay. Thanks for your candour."

He smiled and leaned in, putting his hand on my shoulder. "You're from Edmonton, Alberta, correct?"

"That's right."

"Do you by chance know a Ronnie Wigmore?"

I looked at him in shock. "Yes! I've done a couple of shows with Ron at the Walterdale. He's the voice announcing the beginning of the show and the end of intermission at the Jubilee Auditorium, Edmonton's largest touring theatre. Why?"

"I knew him in London years ago. He was a mod. Oh, we got up to some fun, Ronnie and I."

My jaw must have dropped. The Ron Wigmore I knew was a rotund middle-aged man with a red face and thinning hair, affable and a bit of a ham, happily married with a daughter.

"Do say hi to him for me, would you? We had such fun," Crisp repeated, then turned back to his companion.

Sometime later I saw Ron Wigmore at some theatre function and related this encounter to him. His face flushed nearly purple and he laughed with an infectious, plosive surprise, slapping my shoulder too hard and whispering in my ear, "We all sowed our wild oats, my friend. That's what being young is for."

Someone invited me into the bathroom. We smoked something I drunkenly thought was pot but suspect was actually crack and I was off my nut for the rest of the night. Thankfully my Edmo friends knew how to get me home before things got messy.

I was slated to fly out mid-afternoon the next day. I was hungover when I woke up and grumpy. When I met the Edmo gang for breakfast I made it clear I was not reading the reviews and there would be no talk of the show. I wanted to leave New York and this experience feeling good about both. The reviews could wait a day or two while I recovered.

Du 22 mars au 17 avril 1993

# L'HOMME LAID

# PART THREE

# THE UGLY MAN

THE NEW YORK REVIEWS FOR *Remains*, particularly from the dailies, were not great. While certain elements of the show were praised, other elements left the reviewers cold. The *New York Times* didn't like it at all, which would remain true of everything I wrote after. The weeklies and glossies were kinder. The *Time* magazine review that came out in the second week was a rave, and later in the year *Remains* would be in their top ten plays of the year.

The Canadian press seemed to take delight in the less-than-laudatory reception the play was getting, giving birth to a number of articles dedicated to why it wasn't a hit. The *Globe and Mail*, true to form, ran a blurb about the opening and identified me as Bud Fraser.

The producers were committed to making it work and spent money on promotion to counteract the more hostile reviews. I found many of those reviews had a patronizing "isn't it cute when Canadians write about sex" tone that said more about American hang-ups than ours. Ticket sales were brisk for the first five weeks, then began to drop off. A couple of cast members left and were replaced by actors who turned out to be every bit as good as the people they'd replaced.

It was announced that I was one of the winners of Toronto's prestigious Chalmers Award for best new play. The prize included a couple of nights at a good hotel, a celebratory dinner and a cash prize of $10,000. (Cash has always been my favourite prize.) The award got the show more international attention but didn't help much in Manhattan.

*Remains* got through nearly three months of performances before quietly closing. Late in the run, the producers had called Shain and told him they wouldn't be able to continue running the show if they were required to pay me the very small amount I was receiving weekly. They could run the show for a couple more months if I'd give up my royalties. No one else was being asked to defer their livelihood to keep the show running, so I declined. After the show closed *Stomp* moved into the theatre and ran for years. Oh, to have had that sort of success in New York.

Because the show closed just shy of the deadline that would've given the producers a major slice of my rights to *Remains*, I came out retaining full ownership. This would prove crucial if I were to find myself negotiating film rights. I'd been talking to potential producers from the moment the show opened in New York, and their interest wasn't at all dulled by the mixed reviews. The filmic possibilities were inherent in the play from the very beginning.

Before I left New York I met with a few producers' representatives who wanted to buy me lunch at some swank restaurant I mostly felt uncomfortable in and blow smoke up my ass, which I was also uncomfortable with. When I got home, Shain was constantly calling me to hook up introductory calls with studio reps. My fave conversation made the subtext of nearly every discussion I'd had so far vividly clear:

Producer—"Hey, Brad, it's [NAME REDACTED]. I produce for [STUDIO REDACTED] and I just want to say I saw the show in New York and I was blown away, man."

Me—"Thanks, [NAME REDACTED]. Nice of you to say so."

Producer—"It's so now, you know. I mean it's really in the zeitgeist—serial killers, prostitutes, urban legends, it is *today*."

Me—"Thanks."

Producer—"I see this film, Brad. I see it. And it's a money-maker. But there's just one thing, Brad."

Me—"What's that?"

Producer—"Hey, I'm an open-minded guy. Maybe I've even, you know, walked on the wild side or something. But we're talking money here so I'm just going to ask—how would you feel if we made David straight?"

I paused, not because I was considering anything but because I wanted him to think about what he'd just said.

Producer—"You there, Brad?"

Me—"I am."

Producer—"I've offended you."

Me—"You've made it clear why you're not the person for this film."

I thanked him for his interest and hung up the phone.

I hated, HATED, the erasure of queer people by the majority on any level, and making David straight would be the most profound betrayal I could inflict on queer people. If David couldn't be gay, there would be no movie.

Another afternoon Shain rang me and said, "Denys Arcand wants to talk to you."

There was a flutter of excitement in my belly. I'd loved *Jesus of Montreal* and had great respect for *The Decline of the American*

*Empire*. Arcand was an internationally recognized director and a Palme d'Or winner. He seemed the perfect fit for the *Remains* adaptation. I couldn't wait to speak with him and told Shain to give him my number. Shain also revealed that despite its short run in New York, *Remains* was being picked up in a great many other places.

I was having lunch with Pete one day as I related all of this to him. He shook his head in disbelief.

I said, "It's really happening. The play's a worldwide hit."

He said, "Be careful. You know what they say about being at the top."

"I get it," I said. "Nothing lasts forever. Just give me ten years. That's all I ask."

He smiled, but behind it I could see that flare of resentment I'd been seeing in the eyes of many of my peers around Edmonton. When the play had been listed in *Time*'s top ten it had made national news and I was getting calls to appear on pop-culture commentary panels on various TV and radio stations. I did everything I was asked to do with good humour. It rarely paid, but I was usually promoting a project of my own and it helped my profile. I was known as a good guest, articulate, blunt and often humorous. I was the right gay dude with an attitude and edge at the right time.

Denys and producer Roger Frappier flew me to Montreal for a couple of days, wining, dining and charming me with their plans for the film. They wanted me to write the screenplay and they wanted to honour the production they'd seen at Quat'Sous. By the time I'd flown back home Shain had started negotiating a contract.

Movie contracts are a nightmare of minutiae and theoreticals; the one thing I insisted on was retaining the rights to the play. The film had a very healthy budget for the time and I was well paid, but it wasn't enough to get me to share or sign over the stage rights. The production company agreed and the deal was signed.

Denys Arcand is one of the most articulate, charming, talented people I have ever met. As I wrote the script over the next six months, he would make frequent encouraging phone calls, offering all sorts of helpful suggestions to make it more filmic.

In early December I flew to Calgary as we started rehearsals at ATP for *The Ugly Man*. Casting the show had been problematic because of the commitment and location. This was often the case when casting on the prairies, where the actor pool was more limited. The cast were a mixed lot, although Pete stood out as the damaged brother with the cleft palate. After the first week I was no longer required, so I flew back to Edmonton to continue to work on the *Remains* screenplay.

Shortly after New Year's, Pete phoned me. He was sobbing and said some words that made no sense at all. I tried to suck air into my lungs. My eyes hurt.

"What did you say?"

"There was a house fire. Susan died."

Even with so many gay men dying around me, Susan Wright's accidental death in Stratford was still beyond shocking. She'd come home late one night and fallen asleep on a daybed on the main floor. A space heater had been too close to the blankets. Her parents, who were visiting, died in the same fire. The community was stunned. Brent was stricken. Canadian theatre had lost one of its most amazing talents.

It was a terrible way to bring in 1992.

That January, *Playboy* listed the Chicago production of *Remains* in its year-end roundup of sex in the media, which pleased me more than most of the awards the show had won.

*The Ugly Man* was just about to go into tech when I returned to Calgary. That year, all the shows were done on a thrust stage (protrudes into the audience, who sit on three sides of the stage), which worked well considering the show's Jacobean source material. Bob kept the pace moving along nicely and had a good time with the murders, which were as graphic as the show would get. The reviewer for the *Calgary Herald* wrote, "I have seen the future of English-Canadian theatre and it is Brad Fraser."

On my return home it was publicly announced that the *Remains* movie would be made by Denys Arcand. It was big news. The British production of the play, featuring Dougray Scott as David, produced by the Traverse Theatre in Edinburgh and then transferred to the highly respected Hampstead Theatre in London, was a huge hit and generated a lot of buzz. It would eventually win me a London Evening Standard Theatre Award for Most Promising Playwright, putting me in the company of my hero Joe Orton, who had won the Best Play award twenty-odd years earlier. Around the same time, a Japanese production opened in Tokyo, so the play was all over the news. All this offset the overall reaction to *The Ugly Man*, which, as I'd expected, was criticized for not having any "likeable" characters.

Late that winter *Saturday Night* magazine, which was quite huge at the time as Canada's slightly arty-literary/pop-culture magazine, contacted Shain to ask me to be on the cover of their May issue. I was elated. This was big-time. The only thing better would've been being asked to be on the long-running Canadian panel game show *Front Page Challenge*. Sadly, that never happened.

I flew back and forth between Edmonton, Toronto and Montreal so much I began to feel like I was living in all three cities. On one of those trips to Montreal I had arranged to finally meet Pierre Bernard, the AD of Quat'Sous, and Maryse Warda, the brilliant dramaturge I'd been corresponding with for a couple of years by then. I loved the theatre and its people immediately and was always tremendously proud of my association with them. Pierre promised to read *The Ugly Man* and get back to me about a possible production.

Meanwhile, my generation of gay men, and members of minority groups all over the planet, were dying in droves.

Sam, the hairdresser who'd given me such good advice about being nicer and working out more, had died. His ex, Russ, whom I'd known since I first came out, was sick as fuck and being cared for by his bewildered family. Every time I went to the bar someone would give me the bad news about someone we both knew.

And always there was someone in the bar who was manifesting visible symptoms of the disease: skin lesions, extreme weight loss, palsied limbs. These people stayed in the darker corners with the friends who'd brought them, both visible and ignored within a social structure that was almost entirely based on health and beauty.

One night at the Roost, the hairy Greek bartender who'd been unsuccessfully cruising me for twelve years handed me my change for a beer and whispered, "You hear about Benny?"

I shook my head.

"About a week ago. His lover died last night."

I tipped him too much and walked away, pushing my grief and fear and pain into the compartment I'd made for them over the last few years. It felt like pieces of my life were disappearing.

A few months later John Moffat called to tell me his lover Larry Lillo had died. The theatre community across the country mourned collectively. People like Larry and John were the first generation of out queer theatre-makers in this country. Sadly, as is the case in times of plague or war, the best and bravest died first, and far too often the less brave remained behind to run things. I often wonder what the Canadian theatre would be like today if all of those astounding queer artists we lost had survived.

I never went to funerals. People would say, "Oh you should, for closure." But I didn't want fucking closure. I wanted the rest of the world to know what we were going through. I wanted the disease and death to stop. I was tired of being afraid. I didn't want to mourn, I wanted to fight.

Straight friends and family seemed to think I lived some kind of charmed existence filled with fame and fun. Every attempt I made to talk to them about AIDS and what was happening in my life, in the gay community, was invariably greeted by a glassy indifference, as if I'd just started speaking to them in a foreign language. They smiled and nodded and pretended to understand. Their indifference had a profound effect on my opinion of straight people. It made me angry. It made me bitter.

I was invited to an Italian translation of *Remains* being presented in Milan. I accepted happily. Tad knew someone who was working the flight and had me upgraded to first class for free. I just had to be sure to wear dress pants and not jeans.

I was met at the airport by representatives of the theatre and driven to my charming neighbourhood boutique hotel, which took nearly two hours—a nightmare after my first, sleepless transatlantic flight. They said they would pick me up around six for dinner before some event I was expected to attend. I stumbled up to my room and did the worst thing I could have—I fell asleep. I woke just before six feeling like a sack of jet-lagged shit.

This pretty much set the tone for my first trip to Europe. No one had any time to do anything other than take me to where I needed to be, where I was interviewed through a translator, photographed and then taken to the next appointment. Otherwise I was left entirely to my own devices in a city where I didn't speak the language. To make matters worse, my always problematic circadian cycle was completely fucked up. I couldn't sleep at night and could barely stay awake during the day, stumbling blearily through the various sights Milan had to offer.

After a few days Tad showed up just in time to see the show with me, and it was fucking amazing. Unlike anything I'd ever seen. The acting was broad, simple and very loud. The direction was fearless, expansive, with sound and video woven throughout and set pieces that rose from the floor and descended from the ceiling. The choral work I'd written for the play was interpreted as music, almost like backup vocals. And yet the play, the characters, the dialogue, the action were all still mine. The audience's response was very positive. I was ecstatic and thanked the cast and both directors enthusiastically.

When we got back to Canada I stayed with Tad in Toronto for a few extra days. While cities across the United States had closed their sex hookup places, Canadian clubs had chosen to keep their doors open and offer comprehensive and constant educational information about how best to avoid spreading HIV. Tourists from all over America would fly in to take advantage of the weak Canadian dollar and the strong Canadian commitment to sexual freedom.

Pete was also in Toronto, on business, and we had dinner and caught up. He and the girlfriend he'd met, supposedly shortly after our breakup, had recently moved in together, but he was clearly enjoying his time away. I got him high on E and took him to the Barn, which had taken over the entire building on Granby Street. There was now a dark room and maze on the third floor, with the usual dancing and cruising on the second. By ironic happenstance, a number of gay guys we knew from Edmonton and Toronto were there, and it was like old times as we did some blow and drank too much. It got even more like old times when we ended up crashing on Tad's hide-a-bed, and indulging in some light oral before passing out.

Before we parted, Pete gave me a moist lingering kiss unlike any he'd given me when we'd been together and an intense hug. I whirled away with my imaginary skirt of happiness spinning madly about me to be confronted by Tad, arms folded, regarding me skeptically.

"What?" I said in a voice that was two octaves too high.

Tad said, "We've seen this movie and we know how it ends."

"We were too high, he needed someplace to crash."

"I heard." Tad moved into the Mary Tyler Moore kitchen and put the coffee maker on.

I stripped the fold-out bed and put it away. "He's with a woman now."

"And you're famous now."

"Pete's not like that and you know it."

Tad smirked. I packed.

A day later I was back in Edmonton, paying off a cat-sitting friend and catching up on all the mail that had collected while I was gone. The mail was very important in those days. It controlled my future as I waited for cheques to arrive from my agent after the commission had been deducted. If someone defaulted on a contracted payment, as was the case with a new theatre in London, Ontario, which had been brought down by internal financial malfeasance before I was paid, it could throw my financial situation off balance for months. A postal strike or slowdown could cripple me fiscally. I turned to Randy, offering him 10 percent of whatever I earned if he'd handle the money and keep me informed of what was coming up.

That May the cover story in *Saturday Night* came out; Scot Morison, an Edmonton writer, had been given the assignment, and I was open and honest with him about my background and about the abuse in my past. The story was fair and controversial. That they would feature a fag on the cover was unheard of; that that fag would speak candidly and eloquently about the sexual, physical and emotional abuse that had happened in his childhood was even more surprising. My immediate family had issues with the story, but I stood my ground. Members of my extended family would express their disapproval of what I'd said, but none of them would refute my narrative's veracity.

A few weeks later Randy and I flew to L.A., at the urging of Shain. Since it had been announced that Denys Arcand was shooting my first screenplay, I'd become a hot commodity and people wanted to meet me. This first, three-day trip was to interview agents. Once I had American co-representation, Shain wanted me to meet the development people at all the studios. I paid Randy's way, as I needed someone who could drive and provide moral support. I felt like things were suddenly way out of my league.

We both agreed that L.A. was unlike any other city we'd been to. It was flat and sprawling, an endless network of freeways and roads through a maze of low-slung buildings and palm trees.

The agents were all polished and pleasant to a fault. I became painfully aware just how beautiful people were in this industry and felt second-rate. This was not helped when the agent I finally signed with, who was at MCA, turned out to be perhaps the most handsome man I'd ever seen in my life. That was not why I chose him. He was a good agent and made it clear he knew my strengths and where they would be best utilized. He was just incidentally intimidatingly handsome.

In the evenings we saw the sights and hung out at landmarks like the Viper Room, House of Blues and the Comedy Store, and hit the clubs. I found the tiny run of gay bars on Santa Monica Boulevard rather ghettoized and varied in levels of the attractiveness of the clientele. In Hollywood the beautiful and ambitious often don't want to be seen in gay bars. Many in the business were in the closet and did their socializing primarily at private parties and functions.

George Boyd, my stage manager friend from New York, was living in L.A. and stage managing a show called *Distant Fires* at the Coast Playhouse. He was pitching the theatre a production of *Remains* he wanted to direct, so he invited us to the show. Afterwards George introduced us to all of the actors, whom we'd loved, including D. B. Sweeney and Samuel L. Jackson just a couple of years before *Pulp Fiction* made him a household name. Both actors mentioned they'd heard of my play and were looking forward to seeing it in L.A.

I returned to Alberta with a new agent and a bit of a tan. I also returned to an absolute shit storm in the press.

Originally I had publicly insisted that the *Remains* film should be shot in Edmonton, and Denys Arcand and Roger Frappier had reluctantly consented. A continent-wide casting tour to audition actors had been going on for months. Denys and Roger had been to Edmonton a couple of times to scope locations. Some kind of agreement had been made concerning funding from Alberta as well as Quebec and Ontario to complete the film, but while I was gone, the Conservative Alberta, government, many of whose members resented my success because they hated gay people, had decided against the funding. Denys and Roger basically said, "Fine, we can't afford to shoot it in Alberta then," and moved the setting to Montreal. This created a great outcry from many progressive Albertans. Once again I was the subject of controversy.

Denys and Roger started filming the movie—now dubbed *Love and Human Remains*—in the fall. Partway through the shoot they brought me to Montreal to see what was going on. Denys and the entire team had been more than respectful with the screenplay, even having an assistant call me at home a couple of times to okay a change in the dialogue an actor had requested. The production company got me a good room in a good hotel and I was driven to the set with the actors each morning. On my first day, the first assistant director made a lovely speech about the impact of the play on Montreal and how honoured they were to be working on it. It was a beautiful, gracious moment and I could only stammer a clumsy "Thank you, merci."

Watching take after take, shot after shot, I began to grow concerned. Denys was giving the actors very little psychological direction, and I felt everyone was getting away with their first, safest choice. David and Candy, as portrayed by Thomas Gibson and Ruth Marshall, were making all of the mistakes theatre actors made in their first reading of the play. They see David and Candy as best friends, star-crossed but ill-matched lovers when in fact, if one looks just beyond the obvious, they are far more angry and hurtful with one another than might be immediately apparent. The pacing was wrong. The actors didn't seem to be listening to each other. The scene lacked the tension and therefore the humour of the stage show.

When I asked Denys about this on a break, he explained that

I wasn't seeing what the camera was seeing. What I was talking about would be found in the editing. "Even the energy and pacing?" I asked. He nodded, "Of course." I was skeptical. Ulla Ryghe had taught me that the only thing that couldn't be fixed in the editing was the energy of the performance, but who was I to question Denys Arcand?

Pete was in the same part of the country at the time, and I'd offered to host him on the set if he came out, which he did. As fate would have it they were filming the restaurant scene where David and Kane encounter one another for the first time, something that reflected our own relationship. Pete met Denys and the cast at dinner and we both drank quite a lot before we ended up back at the hotel, passing out fused to one another in sleep as we had been when we'd first fallen in love.

I woke long before the sun had risen and immediately knew he was also awake.

He said, "So—what?"

"Not sure."

"Yeah."

"Should we have done this?"

"You're the one with the girlfriend you're cheating on."

"This isn't cheating."

"Why not?"

"You're a man."

I rolled onto my back, carrying him with me so he ended up on my chest in our old life-raft configuration. He nuzzled his chin into my neck and whispered, "I don't know what it is. I love women. But you and me. There's this thing. We'll always be connected."

A spark in my heart went out. I pushed him off me gently and sat up.

*We'll always be connected*—those words reverberated through my consciousness and some primal survival thing that lives deep inside of me said very decisively, *No.*

I didn't want what he was offering. I'd been fuck buddy on the side to a couple of attached guys in my life but not with someone I'd already lived with. I also knew how seductive it would be to settle for this, to stay with something comfortable right when I knew I should be exploring things that made me uncomfortable. I didn't say anything, though, as we still had one more show to do together.

For the Workshop West production of *The Ugly Man* we only had two weeks in the rehearsal hall before moving into the theatre to open five days later. It was a gruelling schedule. I gathered the strongest actors I had available to me. I had worked with most of them before and knew I could rely on them. They understood what I wanted and knew we had no time to fuck around.

I'd asked David Skelton to design something with rooms and windows; he came back and suggested a tall wooden post, a giant boulder and a small wood-enclosed pond downstage. As usual, David had used his design choices to push me beyond my usual mode of direction, and my half-formed, slightly naturalistic ideas were rendered moot as I was forced to re-evaluate everything. I said to David, "I'll work with that."

David's design forced me to look at the violence in the play in a new light. Everything was suggested. Nothing was literal. When the maid had her throat slit, no blood came from the actor, but a huge gush of it from the downstage fountain made her onstage death even more grotesque as she gurgled and writhed on the floor. When Veronica was shot in the head, a bucket of blood hidden near the fly gallery was dumped over her, soaking her entirely. I expanded the production throughout the space, with characters appearing at the doors into the theatre and in the aisles, playing scenes with actors on both sides of the intimate theatre.

The press response was surprisingly positive, although all remarked on the lack of sympathetic characters, which was my point. It also sold well.

A few days before opening, Pete had finally confronted me about my rather cool demeanour since we'd started rehearsal, and I told him about my epiphany in Montreal and that I'd come to the conclusion that the relationship we had wasn't healthy for me and the only way I could deal with it constructively was not to see him at all anymore.

He was hurt. He was angry. I felt terrible, but I also knew I was making the right choice.

In the final dress rehearsal Pete gave a brilliant performance as the damaged but essentially decent Leslie, who is transformed by the evil of others around him. It was a performance that resonated emotionally with what had happened between us, and in our final note sessions I praised his work unconditionally. I knew he hated me, but I also knew he was strengthened by my acknowledgement of his work.

At the opening-night party he ghosted early with his girlfriend, saving us both a brittle goodbye. Whatever resentments we might've harboured at the end, I still think of him as one of the bravest people I've ever met for following his heart with me, rather than caving to what society told him he should do. Our entire relationship was a mostly wonderful experiment.

I never saw him again.

# PART FOUR

# POOR SUPER MAN: CINCINNATI

IMMEDIATELY AFTER OPENING *The Ugly Man* I made my second trip to L.A. to take the various studio meetings my agents had set up for me. Randy came along again, but this time we stayed at the notorious Holiday Inn on Santa Monica, in the heart of West Hollywood—it was really one step above a bathhouse. I did at least two meetings a day over five days, and they were often quite far apart, so the driving was endless. We were both thrilled to get onto the Fox lot and walk through the still-standing *Hello, Dolly!* street set.

One thing I learned very quickly was how relentlessly heterosexual Hollywood was. While everyone expressed admiration for the *Remains* script, anything I pitched with a queer theme was quickly shot down.

I had been working on a sitcom pitch based on *Remains* without the darkness. Basically a smart-mouthed gay guy (David) and the straight female best friend who once loved him (Candy) share an apartment and various adventures, often aided by their eccentric friend down the hall who was perhaps a drag queen or a trans person. Whenever I tossed this pitch out, it was shut down immediately. I guess it was still too early for a *Will and Grace*. At the end of the week I left with a suitcase full of scripts that could be rewritten and video versions of European films that could be remade.

I had met a number of writers already working in Hollywood. They seemed to be well-paid, bitter people who worked a lot but rarely got anything made, and on those rare occasions when something did get made, the property was so changed they barely recognized it. I resolved to never take Hollywood too seriously, whatever might happen.

That isn't to say I was happy to get back to Edmonton. I was feeling very limited in the city, and there was also an anti-Brad thing going on—the inevitable backlash, I suppose. The press, whom I'd sparred with over reviews and articles throughout my career, was getting hostile, with one journalist asking, "Is *The Ugly Man* Brad Fraser's autobiography?," and another referring to me as "Bad Phrases." There was also a certain contingent within the theatre community who seemed particularly put out by my success. I knew it was time to move on again.

I gave my notice at the bungalow, put everything into storage and talked my sister into fostering my cats until further notice. The world was wide open to me and I could've moved to any number of cities, but I chose Toronto again.

I'd been spending a lot of time in Toronto anyway. I'd recently started talking to Robert Lantos's company, Alliance Films, about adapting for film a prominent magazine story about an infamous journalist's descent into madness in a foreign country. I was also meeting with various TV and stage companies and pitching them ideas. I usually stayed with Bob O or Tad.

For the next two years I would base myself casually in Toronto while flying all over the continent to take meetings and consider projects. I stayed with friends and acquaintances until they got tired of me drinking their booze and fucking their friends, at which time I would cheerfully move on. I always left an expensive gift behind. My mail was all sent to my agent, who knew how to reach me. No one really knew where I lived, and I liked it that way.

This was a golden age in Canadian theatre consumption in Toronto. George F. Walker's *Love and Anger* had enjoyed great commercial success, transferring into one of the large houses for a limited run. Tomson Highway's *The Rez Sisters* played on the stage of the Royal Alexandra Theatre, not known for its production of Canadian plays, let alone ones by First Nations writers. The uptight, snatchy old reviewers from the eighties had been replaced by some truly interesting critics who happily championed Canuck writers. I was a name. Academics and critics used the term "Fraserian" unironically.

One day I got a call from Denys and Roger; they had a director's cut of the film and would be showing it at a prominent director's theatre in New York for an audience that would fill out reaction cards. Would I attend? Of course I said yes, and arrangements were made for a quick trip to Manhattan.

That initial viewing with the film's first audience was painful. I found the film slow and ponderous. Every scene opened with a wide establishing shot and then gradually moved closer in as the scene progressed. The actors were all kind of doing a method thing that really didn't work well with my sharp dialogue, and that lack of energy I'd noticed on the set permeated the whole film. The play had been all snap and sizzle; the film was slow pan and fizzle. But, of course, the biggest problem was the screenplay.

Writing the first draft of the film, I had really let myself go. I saw it as a satirical horror film in the Tobe Hooper/George

Romero fashion with a soupçon of Noël Coward thrown in. I really did try to make it cinematic and off the wall, to come up with a kind of storytelling that did on film what I'd been doing in the theatre. It was edgy, scary and rude. I recall one scene had a naked Bernie slicing open the chest of one of his victims to remove their beating heart and squeeze the blood from it over his erect cock.

Denys and Roger had been so alarmed by what they'd read that Denys had actually flown out to Edmonton for a couple of days to work on the script, which he decisively wanted to bring back closer to the style of the source material.

Having gotten the crazy one out of my system—and my first drafts traditionally would be crazy—I followed their directions and did a more faithful adaptation. Interestingly, we discovered that many of the scenes in the play were too short to register on film. That's because film lacks the peripheral knowledge a live theatre audience has with a show like *Remains*. That knowledge lets them hold the storylines and scenes together unconsciously in a way film, with its constantly subjective point of view, cannot. Even then I could feel the theatricality of the dialogue thudding against the visual needs of film.

I was candid with Denys and Roger with my feelings about the film, and wrote up a point-by-point analysis suggesting a lot of specific cuts that I felt would improve it. They said my reaction to the film hadn't been what they'd hoped for and that there would be further editing and technical work, since it was slated to open at the Toronto International Film Festival in a few months. Disappointingly, Cannes had passed on premiering the film.

In the meantime *The Ugly Man* was showing signs of life. In Toronto everyone passed on it for a variety of reasons—Toronto

Canadian theatre had not found great success with satire or style. Thankfully, Théâtre de Quat'Sous in Montreal had decided to do it and had hired Derek Goldby to direct.

That spring a friend from Toronto, who would die from AIDS in a few months, drove me to Montreal, where I put us up in a cheap hotel overnight. The friend, who didn't speak French, was mystified by the show, but I was absolutely stunned by Derek's production. He'd set the play in the Edwardian period and given it a highly stylized, cinema-noir-meets–Aubrey Beardsley aesthetic that elevated the material in a profound way. The design and the cast were exceptional, and included actress Micheline Lanctôt, whom I'd admired in *The Apprenticeship of Duddy Kravitz* at the Banff Centre fifteen years earlier.

However, the reaction from the press, many of whom had hailed *Remains* as a work of genius, was mostly angry. I heard that one critic had pointedly ripped his program in half and thrown it on the stage in contempt while the cast were taking their bows. But I didn't care what the fucking reviewers said; I thought the show was brilliant.

I flew to Vancouver for work and had lunch with Cam. As we were walking down Davie Street afterwards he brought up a long-time close friend of his. "Dwayne and I always had a deal. When one of us got too sick and were in a lot of pain the other one would help them out." I knew exactly what he meant by "help them out."

Cam said, "He's been in the hospital for the last few months. They can't do anything for him."

We stopped at a light. It was a bright day. All around us the heteronormative world was bustling about its mundane business.

Cam kept his eyes fixed on the traffic light across the street as he said, "He was coughing up this—stuff—it smelled so horrible—he'd choke and gasp for air. One time part of his lung came up through his throat and I had to—poke it back down with my finger."

The traffic light told us to walk and Cam continued. "I kissed him and picked up the pillow next to him and held it over his face. He didn't fight or anything until at the very end when it was like his body had to do it even if his brain didn't want to but he was too weak. Eventually he stopped."

The sun was still shining. People flowed around us obliviously. I was stunned by the conversation we were having. I wanted to accost the people around me and say, "He just killed someone he loves to save them greater pain and you assholes don't know anything about it! We are invisible to you. Our pain means nothing."

Instead we walked on and I said, "Can't they tell? Detached retinas or retinal hemorrhages or something?"

Cam said, "The doctors knew. The nurses knew. No one said anything."

I nodded and we continued on to wherever we were going as if everything he'd told me was the most everyday thing in the world.

I flew back to Toronto, where I was squatting with a lawyer friend (oddly, I've always known a number of lawyers) who lived in an illegal loft that was part of his office on Richmond Street. *Remains* was slotted to open at the Toronto International Film Festival and the city was atwitter. I went to an endless number of parties where I was photographed for the local media and my opinion sought on whatever it was we were doing. There was a pre-showing screening and I invited Bob O and an entire circle of his friends I'd met since knowing him. They were all effusive and friendly before the showing. Most of them disappeared without commentary after.

The night of the premiere, my old friend David Wright and I shared a limo with Thomas Gibson and his brilliant wife Christine. Somewhere there's a picture of David and me in the back seat looking totally like people who belonged in limos. Thom and I would stay in touch over the years as he starred in *Dharma & Greg* and *Criminal Minds*, and he was always a terrific friend. At the Winter Garden Theatre we walked a red carpet lined with klieg lights and reporters sticking mics in our faces every few feet. I watched the first few minutes of the film, then left David Wright, who hadn't seen it, so I could slip out the stage door and smoke a joint in the alley with some of the technicians and featured players who'd worked on the movie.

When the film opened commercially just a few weeks later, critical reaction was mild. I wanted to disagree with the reviewers but I couldn't.

I took the failure of the film amazingly well despite the fact there would be no big profit-share cash for me. I had a new project ready to roll.

The new play was something I'd started shortly after Pete and I broke up. I had no idea what I was working toward, though I had this vague idea about a successful artist who gets a job as a waiter because he's out of touch with his muse.

It had been three years since I'd worked a regular job and it was getting on my nerves. Although I'd spent my twenties wishing I was something other than a waiter, once I stopped doing it I realized how much I enjoyed the constant mix of challenges and personalities that came with working in a restaurant.

I also wanted to write something about AIDS. By 1993 the AIDS play had become its own sub-genre in theatre. William M.

Hoffman's *As Is*, which I'd seen years earlier in Edmonton, and Larry Kramer's *The Normal Heart* were the most famous American examples. They both came out of New York City, the epicentre of the plague. Canada had Kent Stetson's underappreciated *Warm Wind in China*, produced in 1988. I'd seen or read all three of these scripts and admired them, but I also came to dread AIDS plays because so many of them were obvious and maudlin—a variation on the seventies plea-for-acceptance plays.

I knew my play would not be about the gay guy dying of AIDS. I also knew I wanted to write something that explored elements of the relationship I'd known with Pete, something that was an honest look at the situational and complicated dynamics of same-sex attraction that went beyond the trinary of gay, straight or bi. I knew I wanted David McMillan from *Wolfboy* and *Remains* to be the lead and to be, like me, HIV-negative.

If David didn't have AIDS, then obviously someone close to him would have to be dealing with it. Instead of that being another gay friend, I wanted something that was more thematically evocative. Because the script was about the intimate love between a gay man and a straight man, a meeting of the gay world and the straight world, I needed someone who somehow belonged in both those worlds.

And so Shannon, the incomplete trans woman, was born. Shannon and David, like Candy and David, had a complicated backstory that is only hinted at in the play. I had met quite a few trans women after I came out and, unlike many in the gay community, I had no problem with them. Trans people had always been as much a part of the queer community as anyone else. I found the entire idea fascinating and had devoured any trans stories and characters I came across over the years. Shannon was the heart of the show and remains one of my favourite creations, despite the criticism I've taken from some quarters for daring to imagine someone so far removed from my own experience.

To sharpen the gender/sex divide I added two women: Violet, Matt's no-nonsense wife, who was like every hard-edged, man-desiring girl from a working-class home I'd known in northeast Edmonton, and Kryla, the glossy, fast-talking-broad-with-a-hat, over-educated downtown gal who was David's best friend.

The characters had a lovely symmetry and balance and I had no trouble writing scenes and vignettes for them, but I hadn't yet found that central metaphor that would hold the concept together—the serial killer in *Remains*, the werewolf possibilities in *Wolfboy*—so everything I wrote felt fragmented and loose.

Then one morning one of my nephews called and woke me up. He was five at the time, and I'd ensured my niece and nephews were steeped in comic-book lore from an early age.

He said, "Is Superman dead?"

I realized he was referring to a recent publicity ploy by DC Comics to reawaken interest in their aging property. Superman was going to succumb to a creature named Doomsday and finally shuffle off this mortal coil. Despite the fact there'd been many stories about Superman being killed throughout his history, the mainstream press picked up the story.

I assured my nephew that no one ever really died in comics and that this was all a publicity stunt, and that Superman would be back in about six months when the stories about who would replace him got stale. I assured him all would be well.

After I hung up I thought, "This is my Superman. They're killing *my* Superman. The one I grew up reading in the sixties." I'd found the missing metaphor: the death of the silver-age Superman was the end of an era. After that, the writing came quickly. The play was meant to be as funny as it was tragic, as brutal as it was poetic, moving without being sentimental. And there would be captions.

In interviews over the years I'd often talked about how comics had influenced my work, and with this new play I wanted to explore that more deeply. I always found watching subtitled films or silent films with title cards interesting because I personally found the act of having to read while watching brought me more deeply into the narrative. I wondered how this would work in the theatre and how it would affect my writing. The captions became a kind of sixth character in the play who was actively participating in, and commenting on, the words and actions of the living characters.

Initial reaction to the early drafts was strong. This was the play they'd been waiting for, the true follow-up to *Remains*. Because it featured David McMillan, some called it a sequel to *Remains*, and it was in a way, but not literally. To me, all the David McMillan plays, while discrete, are linked.

This play's connection to what was going on in my life at the time was uncanny. It sometimes felt that what I wrote took shape in reality a short time later. The scene where Matt and David are dealing with the fallout of just having had sex and discussing the ethics of it and Matt says, "This is different. You're a man," was almost exactly what Pete would say to me a few months later when we were in Montreal after our initial break-up.

As I was writing, the deaths of people I knew continued. I kept a list of the names and added them to David's roster of his dead friends in the play. Imagination and experience were woven together in a way I'd been seeking from the beginning of my career. I kept altering the dialogue, working always to make it more specific and more true to the way people actually communicate with one another.

I was immensely proud of what I'd written and felt I'd answered those critics who said I didn't so much write plays as create novel theatrical experiences. Both are equally valid, but I wanted this one to be seen as a "real play."

Shain shopped the script around to a number of theatres, and there was a great deal of interest, but it was Ensemble Theatre Cincinnati's Mark Mocahbee, whom I'd met in Calgary a few years earlier, who beat the others to the punch. He secured the rights to the premiere production after Ensemble flew me to Cincy to check out the theatre. I liked the space and the vibe of the city. Also, my financial situation didn't give me time to wait.

A few months later, while I was again taking meetings in L.A. with Randy, I picked up a Canadian paper at a newsstand and found out the Ensemble production had been cancelled "due to unforeseen circumstances." I raced back to the hotel and called Shain. He said the board of directors at the theatre had reconsidered and overruled Mark and the AD. Apparently some board members had been made nervous after a 1990 exhibit of work by the photographer Robert Mapplethorpe and related artists had met with a virulent reaction in the city. My show was being cancelled because of the possibility of a homophobic backlash that could jeopardize the theatre's future funding.

This happened at the same time a professor was fired for daring to do a production of *Remains* at a university in Montreal. Suddenly I was in the headlines again, this time for being censored. While Canadian artists did nothing to support the Montreal prof, the theatre artists in Cincinnati were not so reluctant. They spoke out volubly against the artistic director's decision, and Mark assured me some grassroots action was about to happen. I told him if he didn't get the play back on track, the premiere production would be in either Edmonton or Toronto, since theatres in both cities had made bids on the show.

DC Comics had gotten wind of all the press and Great North received a letter from them reminding us they held the trademark to Superman—despite the name being used by both Shaw and Nietzsche years earlier. It was a hassle, but ultimately we were barred from using the name Superman but free to air whatever commentary about Superman we wanted to. That's when I decided to call the show *Poor Super Man*—"Super" and "Man" had to be separated for legal reasons, although almost every producing theatre thereafter would overlook this legal proviso and call it *Poor Superman*, as would many in the press.

After a few weeks of waiting while Shain back-and-forthed with the Cincinnati AD and the board, the artists scheduled to work at the theatre throughout the season wrote an open letter threatening to withdraw from those shows if the theatre followed through with their cancellation of the production. Management realized they could not come out of this debate looking good and relented. Mark was ecstatic; that kind of publicity can't be bought.

I had sent an earlier draft of the play to Canadian Stage, which was Toronto's biggest theatre with both an A (large) and B (smaller) house and a generous budget. It was being run by Bob Baker, who'd run the Phoenix Theatre in Edmonton ten years earlier. He'd had no interest in my work then, but I was hoping the success of *Remains* might have gotten his attention. It had. The theatre's dramaturge, Iris Turcott, set up a meeting with me.

She was unconditional in her love for the play, and she had a number of canny observations and questions that helped immensely in the early development of the script. I would work with Iris on every play I wrote for the next twenty years. We also became great friends. She had a huge effect on my life and work.

Canadian Stage did the first reading of the *Poor Super Man*. It was in the downstairs space of their Berkeley Street complex, which contains two theatres that were once parts of a gas pumping station. No one had heard the play before and only Iris and a few others had even read it. We hired a group of actors I trusted and invited a few people to watch. Bob Baker and a few other theatre employees were also there.

Everyone in the room had been personally affected by AIDS in some way and their attention was intense. Right as we got to the part of the play where David's out drinking by himself while Shannon commits suicide and he is listing the names of all the men he knows who have died of AIDS, at a moment when we were all lost in our emotions, a thin black bar appeared on the back wall of the stage, from floor to ceiling, and began to grow wider.

I thought I was hallucinating. Then I realized everyone else in the audience was stirring in their seats. The actors had no idea what was going on because they were sitting with their backs to the wall as the blackness grew wider and wider. We were suddenly looking into the street, where rain was falling from a dark sky. A hard wind whipped into the room. There was a rumble of thunder and a few seconds later a flash of lightning in the distance. No one knew what was going on or how to react.

The stage manager made an annoyed noise. "What the hell?! Those doors are never unlocked." She got up from her chair, and rushed to the large double barn doors on the back wall of the theatre. One of the actors helped her close the door. The stage manager locked the doors and returned to her seat with an apologetic smile. "I have no idea why that happened."

I said, "Maybe our friends we lost are joining us for the end of the reading."

I could tell everyone present, like me, felt the theatre was suddenly filled with ghosts.

The actors finished reading. There was no applause. No commentary. Actors, theatre staff, my friends, we all sat there in a prolonged moment of silence, too moved to speak.

I finally cleared my throat, wiped away my tears and thanked everyone for coming. Then they all applauded.

Ben Henderson in Edmonton, who'd taken over running Theatre Network, had agreed to a co-production of the show with Gerry Potter at Workshop West. I would direct. The show would open a few months before a co-production between the Manitoba Theatre Centre (which had a huge hit with Crow's production of *Remains* a few years earlier) and Canadian Stage's second space to be directed by Derek Goldby. Shain was meanwhile fielding expressions of interest from various theatres all over the world.

Producing the *Poor Super Man* in Cincy had its issues. The theatre was called semi-professional because no one was paid except the playwright and director. The acting talent pool was limited. Theatre is often a compromise, and this production was full of compromises when it came to casting and technical ambition.

Opening night, knowing I might be facing cameras and reporters, I didn't smoke a joint when I left the hotel I'd been living in for the last three weeks. Laurie Brown and a CBC crew had been shadowing me for an upcoming story, but I'd asked them to leave me alone before the opening.

As I strode up to the theatre I could see a large crowd gathered in front of the steps as well as many camera crews. All the major networks were there, along with a smattering of Christian protesters with signs condemning my lifestyle and my writing. Helicopters circled overhead and far more cop cars than can reasonably be expected at a theatre opening were in evidence. There were armed guards at each side of the entrance, which had a storey-high banner on one side emblazoned with my face and name along with the title of the play.

I thought, "Fuck, girls, it's only a play," and skipped up the steps and through the doors before the people with microphones registered my presence.

Mark was pacing in the lobby, a slightly crazed gleam in his eye. He said, "The vice squad is coming."

I laughed. "That's amazing!"

"Someone read the preview in the paper and complained that we were producing pornography." He threw his arms around me, whispering, "Thank you for this play."

I hugged him back and said, "Thanks for doing it."

The ushers opened the doors to let the surging crowd and the vice squad into the theatre. The entire experience was intoxicating, and the energy among those presenting it and those experiencing it was mystical. The members of the vice squad who were asked to comment afterwards all remarked on the power of the show. Not one of them had an issue with the ass-fucking scene, which I'd saved for act two so no one could walk out. Context is everything.

After the opening party and a few beer and joints I walked back to the hotel through the dark, mostly deserted streets with this strange sensation of both tugging and releasing in my heart. I stopped and leaned against a wall. I started to cry. I let it go, sinking to a squat in the street, one hand over my eyes, the other on the sidewalk keeping me steady. I sobbed like a crazy drunk for a long time.

That night I slept the deep sleep one attains only after the dead have left them alone for the first time in a long time.

# PART FIVE

# POOR SUPER MAN:
# EDMONTON/MONTREAL/TORONTO

THE PRESS RESPONSE TO *Poor Super Man* was highly encouraging. Most of the reviews were solid raves, and there were a lot of them from the major American media outlets—but not a single reviewer from Canada. The naysayers were, as usual, straight people who didn't believe a relationship like David and Matt's could actually happen. *Time* magazine gave it a rave, and *Poor Super Man*, like *Remains*, appeared in their list of top ten plays of the year.

Back in Toronto I was spending my days taking meetings, writing endless drafts and working out; my nights were spent hanging out with the Davids (Gale and Wright), Tad or any of the new friends I'd made since becoming famous—there were many of them at this point and they came and went with casual ease. I smoked a lot of weed, I drank a lot of beer and I took a lot of E for my nights dancing at the clubs around town where I was known to the doormen and always waved past the lineup.

The look had changed: the eighties' 501s and polo shirts had been replaced by shaved heads (putting me well ahead of the curve), muscled bods, army boots and heavy socks worn with short shorts and an ironic T-shirt.

AIDS wasn't killing people as fast. New drugs were prolonging lives and helping alleviate the symptoms of opportunistic diseases. Some guys developed terrible side effects, like buffalo hump and facial wasting. Some of them were prescribed steroids to counter the weight loss and wasting and ended up with better bodies than those who were negative.

There was a sexual split in the community as well. Many of those who were positive wanted to have bareback sex with other positive guys. Doctors warned against this, as the virus had strains of different strengths, but many said when you're facing a death sentence, it was worth the risk. Meanwhile, those who were negative and wanted to stay that way were vigilant about using condoms. People were fucking like crazy again, and every warehouse party had a designated sex area, the baths were doing business like they'd done in the late seventies, a number of the bars had dark rooms/back rooms, and the foam-and-underwear raves were hotbeds of hard cock and playful sex. (With my new-found public self I avoided public sex places.) Rates of new infections plateaued and even fell in some areas where safer sex was constantly promoted.

Generally, with the partners I met, I didn't ask about their status unless they volunteered that information, because if there was fucking it was with a rubber, so their status was irrelevant. During that period I refused to give an answer if an interviewer asked about my HIV status, saying whether or not we were infected, we were all affected.

The panic in the community had subsided and even the straight world had learned it wasn't that easy to pass on HIV through casual contact. I don't think people's families rejected them less for being gay or being sick, but I do know the medical community became more responsible. The community had developed tactics and hospices for dealing with the sick and the dying. We had learned. We had organized.

I kept track of the loss of old friends and acquaintances through a column called "Proud Lives" that ran in every issue of the free gay biweekly *Xtra!* and featured the pictures, names and life dates of those who'd passed. I recognized someone in almost every issue.

ACT UP, a radical queer protest group started by Larry Kramer and a group of other radical gays in New York, had been staging large public demonstrations and protests in order to get potentially life-saving drugs expedited through the approval process, which ordinarily took many years, if there was a chance they would spare someone's life. They were militant, angry and exactly what was needed at the time. From publicly shaming homophobic politicians to opening their veins and spraying blood on those who wanted them dead, ACT UP changed the way treatments and medicines are tested and approved for people with life-changing diseases in a manner that would benefit everyone in society, whether suffering anything from breast cancer to heart disease.

Their tactics informed our behaviour, and those of us who survived the eighties saw ourselves as seasoned warriors who'd seen the worst years of the disease and the worst behaviour from the straight majority with their hostility or indifference. We were not about apologizing and we were not about hiding. And we were taking advantage of every moment life gave us.

The survivor's guilt I'd been feeling since the beginning of the plague kept surfacing. Late at night I'd lie awake in bed thinking about the ones who'd died, the ones who were positive, and wondering how I was not one of them. We had shared every intimacy and yet I was healthy and thriving, doing better than I'd ever done in my life, living the dream I'd always held in my heart while losing those I cared about most.

I suppose it was this constant sense of loss and grief that kept me from becoming a total diva as my fame grew and productions and contracts kept rolling in. To be sure, I was full of myself and very pleased with everything that was going on, but I'd always been something of an asshole and I don't think that amped up perceptibly with the changes in my life. I was very impatient, as I'd always been. I didn't like to be kept waiting and I didn't like being treated as if my time was less valuable than anyone else's. I was punctual. I was professional. The reputation I had in some quarters for being "difficult" came only from my willingness to call out mediocrity and ask for more. If I'd been straight I'd've been known as "uncompromising."

I'd delivered the commissioned script, based on the magazine story about the wayward Canadian journalist, to Alliance and they were less than impressed. Coming from the theatre, I was used to people reacting badly to an early draft, listening to their concerns and then rewriting to address those concerns. I learned quickly that this was not how the film world worked. They simply passed on the screenplay and future drafts of it. There would be no notes and no opportunity for me to improve things.

I didn't dwell on it too much. Many films got written, few of them got made—and I was working on a couple of spec scripts, which I took with me to L.A. when I flew down late in the fall of 1994, meeting Randy, who was now living in Vancouver. We may have been separated by the continent but we remained on the phone with one another a couple of times a week. He was then developing the business that would eventually take over his career, but at that time he still looked after my money, which tended to ebb and flow dramatically. Randy set up enough credit to see me through the rough times.

The producer of the recent hit Tina Turner biopic *What's Love Got to Do With It* had liked my samples. He had a deal with Touchstone Pictures, a Disney subsidiary, and I met with his people on the Disney lot. I also met with a number of other studios and was given a large number of novels and galleys of unpublished work that the studios were looking for pitches on.

I was approached by NeWest Press in Edmonton who wanted the rights to *Remains*, which had recently come up after having lapsed with another publisher. They would publish both the play and screenplay version of the property as a flip book, and also wanted to publish *The Ugly Man* as well as *Wolfboy/Prom Night of the Living Dead* in one shared volume. It was odd to go back to *Wolfboy* after so many years, but I cleaned the script up and finally cut poor Dr. Sherrot, who'd never lived up to her potential as a character.

I was getting tired of living like a gypsy. I missed my cats and I was hoping to make enough money to get my own place somewhere. I was looking at all the potential Hollywood properties very seriously, writing up proposals and pitches to adapt the most interesting as films and running them past Randy and Shain over the phone for their feedback. I eventually narrowed everything I'd been given down to three projects. The first was an American remake of Wim Wenders's sublime *Wings of Desire*, a movie so good and highly regarded it had nowhere to go but down. The second was some kind of adaptation of Georges Franju's 1960 atmospheric horror movie *Eyes Without a Face*, but I found the source material wasn't quite as rich as I'd hoped. Third was an adaptation of a novel that combined elements of both the others called *Beauty*, by Brian D'Amato.

This book was right up my alley. It was a smartass combo of Bret Easton Ellis and Mary Shelley. The lead character was a surgical/mystical genius who uses his abilities to turn his girlfriend into the most beautiful woman in the world and a huge movie star. As expected, things go wrong, with many horrifying complications. I loved the satirical scary/funny tone of the book and sat down to write up a treatment for it as a feature.

A few weeks later I delivered it to Shain to look over and then flew to Edmonton to start rehearsal for *Poor Super Man*. I went there a week early to prep and visit family and friends. A few days before we started I got a call from Shain, who'd just spoken to my L.A. agent and the Touchstone people. "They loved the treatment," he enthused. "They want you to come in and pitch it."

"I'm in rehearsal," I protested.

"You've gotta jump on these things when you're hot, Brad. They'll cover everything."

"Do you think we can cram it in on my day off?"

"Let me see what I can arrange," he said.

The next morning a FedEx package arrived with an itinerary and a plane ticket. Everything had been arranged for our day off.

I got up at 4 a.m. and was picked up by a limo for the nearly hour-long drive from downtown to the Edmonton airport. From Edmonton I flew to Salt Lake City, and from Salt Lake I flew to L.A., where another limo was waiting to drive me to the Disney studio for the pitch meeting. I'd been through my notes multiple times on the plane and felt comfortable.

My handsome L.A. agent was waiting for me at the studio and accompanied me into the boardroom, where eight studio executives sat looking at me expectantly.

I smiled at them and delivered my pitch carefully, starting with a breakdown of the book's plot and how I would change it for film. I spoke for about twenty minutes, taking them through the story from the comedic beginnings to the shocking ending. When I was done they all applauded. There were a few questions but nothing profound. I thanked them all for their time. They thanked me for taking the trip.

I shook my agent's hand outside before getting into my limo. He said, "That was one of the best pitches I've ever seen."

I thanked him, got into the limo and repeated the entire process in reverse, arriving back at my hotel in Edmonton at 4 a.m. There was nothing to do now but wait for a response, and I was grateful to have a show to keep me occupied.

*Poor Super Man* opened and received great reviews, although an ultra-right-wing magazine published one of the most homophobic "reviews" I'd ever read, and I'd read a lot of homophobic reviews by this point. But this only increased the play's visibility once the mainstream press picked up on the controversy, as they always did.

From long before I was recognized in any way, I had written responses to articles and reviews I disagreed with, or that I thought were particularly well-written and worthy of praise (rare). I felt it was better for criticism to lead to dialogue between artist and reviewer, and reacted accordingly, often with quickly typed, badly edited letters to the editors or to the reviewer themselves. I learned that a bad review, if responded to in the right way, could actually be a boon for the show, particularly if I could honestly call someone out for being homophobic or biased.

I learned quickly that despite the press's lip service to balance and fairness, the predominantly slightly right-of-centre journalistic elite in Canada did not like being subjected to the same scrutiny and tone they themselves almost always used. Many of them were far more sensitive than the people they wrote about when treated the same way, and I delighted in exposing that.

I could tell my cockiness irked some of the journalists I was speaking to—and not just the straight ones—and they'd often bait me with questions like "Does it bother you that so many people dislike you?" or "Is the subtext of your work that gay people can't make relationships work?" I learned to anticipate these questions and had a cutting response to each. ("Universal popularity has never been an objective of mine" and "It's called conflict. You also don't see a lot of plays about straight people in 'working' relationships.")

But I was genuinely shocked one day when an Edmonton television personality asked me during an interview, "Okay, Brad, all of this gay stuff is fine. We get it. But when are you going to write something for straight people?"

I said, smiling, "Do you have any idea how offensive that is?"

He looked at me, confused. "What? Why?"

"If you were interviewing Spike Lee, would you ask him when he's going to write something for white people?"

"Oh, that's hardly the same thing. Gay isn't a race—"

I cut him off, but not too angrily because that can be dangerous for queers. "No. But it is a historically persecuted minority that until very recently was systemically wiped from history, tortured and killed. Currently we're in the middle of a plague the straight world is oblivious to."

"But, Brad, do you have to be so angry about it all the time?"

"Yes. I do. It's the only thing that keeps me going while everyone around me is dying."

He laughed and nodded, dismissing the entire digression, which would be edited out of the interview, and we went on to other things. Decades later when he interviewed me for another play opening the same journalist said, "We baited you a lot in those days. You stood up to us, but it really wasn't fair."

The negative feedback wasn't entirely from the right. There was a contingent of university grads redolent of developing identity politics who insisted the "sex and drugs/hard living/hard talking" world I depicted was not conducive to the creation of aspirational queer/feminist role models. When I explained that I wasn't writing role models, I was writing characters for popular culture, I was denounced as callous to the minoritarian representatives I was writing about. I found it hysterical that people who could afford to go to university would lecture me about privilege. For me, there is no more fascistic an impulse than to try to limit anyone's imagination, and I refuse any such attempt under any circumstances. My imagination has always been both an extension of my empathy and my greatest gift.

After opening *Poor Super Man* in Edmonton I flew back to Toronto, where I learned that Disney wanted one more meeting. I hopped a plane two days later and was back on the Disney lot in another room full of studio executives who listened to my pitch, which was much more polished than the first time. Their questions were much more penetrating, my responses much more specific. I could tell they were close to making a decision.

In Toronto I despaired because of my lack of a lover or life partner. I prayed for the right guy to come along who was ready to share the madness that was my life at that time. In truth I was in the worst possible condition for having a boyfriend. I was too full of myself. My inspirational bulletin board that I'd curated for so many years was no longer filled with ideas, images and articles for further inspiration for my work, but covered in articles about me and photos of me.

I worked out for at least ninety minutes four days a week religiously. I tried to limit my carbs and obsessed about my weight. I had a membership at a tanning salon. I flirted with the circuit party scene, but found that underneath the steroid-fuelled macho bravado and the "fuck you, we're not fairies" attitude there was a dark nihilism—an attitude of "If I'm going I don't care who I take with me" that creeped me out. It was a movement fuelled by drugs and dance music, and I found myself increasingly tired of both.

I was sleeping somewhere in somebody's home, probably in Toronto, when the phone rang.

"They want it," Shain said.

I said, "Who wants what?"

"Disney wants the screenplay for *Beauty* and they're willing to go pay-or-play"—meaning I'd get paid a high rate regardless of how many drafts they wanted and regardless of whether the film was ever made.

Two days later it was all over the news that Brad Fraser, king of the rude, alternative theatre scene, had signed a deal with a subsidiary of the Walt Disney Company to write a screenplay based on a successful novel. The Canadian media gave this a lot of play, as the juxtaposition of my aesthetic with the Disney style was fascinating to consider.

Disney offered Shain a three-year, three-picture contract if I would sign my entire back catalogue—literally everything I'd written prior to that moment—as well as anything I would write for the next three years over to them, across the universe in perpetuity. The money they were offering was more than I'd ever contemplated but wouldn't take care of me for the rest of my life, so I politely declined, happy to adhere to the original one-movie deal we were discussing and retain the rights to my plays.

The final contract brought me the largest payday of my life up to that point. I decided it was time to do something no one in my family had ever done before: buy a house.

I struggled with where to buy. Toronto was in a downturn at the time and property was relatively cheap. I could've gotten a smart, compact downtown condo for my budget, but the same amount of money in Edmonton could get me a substantial house. I still distrusted Toronto. It was a great place to sort of live, but I feared a repeat of my early-eighties experience if I should commit. In the end, Edmonton won.

My new house had a spacious, modern layout on a nice-sized, undeveloped lot. There were three bedrooms and two bathrooms on the main floor, an attached double garage and a huge basement space just waiting to be developed. I approached an old friend from my early days at Flashback who was still living with his parents and struck a deal with him to live in the house and care for my cats when I wasn't there.

While settling in I heard that I'd been nominated for Best Adapted Screenplay for Canada's version of the Oscars, then called the Genie Awards. Given the critical response to *Love and Human Remains*, I figured it was unlikely I would win, but since the Academy of Canadian Cinema and Television would spring for my airfare and hotel for two nights in Toronto, I decided I'd go. David Gale consented to being my date. I wore an expensive pair of skin-tight tweed pants that would now be called leggings with a sumptuous high-collared Egyptian cotton shirt and a grey herringbone vest—very on trend at the time—with a heavy pair of black Harley boots, looking way more rock star than film writer. To my surprise, I won.

I made my way to the stage with as much poise as I could summon, made some vulgar joke about the obscurity of Canadian celebrities and gave Denys and Roger my genuine and heartfelt thanks. It was lovely to win a statue, but the real reward was the $10,000 cheque.

When the news of my Genie win was announced, the New Democratic Party in Alberta, who were in opposition at the time, put forward a motion in the legislature to congratulate me on my win and the prestige it brought to Edmonton and the whole province. The Conservative party, which had ruled the province for thirty years at that point without a challenge, declined to support the honour because I was a well-known homosexual and therefore not someone Alberta could be proud of.

The outcry at the blatant homophobia was mild, but the press picked up on it and within a few days it was the subject matter of radio call-in shows and TV interviews with the religious element overrepresented, as it still is in the Canadian press, and a few progressives and gay-positive allies sprinkled in to maintain a scintilla of objectivity. When the news of this scandal finally filtered back to me in Toronto, I laughed it off. I'd been dealing with Alberta's homophobic bullshit my entire life. I was proud of my accomplishments even if they weren't.

During this period I watched five films a week for months, mostly contemporary but with classics thrown in here and there, as I worked to more completely understand how film scripts worked. Whenever I was hired to write a screenplay the producers would always go on about how hip and edgy I was and how they wanted a hip, edgy script. So I'd write a hip, edgy script and their reaction was invariably, "Holy fuck, this is way too hip and edgy. No one will ever buy this." I'd dutifully integrate their notes in a new draft and they would inevitably respond with "It's lost something . . . ," and I'd think, "Yeah. Originality, courage and surprise because your notes were stupid." I learned what I could and cashed the cheques.

———

That summer I went to New York with my Trinidadian/Canadian friend Gordon, an executive at a large cosmetics company, for the 1994 Stonewall 25th Anniversary celebration, which included the Gay Games and a huge arts festival celebrating the gay community. People came from all over the world, and for a week New York was gayer than it had ever been—which was saying a lot.

Gordon had use of a company apartment at Columbus Circle with a pullout couch in the living room for me. We spent our days sightseeing and hanging out with his friends from the world of fashion and cosmetics. Our evenings were spent at the many dance parties at the Palladium, the Tunnel and Club USA and attending nostalgic concerts featuring stars of yesteryear.

We'd also taken advantage of a special deal on tickets for the Broadway production of *Angels in America*, both parts on consecutive nights. Although the play had been in development and limited production as early as 1993, I hadn't heard a thing about it until we were opening *Poor Super Man* in Cincinnati. There were many plays about AIDS at the time, what did one more matter? In the case of *Angels* it mattered a lot, and, unfortunately for many gay artists dealing with similar material at the time, it would become the defining theatrical offering on the epidemic.

The night before the Gay Pride parade, Gordon and I did all the drugs and all the clubs until we ended up at the Sound Factory, which was the hottest club of the day. I kept running into guys I knew from Edmonton, Calgary and Toronto. I got sidetracked by some hot young thing and spent most of the night necking with him on the dance floor or in a dark corner. At what I assumed to be about around five or six in the morning I bade him goodnight and headed out to skulk home just before the sun rose.

I had seriously fucked up my timing. Wearing only ripped jean cut-offs, a jockstrap, army boots and the large wool socks that held my wallet and keys, I stumbled out onto West Twenty-Seventh Street to full-on sunlight and Sunday-morning traffic with pedestrians on their way to brunch and church. I walked down the street with my head held high despite the stares and got a cab as quickly as I could.

When I got up to the apartment Gordon was there, passed out. I stretched out to catch what sleep I could. Two hours later I was apologizing to Thomas Gibson on the phone. He had invited me to walk in the parade with a group of actors from *Tales of the City* and its author, Armistead Maupin, whom I greatly admired, but I was too fucking hungover. Thomas was disappointed but understanding. I would later regret not having taken the opportunity to meet one of my idols.

It was late afternoon before Gordon and I came to life, and the parade, which would last for hours as all Pride parades do, had begun its long walk up Fifth Avenue to Central Park. We could see the floats and the tops of flags a block away from where we had a hungover brunch, nursing Bloody Marys.

Gordon made a dismissive gesture with both hands and said in his soft Trinidadian accent, "I am done with the drugs."

I reached into my pocket and pulled out a folded piece of paper. Gordon watched carefully as I opened it up and revealed two very small purple pills. "These were in one of my socks this morning. I think it's acid and I think I bought it last night."

Gordon looked at me over his sunglasses, impressed, and said, "You are *wild* . . ."

Two hours later the drugs kicked in, after we'd fallen in step with the crowd who'd watched the parade and was now making its way to the park. The sun was getting low in the sky, we were surrounded by beautiful people blowing on whistles and screaming defiantly—it felt like being in a movie.

Every few blocks we'd pass an isolated crowd of six to ten badly dressed people, men, women and children, brandishing signs denouncing homosexuality, liberalism, sex, everything we were celebrating. Often they were screaming at us, their faces twisted with hate, spittle flying from their lips—but their contempt was always tempered by the fact they were so radically outnumbered. When we were all gathered together, these bigots were no threat.

We arrived in hordes on the Great Lawn, gay men, lesbians, trans people, bisexuals, our allies, of all colours, all religions and all races, luxuriating in the rare power we were feeling in all being together.

A moment of silence was called for to remember those we had lost. An electric wave of recognition ran through the crowd as the hush fell over the park and seemingly across the entire city. It wasn't just a moment of silence—it was a moment of blankness, a moment of non-existence, of negative space where those who were lost had once existed. No other city on the planet knew this feeling as well as New York.

People wept without inhibition; strangers hugged one another. I put my arm around Gordon and pulled him close. The sounds of the city were muted. The shadows crept longer on the grass. Eventually the moment dissolved, but the energy afterwards was gentle, careful, like lovers after a particularly savage fight, like a parent finally realizing their punishing behaviour is only making their adolescent child's issues worse, tender, open, wounded.

In August Bob O accompanied me on my second trip to Edinburgh (I'd gone the year before for a One Yellow Rabbit production of *The Ugly Man*), where *Poor Super Man* opened at the Traverse Theatre before transferring to the Hampstead in

London. We arrived at the end of the festival so we could attend the opening in London. Ian Brown's production there was solid, although some of his actors fell into the trap of editorializing their internal pain for the audience, making the experience too maudlin and sentimental for my taste.

I loved London. Like New York it was a place that had been mythologized in my mind through popular culture, and particularly the history of the theatre, for decades, and to be not only visiting but also opening a show there was amazing. In the days leading up to the opening I spoke to a lot of journalists. Britain's tradition of a wide and varied array of newspapers and magazines provided many opportunities to plug the play and remind people of the success of *Remains*. *Poor Super Man* would also be a hit in London.

Early in the spring Derek Goldby's production of *Poor Super Man* opened in Winnipeg to ecstatic reviews. The Manitoba Theatre Centre hadn't invited me to the show, but I read about it in the papers. While it was running I met Randy in Montreal, where we saw the French production at Quat'Sous. It was brilliantly translated, directed, designed and acted. The Quebecois did not judge my characters according to the same questionable standards the university-educated "liberals" subjected my work to in English Canada. David was unapologetically gay and horny, and the women were unapologetically dedicated to and fucked over by the men in their lives. It was earthy, urgent and horny. The captions, projected across the back of the stage, were highly effective. After the show we ate with the cast and crew at a restaurant that served us late into the evening with delicious food and fine wine.

The Toronto opening a few months later was not so sweet. I arrived dressed to the nines and accompanied by one of the hottest men in town, whom I'd met a few weeks earlier. The audience was responding exactly as a playwright might hope, the actors were killing it, and Derek's direction worked brilliantly against any hint of sentimentality in the script—but the captions were nowhere to be seen.

I was horrified. It was as if an integral character had been excised from the script without my consent. The audience had no idea what was missing and stood at the end as they almost always do at Toronto openings regardless of what they've seen. As the audience was filing out of the theatre I ran into Shain and asked through clenched teeth, "What the fuck happened to the captions?" Shain said, "I have no idea, but I'll find out."

As we all converged in the rehearsal hall for the post-opening party, I saw Derek. "What happened to the captions?" I hissed.

"Don't worry about it," he said. "The show's a hit." And then he scurried away.

The handsome date had been very aware of the transition in my mood from the moment the play started. Many of my friends were there, and those who knew the play all asked me what had happened to the captions. They could tell from my expression that my response was best left unspoken. The handsome date wisely made an excuse and left.

David Gale and I ghosted from the party at the earliest opportunity. As we cabbed uptown I railed against Derek's betrayal while he patiently listened—which was really all one can do when I'm like that.

Unknown to me, Shain had a screaming match with AD Bob Baker in the lobby while the party was still going on. When I spoke to Shain the next morning, he informed me that Derek's way of dealing with the captions, which he'd never liked although he never articulated why, and which I'd made clear were non-negotiable, was to have them projected at the same light level as everything around them, so they were effectively invisible. This meant he wasn't in contravention of the "no changing the material" clause of his contract because, officially, the captions were still there.

I was having none of that shit, and by the next show adjustments had been made to the lighting so the captions were visible. Derek left an abusive message on my voice mail telling me the captions were a cheap gimmick. This was the last contact we have ever had.

I flew to New York immediately after the opening for meetings with a producer about a TV series he wanted to pitch to Fox. I also saw Brent Carver in his Tony-winning performance in *Kiss of the Spider Woman*. We had time for only a quick hello after the show. We kissed and I assured him he would win because he seriously was fucking brilliant. Everyone in Canada who cared about theatre celebrated when he won.

While there I also recorded a television interview with the CBC's Hana Gartner for a special the network was doing on prominent Canadians. Hana seemed particularly put off by my questioning of the idea of love as anything more than the heteronormative pair-bonding template. I enjoyed the conflict and gave sharp answers to her sometimes slanted questions, but when she said something like, "But doesn't it bother you, knowing you'll be denied a lasting love like normal couples have?," I was so taken aback I sloughed the question off with one of my patented smartass quips—but I was angry at myself later for not having pushed back. I should've asked her what kept long-term gay couples from knowing what "normal" couples have, or how she could be so certain her own relationship would be "normal" and last the rest of her life when so few hetero relationships did. Many gay people who later watched the interview expressed their disgust with her.

I was staying in Bob O's apartment while he was away, putting the final touches on the Disney script one afternoon, when the phone rang. I picked it up, still focused on my laptop, and said hello distractedly.

"Hello. I'm looking for Brad Fraser." It was a woman's voice I didn't recognize.

"Speaking."

"Oh hi, Brad, you've never met me, but I'm Ellie Moffat, John's mother."

I pulled away from the computer, giving her my full attention. "Of course, Ellie. How are you?"

"I'm—oh, you know—I'm not that good."

"How is he?"

"He's right here. He wants to talk to you." There are no words to describe the broken-hearted edge to Ellie's voice. "We'll talk again," she said as she handed the phone to her son.

John once had an actor's voice, rich, sandy and adroit. He could sound like Marilyn Monroe or Clark Gable. On the phone that night his voice was flat and as thin as a fading radio signal on a dark prairie highway.

"Hey, Brad. How are you?"

"I'm fine. How are you?"

There was a long pause and the dry, laboured sound of his breathing before he said, "I'm really sick now."

I said, "You are one of the best actors I've ever known. I would've written parts for you for the rest of your life."

"Actually, you did."

We both laughed—him weakly. "I don't know if we'll talk again."

"We will," I said, "I know we will."

"I love you, Brad."

"You know I've always loved you."

A slow, whistly sigh. More laboured breathing. A low moan, and then, "I have to go."

"Okay."

A moment of nothing as his mother took the phone. "He's going to sleep."

"Thank you so much for doing this. Please keep me posted."

Ellie said, "I will."

It was humbling to think that whatever emotion I was feeling about losing John was insignificant compared to whatever his mother must've be going through as she cared for him. John was blessed. Many of the people who died of AIDS died alone because their families rejected them.

It had been twelve years since I'd met John. I'd hoped we'd collaborate well into the twilights of our careers. Now he was another friend dying of AIDS I spoke to long-distance on the telephone.

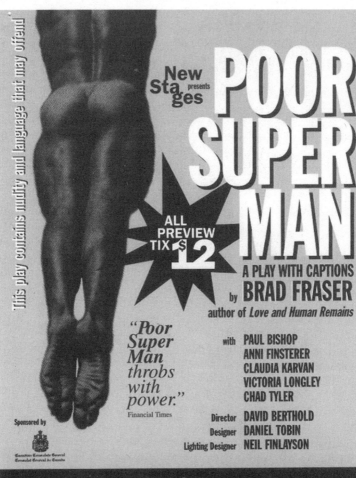

This play contains nudity and language that may offend!

New Sta*ges* presents

# POOR SUPER MAN

**ALL PREVIEW TIX $12**

A PLAY WITH CAPTIONS

by **BRAD FRASER**

author of *Love and Human Remains*

*"Poor Super Man throbs with power."*
Financial Times

with **PAUL BISHOP**
**ANNI FINSTERER**
**CLAUDIA KARVAN**
**VICTORIA LONGLEY**
**CHAD TYLER**

Director **DAVID BERTHOLD**
Designer **DANIEL TOBIN**
Lighting Designer **NEIL FINLAYSON**

Sponsored by

Canadian Consulate General
Consulat Général du Canada

**SYDNEY THEATRE COMPANY** *australia*

**Wharf** ② *Previews 31 March - 4 April*
*Plays from 5 April*
**Bookings 250 1777**

# PART SIX

# THE "BIGGER THAN
# JESUS" MOMENT

THAT NIGHT AFTER TALKING TO John Moffat I went to Dudes, which still had a dance bar upstairs. It was a middling busy night and, as usual, I was dancing by myself at the edge of the dance floor when I was approached by a man I'd had my eye on for nearly a year. He was about five nine or ten, with a muscular but wiry build and a very Warren Beatty face, particularly across the bridge of the nose and the cheekbones. I'd first noticed him at Katrina's, but he always seemed to be haunting the young guys, so I assumed he was a chicken hawk, which left me off his list.

His name was Grayden John. He was successful, articulate and, unlike many of the people I met, not at all intimidated by me. We had a lovely chat that night, and as the bar was closing we exchanged numbers.

He called me before I called him, which was a great sign. We were affable on the phone, very comfortable, getting each other's humour and references easily. We made plans to have dinner on the weekend. I was encouraged.

Two nights later I was out for dinner with Gordon at one of the trendy restaurants we frequented on Queen Street West when Grayden entered with a handsome young guy. They were seated at a table that allowed us to observe them without them seeing us. Just before they walked in I'd been raving to Gordon about how amazing Grayden was. From my seat I could see every time Grayden touched his companion's hand or rubbed his ankle with his foot under the table.

There was no way to exit the restaurant without going directly past his table, so when we did I forced a hearty, casual smile as if I was surprised to see him. His surprise was more genuine.

When we got into Gordon's jeep he said, "He's a popular guy."

I said, "He sure is," and we drove the rest of the way home in silence.

Grayden called me two days later. He made no reference to the meeting at the restaurant. Our dinner date was still on. I was happy to go.

He knew who I was, had seen a couple of the plays. I learned he was ten years my senior, well-educated and cultured, from that upper-middle-class background that only white people from central Canada really understand. He was an expert bureaucrat who had worked his way to the top of a major agency after a decade working in the public service.

I loved his face. The sound of his voice. The things he said. Our eyes sparked when they met. We laughed often. After dinner we went to a bar for a few drinks and to dance. After an hour or so, as we were taking a break, he leaned into me and said over the music, "I'm HIV-positive."

I could feel him watching my reaction. While I always told myself I should assume everyone was positive, I was surprised, but I shrugged, saying, "Thanks for telling me."

"Just so you know what you're getting into."

For a few minutes we said nothing, both of us moving to the

music. I'd had sex with positive guys over the years but hadn't been involved intimately. It wasn't the fear of infection that kept me at arm's length; it was the fear of getting involved with someone who was probably going to get sick and die. At the back of my mind the same unspoken question lingered: "Were you infected before or after we found out what caused it?" For the men who were infected before we learned how the virus was transmitted, I felt great compassion. But for the men who tested positive after understanding where it came from, I was less generous.

"Is it a problem?"

"Not at all."

He put his arm across my back and squeezed my shoulder. My heart swelled.

He drove me back to Bob O's building, where I was staying, and in the car we kissed. It was gentle. It was exploratory. It was uncommitted. I found it profoundly exciting and my cock grew instantly hard. The kiss grew more insistent. I put my hand on his crotch and he was hard as well. When we finally broke the kiss and reluctantly parted, we made plans to meet again in a couple of days.

After the next date we ended up back at his place. The sex was careful at first, as if we were both hoping to be whatever the other most wanted. When we were done and lying entwined together on the verge of sleep he said, "So what happens now?"

I said, "I go to Australia for three weeks."

He said, "Lucky."

I said, "But let's see what happens when I get back."

*Poor Super Man* was being produced by the Sydney Theatre Company and my presence had been requested. Shain had negotiated a great deal that got me airfare, subsidized by the Canada

Council, accommodation and per diem paid by the producing theatre. I had been anticipating this trip for months and didn't want to take the baggage of a new boyfriend with me. Grayden seemed very understanding. We had sex once more before I left and our goodbye kiss was tender.

Twenty-two hours on a plane was too daunting to face narcotic-free. I'd cadged from Bob O a few lorazepam, an anti-anxiety drug everyone with HIV and everyone dealing with someone with HIV was taking at the time to keep from losing their minds, and managed to sleep most of the trip.

The director of the play picked me up at the airport and drove me to my condo. I'd sent an email earlier alerting them that I was a pot smoker and asking them to get something for me. I usually did this when I was travelling to another country; people in the theatre are generally understanding about that sort of thing. The director didn't disappoint and laid a nice bag of weed on me as he parted. I had to do a photo shoot immediately and did so looking like someone who'd just been on a plane for nearly a day while heavily drugged. Then I was taken back to the condo where I gratefully napped for a few hours.

After waking I ate nearly everything in the fruit and cheese basket in my suite, smoked a huge joint and left the building to experience Sydney for the first time. The entire city felt familiar and strange, more Canadian than American or European, but also deeply different.

I had been told to walk south through Centennial Park toward the harbour, then follow the shoreline on the left to find the theatre. I happened upon the park quite quickly and was terrified by the large grey leathery pods that hung upside down from the giant eucalyptus trees. Initially I took them for nests of some kind, but then realized they were actually flying foxes—bats as large as small dogs—sleeping with their wings wrapped around themselves. From the indifference shown by the many people around me, I understood that they weren't a threat, but the sheer alienness of them still disturbed me.

The sun was setting and thousands of sparkling white lights began to glow from the branches in the trees around me. I could see the Sydney Opera House in the distance and headed toward it. When I reached the shoreline I turned left, passing under Sydney Harbour Bridge. Across the water I could see Luna Park, a tacky amusement fair with a giant clown's mouth for an entrance. On my side of the shore it was all trendy cafés and bars in the old harbourside warehouses. I thought, "I'm so fucking glad I'm high for this."

The theatre was situated on an enormous pier that jutted out into the harbour. I got my ticket at the box office and settled in at the back, entirely anonymous. The director and his cast and crew had done an amazing job on a wide stage that gave the entire production a sort of CinemaScope quality. It boded well for the opening.

The theatre had put together a rigorous promotional campaign that involved me doing a great many interviews and sitting for a great many photographers. There were luncheons with speeches coordinated by *Vogue Australia* and full afternoon lectures/Q&As at the Sydney theatre school and other artistic institutions.

But if I worked hard for my money, I played hard for it too. A few days after my arrival the publicist at the theatre invited me for a Saturday excursion on his yacht through Sydney Harbour with a number of other gay men. Three of the men on the boat— the director, the designer and the designer's lover—were known to me; the two other queer larrikins were obviously taken with me and they'd be my hosts in the end.

Their names were Marcus and Dante. They were about ten years my senior and they were two of the hardest-partying dudes I've ever met. We made plans for them to show me the bars, and when they called to confirm, Marcus ended with, "Clean out your nose."

Cocaine in Sydney? Now that sounded like fun.

When they arrived they laid out a giant rail on the table and told me to snuff it up, before doing the same themselves. I was experiencing a lot of sinus pain. "What's that blow cut with?" I asked. They shared a look.

Dante said, "It's crystal."

Marcus said, "We assumed you'd know that."

I'd never done crystal meth, and I never did it again—but I have to say, that was a fucking fun three days.

The play proved to be a hit. I found Sydney was very gracious to anyone who made the trip. By my final night in town I'd been around long enough to throw a small cocktail party at the condo to thank the people I'd met and the people in the show for the excellent time. It turned out to be a total piss-up and climaxed with all of us at one of the bars high on ecstasy and dancing our faces off. Marcus and Dante gave me some downers to get me home and I decided it was best for me to stay up all night so as not to miss my flight.

I passed out and missed my flight. Luckily another one was leaving the next morning, although it cost me an extra $500.

Grayden greeted me at the airport with a wet kiss. We had some hot sex and he dropped me off, knowing I'd need some recovery time.

I wasn't quite my usual self when Hilda Jurgens phoned me my second day back and said, "Did you hear about the *Star* story?"

"What *Star* story?"

She said, "Sit down. I'll read it to you. It came out just after you left. It's the entire lower half of the front page of the entertainment section."

"What's the headline?"

"'Canadian Playwright Against Government Funding for the Arts.'"

I said, "I didn't give any interviews about arts funding."

Hilda read me the article. The gist of it was that some people considered government funding for the arts controversial but, ironically, homegrown bad-boy playwright Brad Fraser was against it while David Mirvish, producer of the most commercial house in Toronto, was for it. It made no sense to me. I couldn't remember saying the quotes they attributed to me. I was weirded out more than alarmed.

I said, "The last interview I did with the *Star* was when *Poor Super Man* opened months ago."

"Did you discuss arts funding?"

"We might have. But it wasn't the point of the interview, just a sidebar that I was glib about. Along with a bunch of other topics I was glib about. They wouldn't have used that?"

Hilda said, "I think they did."

And they had.

My public stance on arts funding had been consistent throughout my career and I'd expressed it many times. While I absolutely thought it was wise for the government to invest money in the arts and support the careers of artists in the same way they did for any other industry that brought money into the country, I also felt it was important that artists find a paying audience so they weren't reliant on government resources for their livelihood—which could lead to all kinds of censorious complications depending on the government of the day (as I experienced repeatedly through-out my career). I'd been the recipient of the government's largesse a few times in my career and was always appropriately grateful and careful to acknowledge it.

Taken out of that context and without the nuance I usually brought to the subject, my comments seemed harsh and didn't reflect my true opinion.

I was stunned, unable to believe Toronto's largest and most progressive newspaper would do such a thing. Hilda explained it had generated a lot of debate and angry discussion about Canadian artists betraying their own when I wasn't around to respond.

I had become accustomed to saying things that drew public ire. It always blew over. I shrugged the whole thing off. It was the *Star*'s fuck-up, not mine. People would see that.

I was wrong, but I wouldn't know it for a while yet.

One bright afternoon, after my workout, I bought a *Globe and Mail* and went for lunch at the innocuous restaurant in the hotel around the corner from the gym. There were few things I loved more than a quiet lunch while thoroughly reading the paper. After I'd ordered I pulled the entertainment section out and saw the lesser headline lower on the front page—"Vancouver Actor John Moffat Dead of AIDS."

The restaurant was full of people chatting happily; Cyndi Lauper's "Time After Time" was playing, reminding me of every-one I had ever loved. A knot, a growth, a throbbing tumour of anger and sadness was swelling in my chest and I felt like I was going to choke. The words in the newspaper suddenly meant nothing, my lunch was sawdust in my mouth, my hands shook when I paid the bill, but I did not break.

John's death made me question this relationship I seemed to be embarking on with Grayden. He and I kissed deeply and engaged in oral but always used a condom for anything invasive.

Grayden was well known in a number of different circles in the city and was as comfortable in a suit at a municipal meeting with politicians as he was dancing shirtless on a speaker while high on E.

If anything he was too popular. Too many people knew him, too many people wanted him, and too many people lived with him—specifically his two younger ex-boyfriends, one in his early thirties and one in his early twenties. Grayden assured me it was all just friendship and convenience, but I could tell there was more to the story. I could also feel more than a little resentment and curiosity emanate from them whenever I arrived on the scene.

It became apparent to me that there was a negative dynamic to Grayden's relationship with the two exes profoundly connected to who infected who first. This question, I will admit, was also an issue with me at the time.

Despite my doubts, I felt better than I ever had in my life. I remember walking down Queen Street on a beautiful late-spring day, the clockwork madness of Toronto, pedestrians, cyclists, streetcars and vehicles ticking around me, and thinking, "This is perfect. This moment is absolutely fucking perfect. I wish everything could stay like this forever."

Grayden and I took a break from our budding but still uncommitted romance when I flew back to Edmonton to direct a musical version of *Young Art* at Theatre Network that was underdeveloped and under-rehearsed. The best thing that can be said about it is that it featured a young Damien Atkins, who would make his name as an actor and writer across the country a few years later. While I enjoyed being back in my house and among my beloved collectibles, I was distracted, wondering if Grayden was being faithful to me even as I was sure he was not.

The show opened to general indifference and I was glad to get out of town fast. Only later would I realize how tired I was when working on that production. The other shows, the trips back and forth to L.A., the Australian adventure had all taken their toll. I was shocked to discover my formerly endless energy had limits.

To further darken my mood, a right-wing, anti-tax propaganda organization that the corporate press loved to refer to as a "think tank" got wind of my government-sponsored trip to Australia and decided to make it an issue.

That year a great many prominent Canadian artists had travelled with the sponsorship of the government—given because promoting Canadian talent around the world does indeed help the country in many ways—but for some reason I was chosen from among all the other uniformly straight artists to be attacked. The propaganda organization started this whole "why are our tax dollars being used to promote homosexuality?" outcry that the complicit media amplified.

I fought back as I always did, but what was particularly sobering for me was that I got absolutely no public or private support from my fellow Canadian theatre artists. I'd made my reputation by speaking out not just for myself but for anyone I felt was being unfairly treated in the press or the profession, and many of my peers had thanked me for my support over the years. I took on and pissed off some very high-profile and powerful people in the name of denouncing hypocrisy or corruption, but the Star's inflammatory story about my supposed stance against public arts funding prejudiced everyone's opinion, and there was no defence for me.

I returned to Toronto chastened and had a bit of time off, but another project on the horizon I'd been working on with Daniel MacIvor was about to take precedence.

Since our first meeting years before in Calgary, we often hung out, particularly after Nick Sheehan had asked both of us to be in a doc/drama fusion film he was directing called *Symposium: Ladder of Love*, which featured a number of prominent gay men of the time expounding on their ideas of love.

Danny has a great wit and the soul of a true poet. We both liked to drink, smoke pot, occasionally suck up some blow, and talk. One night, while doing exactly that, we had come up with the idea of making an entirely improvised low-budget film on Gay Pride Day. It started as one of those pie-in-the-sky "someday we should . . ." ideas, but gradually we both grew serious about it.

Before I'd left for Australia we had outlined a basic plot for the film and committed to hiring equipment so the camera, sound and other technical volunteers we were enlisting would have something to film with. We also committed to a budget— small in film terms but large because it was our own money. Randy and Hilda came on board as producers.

The project was highly questionable in light of our various union affiliations, which frowned upon improvisational film projects using members who didn't get paid. To get around this we made it a cooperative effort: everyone involved signed general releases as co-producers, should money ever become an issue in what was never meant to be a money-making enterprise. Neither Danny nor I wanted to ask anyone's permission or deal with the endless bureaucracy that came with these kinds of projects.

The plan was to film the exterior scenes on the day of Pride, throughout the Church/Wellesley village. Danny and I each had a crew of a cameraman, a sound person and someone to help them. There would be no lights, no costumes, no fluffers; *Parade* was to be all *au naturel*, raw and fast. We met with the entire crew to find out what they would need and worked out a schedule for the day. We then met with the large cast we'd wheedled into appearing in the film and gave them a breakdown of the day with written instructions of where to be and when as well as a general idea of the situation and their character. We even included a helpful map of the neighbourhood.

Danny and I then planned to schedule a couple of days of interior scenes to fill out the story and see what we came up with in the editing suite.

While all this planning was going on, the Toronto theatre awards, the Doras, announced the nominations for 1995. *Poor Super Man* was nominated for best new play, best production, best direction and best performance by a male.

The *Parade* shoot started at seven thirty. The hood was rife with film crews on Pride Day, so we knew people would take little notice of us. Everyone was in their place at their allotted times, we had a quick confab, then shot the scene, improvising all business and dialogue.

Danny and I played long-time partners who were going through a period of conflict on Pride Day just as Danny's character's hot younger, straight brother shows up on the scene. We each had our separate storylines that only intersected at the beginning, briefly in the middle and at the end. Danny's character, a display artist at the Bay, was having an existential crisis about staying with his inconstant, aging club-boy lover, a brash, outspoken bartender from the Barn, played by me. The straight brother (played by Trevor McCarthy, an alumnus of *Blood Buddies* five years earlier) accidentally takes ecstasy and has his own narrative for the day.

It was a magical, insane experience fuelled by adrenaline and determination. Danny and I were a great team and had organized things brilliantly as we wove our way through the village to the various locations. There were no breaks. We ate whenever we had a moment. When filming was over we met at an after-hours place in the alley behind where the Manatee used to be and most of the cast and crew did ecstasy and partied late into the night.

We then had a two-week break until we reconvened to shoot the interiors for the film, and Grayden and I flew to New York City and Fire Island for our first vacation as a couple.

We spent two days in the city in early July, when NYC was at its most surly. We lunched and shopped during the day and danced at the latest hot bar at night. When we got back to the Gramercy apartment of one of his friends—a literary critic who was in the last stages of AIDS who was already at the island—I fucked him and he purred like a happy cat. As we fell asleep spooning, I felt that we were at that moment embodying everything that was amazing about being gay.

The next day we caught the train to Fire Island. I was excited. This was gay history. I'd been reading about Fire Island my entire adult life, in literature and in porn. Everyone who was anyone in New York's artistic history had summered on Fire Island. If they were rich they did it in their amazing homes; if not, they rented a time-share room in one of the many gay co-operative houses on the island. Grayden and I would be experiencing it mostly in the fashion of those who had money. His friend, whose New York apartment we'd fucked in the night before, had a half ownership of a beautiful but not too ostentatious house on a low-key part of the island.

I was charmed by the endless elevated boardwalks and the fact no cars were allowed there. We stowed our luggage in our bedroom and met our other guests, four incredibly handsome, built, upwardly mobile young white men in their late twenties and early thirties who were making their names in the world of publishing or galleries or something equally fabulous in Manhattan. I felt gauche and clumsy, so quickly defaulted to a quiet listening persona that took no risks in order to avoid embarrassment. Grayden was far more comfortable with these people than I. Positively garrulous.

He gave me a full tour of the island, including the infamous outdoor cruising/sex area known as the Meat Rack, as well as the few bars and clubs that catered to the endless flow of gay men. We did ecstasy and went to a dance, but it wasn't a good trip and neither Grayden nor I were particularly attentive to one another as the drugs made us both internal and silent. The music seemed to be mostly pots and pans.

When we got back to the house the guests were all gathered around the pool having drinks. Grayden joined them, but I begged off and went to the bedroom, where I took my lenses out, stripped off my clothes and climbed into bed. I did that "not quite committed to sleep or awake" thing for a while before Grayden came in to change. He got naked, sat on the edge of the bed and grabbed my cock. He leaned over and devoured it, coaxed it to its full length—and it always seemed to be just a little bit longer for him—and gave me a long, slow hummer. He stretched out on the bed next to me and said, "Why don't you come out and join us?"

I said, "I'm too tired and—weird. That ecstasy went sideways."

"You want a lorazepam?"

I said, "Maybe half. I'll probably skip dinner."

He gave me half of the pill and I swallowed it with some beer I had in a glass beside the bed. He kissed me as I slipped into blackness.

When I woke my mouth was cotton and sand. I felt weird. The E still fizzed through my system but not as intensely. The light was wrong. Things were disturbingly quiet.

I fell out of bed and pulled on a pair of cargo shorts. The clock beside the bed told me I'd been out for hours. In the kitchen I ran myself a glass of water and downed it quickly. I heard distant music, some Frankie Knuckles remix of something significant to my meeting with Grayden at the time. The walls and ceiling were painted by a soft, undulating blue light that emanated from beneath the water of the pool and was cast back into the house.

Through the window I could see the gangbang happening at the other end of the pool. Grayden's friend who hosted us sat in a deck chair and watched with bright eyes as Grayden, bent over the table, was fucked by the swarthiest of our fellow houseguests, with the rest of them lined up waiting their turn. None of them were wearing condoms.

Grayden's face contorted with a smug, savage pleasure as the first guy came in his ass. I pulled farther back into the shadows, angered but also turgid, a thick thread of pre-cum already oozing from my cock as I experienced an arousing mixture of jealousy and desire. They were doing the one thing Grayden and I never could.

I was consumed with resentment as I jerked off indifferently onto the dying literary guy's expensive carpet. They were still going at it when I wandered back to our room and passed out again.

I woke up well before Grayden did, and wandered the boardwalks. Eventually I sat on a rail overlooking the protected dunes and the pounding ocean beyond them. Suddenly Fire Island seemed like a very expensive graveyard to me.

I said nothing of what I'd witnessed as we packed for our return to Toronto. When he dropped me off at my place we shared a perfunctory kiss.

In August Grayden and I flew to Edmonton for the folk festival, which was held just down the hill from my house. The festival was a big deal, and knowing someone nearby where you could use the toilet and freshen up between acts was a lovely bonus. A number of gay male friends from Calgary stayed at my place and mingled happily with my mostly straight, married Edmonton friends, many of whom had children by now.

I had my entire family over to meet Grayden. He was smooth and charming and they were surprisingly intrigued. During the years Pete and I were together they'd essentially acted as if he didn't exist, even when they were all in the same room. My friends were also much impressed when they met Grayden. On the surface we were an ideal couple. We had great sex the night before he left—he topped me for the first time, and when his airport limo picked him up the next day, after a lingering kiss I watched the car pull away and thought, "I think I might really love this guy."

When I got back to Toronto a week later and called him, he suggested we meet at a popular greasy-spoon breakfast place.

The restaurant was packed. We were seated at a deuce in the centre of the room, chattering tables all around us. I could tell right away something was off. After we'd ordered I said, "What's going on?"

Grayden started to say things. They were fragmented. They were general. They were odd. Something about a rise in the virus in his system. Something about not being comfortable with a dominant man because he was a dominant man. Something about not being ready for a relationship.

I said, "Are you breaking up with me?"

He gave me his most charming smile and said, "Yes. Yes, I am."

My face was frozen. My eyes were hard. "Is it something I did or said?"

He flashed another charming smile. "It's not you."

"If it's not me, why are we breaking up?"

Grayden said, "There's so much going on in my life . . ." and let it trail off so it encompassed all possibilities.

Everything in me wanted to say, "Please don't reject me. I don't like it. I've had too much of it. Tell me what I need to do to keep you and I'll do it. I will. Anything you ask." Instead I gestured for the waiter to bring our bill and made a point of paying.

When we walked out of the restaurant I insisted on walking him to his office to further understand why he was dumping me. By the time we got there he'd made it clear that he was originally drawn by my confidence and public profile but, sexually, I wasn't what he craved most of the time. We shook hands at the door.

I said, "I saw you. At Fire Island. With the guys around the pool."

Surprise, shame and defiance flickered across his face, then he shrugged unapologetically and disappeared into the building.

I trudged home, devastated.

With the luxury of hindsight I can now examine my behaviour after this breakup and cringe. I was wounded and angry, and they are a dangerous combination. There were late-night phone calls and accusatory letters that he rightfully ignored, which only increased my fury. I came close to sexually acting out negatively a number of times. I'd been shaken badly as I realized everything I'd accomplished to date, and having so many of my dreams come true, didn't insulate me from failure or rejection at all.

Also, it was time I faced the fact I had terrible judgment when it came to boyfriends.

## PART SEVEN

# MARTIN YESTERDAY

AS ALWAYS MY RELIEF FROM heartbreak and depression came with creativity, and I had a huge project on my plate—the editing of *Parade*. Danny came in for part of the work and we had a lot of laughs getting high and playing with the material while being alternately thrilled and horrified by the performances and shots we were seeing. The incidental footage of Pride Day and the parade itself was quite marvellous, with tons of detail and quirky shots. Danny had a lot on his plate at the time and I had a lot of free time, so the bulk of the editing fell to me.

I worked into the fall on a rented editing suite in my bachelor apartment, which for months looked like a storage room for video cassettes, empty pizza boxes and ashtrays full of roaches. We now had to digitize the material we knew for sure would be in the film so it could be properly cut and processed for projection, but the cost of doing so in Toronto was high. Randy made a deal with the Alberta Film Association to use their state-of-the-art equipment at a fair price. This meant I would be spending November, December and January in Edmonton working with a professional editor for the final fine cut of the film.

On the one hand, it was comforting to be back at the house with my things and my cats healing my broken heart. The editor and I worked in an old building in the river valley during afternoons and evenings and then I'd either head home or off to the Roost for a drink.

It was odd going to the bars in Edmonton now. Just a few years earlier I'd been a local celebrity and my appearance always created a stir. By this time I'd been away for so long, and my work had been distant enough, that only the old-timers had any idea who I was. I could actually have a drink on my own without someone approaching me to talk, express their admiration or tell me what a charlatan I was, as had become the case in Toronto.

In the final week, we spent about eighteen hours a day in the editing suite during one of the worst winters on record. It nearly killed us, but we got a cut that came in at just over eighty minutes, and I flew back to Toronto with a copy of it in my hands.

Danny's reaction was positive, and he had a professional friend of his give the cut a polish while we did a couple of test showings, one in Toronto and one in Edmonton. Randy would take care of setting up the Edmonton event, while Danny had his producer oversee the Toronto showing.

I flew to Edmonton for the screening, which was held in the movie theatre housed in the main branch of the Edmonton Public Library. We'd sent invitations to almost everyone we knew, from our past and our present. There was plenty of laughter during the show because those who knew me knew I was playing a character based on a small part of myself they knew well.

I then went to Toronto for its screening, held in the Canadian Stage rehearsal hall. The audience sat at tables and we projected the film onto a moderately sized screen set up against one wall. The audience here was mostly friends, but also business associates and professional representatives who were looking at the film as a commercial possibility.

Standing at the back of the room, I could feel the chill that descended during my scenes. It wasn't just my performance they were responding to but also the character. Friends would later tell me they admired my brave choice to be so unsympathetic; given Danny's major charm, I'd really felt I had no choice but to go in the completely opposite direction. I've never been afraid to create or portray a mostly unsympathetic character.

A representative from Alliance Films, which was the most influential company in the country at the time, praised Danny's performance effusively to me and then added, "Of course acting really isn't your thing."

A few days later I flew to Vancouver to direct *Poor Super Man* for the Arts Club in their smaller second space on Granville Island. I was looking forward to this project. I'd never worked in Vancouver, but it was a city that was close to my heart and resonated constantly with flickering phantoms of John Moffat and so many other men from western Canada who had gone to Vancouver to die beginning in the early eighties. I never blamed any of them for not wanting to live out their last days in Edmonton or Calgary.

Although I hadn't seen much of Cam since New York, we were in touch by phone every few weeks. But he hadn't called me back the last couple of times, so I was relieved to be in Vancouver to find out what was going on.

When I called his number his long-term partner, Shane, answered and told me Cam had taken a fall and was in the hospital. I hopped a cab to St. Paul's Hospital and found my way to Cam's room. When I entered he looked up in wonder and said, "Brad?"

I sat in the chair beside the bed and took his hand in mine. "Hey, Cam." Shane, who'd been on the other side of the bed, moved away to give us room.

Cam's former steroid bulk was gone. He was like the Cam I'd first known except emaciated rather than thin, and brittle rather than willowy. He still had plenty of light brown hair, although it hung lank and dead around his face. He gave me a loopy smile through unfocused eyes and hiccupped. "Why are you here?"

"To see you, of course. And I'm opening a show."

Cam hiccupped and said, "Your AIDS play."

I nodded. "I'd really like you to be there for opening." I put my hand on his forehead softly.

He said, "I'm sorry I didn't call you back. Something was happening. It scared me. Then I fell down and couldn't get up until Shane came home and called an ambulance."

I said, "I understand," and squeezed his hand. He hiccupped. "What's with the hiccups?" I asked.

In the doorway, Shane shot me a look that said "Don't ask that," but Cam said, "Brain cancer. My dad had it. One of the signs. Hiccups. Hurts. A lot." Then, with some effort, he turned his head on the pillow to look at me directly and said, "I've always wanted to tell you—"

A nurse came in, announcing, "It's time for his pain meds." She plunged a syringe into a plastic shunt punched into the left side of his chest.

I wanted to scream "No, wait, he was trying to tell me something" but knew it would look selfish. Within a few seconds Cam's eyes rolled in his head and his tongue made a dry clicking noise in the back of his throat. Shane moved to the other side of the bed. Cam's hand went slack in mine as the drugs took hold.

I leaned forward, resting my forehead on his bony shoulder, and whispered, "Please don't go."

He fell into a laboured slumber. Eventually Shane moved behind me and put a hand on my shoulder, giving me permission to leave. I walked over the Burrard Street Bridge and down to Granville Island in a daze for a night of barbed-wire memories and broken sleep.

For the next two days we did general auditions for the show and I tried to put Cam out of my mind and concentrate on the performers I was seeing.

Then Shane called me and told me Cam had died quietly in his sleep a few hours earlier. I didn't break down. I asked him if there was going to be some kind of service, but there wasn't. I thanked Shane for calling and offered him any support I might give him.

Alone in the generic condo I curled into a fetal position on the bed and keened and rocked to soothe myself.

A few hours later artistic director Bill Millerd called me from the Arts Club to remind me he needed the names of the actors required for the callbacks after the general auditions. I assured him I'd have a list ready the next day. But when I sat down to compile it I found my brain befuddled, and it was hard to concentrate as I went through the resumés and my notes from the earlier auditions. I was in shock. I was grieving. I was paralyzed.

In the end I shattered one of the basic tenets of professionalism by calling back far more people than I needed to because my situation had kept me from properly assessing their abilities the first time. There was a major backup of actors and audition times, and the process ended up taking most of the day in a cattle-call manner that many of those auditioning took exception to after they discovered they hadn't been cast. The theatre eventually ended up paying the actors' union a fine for every actor who'd been kept beyond a dictated time. What was particularly galling about all of this was that big commercial producers did this sort of thing all the time without hearing a peep from the actors. They tended to take out the frustration of their general power-lessness on the smaller Canadian companies, which didn't hire as many people or pay as much. Nonetheless, this extra cost to the theatre was caused by me and I've always regretted this rare lapse in professionalism.

Cam's essence suffused every bit of my work, which was some of my best as a director. I had a strong cast and an amazing design team. The way the captions were handled on the computer and a projector were what I'd always imagined. I was comfortable with the material and knew how to physically guide the show in the space. Rehearsals were exciting.

The show opened to strong reviews and great houses. Randy came for the opening and had tears in his eyes when he hugged me afterwards. *Poor Super Man* ran all summer.

Back in Toronto, Danny's editor friend had completed her cut of *Parade*. I felt sick when I saw how much better it was than mine. This version went on to play endlessly at gay and lesbian film festivals all over the continent for the next couple of years, but we would never make any money from it.

Whatever its deficiencies, *Parade* captures the Gay Village of Church and Wellesley and the Gay Pride celebration at their nine-ties peak. At that time there were no barriers between the crowds and the parade participants. As those barriers went up a few years later, so did the corporate sponsorships and the gelding and homogenization of what had started as a protest and a demand for recognition. *Parade* also features a number of important artists from that moment: Tracy Wright, Caroline Gillis, Sky Gilbert, Allegra Fulton, John Frizzell, Gale Garnet and many others.

I flew back to Sydney, Australia, this time at my own expense, to experience their gay Mardi Gras, which was legendary across the globe. Dante and Marcus had had an acrimonious split, which put a definite crimp into my hopes for the holiday as I liked them best as a couple. While there I was also working on my newest script, which was to be a radio play.

I had been co-commissioned by the CBC and the BBC to write a radio drama. I wanted to write a show that skipped through time, juxtaposing the most important moments in a relationship between a young, promising cartoonist and an older philanthropic political leader. The politician was HIV-positive, the cartoonist was not. It was loosely based on my experience with Grayden.

This was to be my bookend to *Poor Super Man*. Where that play was about everything that was honourable about the queer community's response to AIDS, *Martin Yesterday* would be about all of the most reprehensible qualities of a community that had been fighting for its life and identity from the very beginning, while now facing a threat few other communities could even imagine. I wanted to take some risks and say some intentionally unpleasant things.

I should've read the signs when, while in Sydney, just as I was adding the final touches to the last scene, a strange black stain appeared in the upper left corner of my laptop's screen and slowly began to spread outward. I desperately and repeatedly pressed the save command until the screen was black and the computer stopped humming. It was dead. The two weeks of work I'd done since arriving in Sydney, essentially the last act of the script, had been lost. It would have to be recreated when I returned home to Toronto, where I had a dated backup on a floppy disk.

A few months later, back in Toronto, we taped the show at the CBC Radio studios on Front Street. Hillary Norish, who'd originally commissioned the script for the BBC, was there to direct, Danny MacIvor played Matt, the main character, and a stellar cast supported him. When it was finally broadcast, not much attention was paid—it was radio, after all—but it was nominated in London for a Sony Radio Award (and did not win).

I was getting low on money, so I arranged for another round of meetings and pitches in L.A. The failure of the *Remains* movie and the oddness of *Parade* had dimmed the lustre of my star, but I was still hot enough to get meetings at the major studios. I would gain a couple of jobs that got me paid, although nothing was ever made.

Tad had stopped speaking to me a few months earlier, and I was hurt and baffled by his refusal to return my calls. I reached out a number of times and got one of those mild passive-aggressive responses that let you know your overture was ineffective.

Randy also withdrew from me around this time. That was natural in a sense, as I wasn't making much money at the time, and I knew he felt *Parade* had been a lot of work for no payback and I couldn't argue that. He sent me the company cheque book and records, suggesting I take control of my own finances.

There was a tension growing within me and with those around me, and I wasn't sure who was at fault.

Sarah Garton Stanley had taken over Buddies in Bad Times Theatre after Sky Gilbert surprised everyone by resigning from the theatre he had started. I'd met with her and left her a copy of the radio version of *Martin Yesterday*, saying I'd like to adapt it as a play. She called me a few months later and asked me if I'd be interested in directing the script at Buddies in the 1996/97 season. I accepted immediately. I'd tried over the years to get Sky to produce my work with no success. Finally I'd been asked to work at Buddies.

I threw myself into reinventing *Martin Yesterday* for the stage. If it was going to be done at the largest gay theatre in North America, then I was going to make it the gayest show I possibly could.

The press around the world and especially in Canada had dubbed me a "bad boy" early in my career. Initially I'd welcomed the title. It was gangster. It was James Dean. And I was being a bad boy with *Wolfboy* and *Chainsaw Love*, intentionally pushing boundaries that kept people from examining too closely my ability (or not) to create two hours of sustained entertainment through the writing alone. But after that I had taken the craft and discipline of writing a play and creating for the theatre very seriously. I pushed barriers, particularly concerning sexuality and gender, with defined intentions that usually came from challenging our ideas of what could be said and done in the modern theatre.

Again and again certain critics had dismissed my work by criticizing the very things about the experience I'd set out to do, to wit: if my intention is to offend or challenge upper-middle-class white people who share the same education and viewpoint, and if that is exactly what happened, then, from my point of view, I did not fail. I would eventually understand that being their "bad boy" diluted my power, it minimized my message, it kept them dominant. It characterized me as a child.

I wanted *Martin Yesterday* to be the most honest play I could write. I didn't want any of *Poor Super Man's* strategic sentimentality and careful modulation of sexual content. I wanted to create something that accurately reflected the gay world that many of us were living in, with all of its squalor and questionable behaviour. I wanted to talk about the self-hatred and abuse of emotion I saw in our community, and I wanted to talk about the straight world's control of how we felt about ourselves and each other and how we let them get away with it by co-operating in their societal narrative rather than creating our own.

Twenty years earlier, *With Love from Your Son* had been denied the production that had been promised when it had won the Alberta Culture Playwriting Competition because of its mild gay content. Now, this Buddies production of *Martin Yesterday* was going to be my response to the psychic trauma I had carried since that decision and so many other transgressions I'd had to endure because of my sexuality.

I intended to respond to every homophobic slight, attack and insult I'd had to deal with from the corporate media throughout my career in the most entertaining and challenging manner I could muster. I knew I was flirting with disaster but figured I'd finally earned the right to take some profound chances.

In the end I cast my usual blend of people I'd worked with before, and brand-new actors found in auditions. As has almost always been my experience, the designers and technicians were a dream team who had done their homework, listened to my challenges and come back with solutions that allowed them to elevate whatever I'd asked for with their considerable thought and talent. We had ample rehearsal time and a healthy budget, and I intended to take advantage of both. The actors were uncertain of the material. It was a challenging rehearsal period.

There's a scene in the radio play where Martin tells Matt he's HIV-positive while they're riding on a roller coaster, and I wanted to find some version of that for the stage. After considering a number of possibilities with the designers, we went with my original proposal—rear projection. Since we were using video elsewhere in the show, I had a designer create opening credits and background video for segments of the show based on ideas we'd tossed around. I knew that showing World War Two newsreel footage of bodies being bulldozed in Nazi death camps would be controversial—it occurs when Martin talks about killing his best friend to save him further suffering from AIDS—and so I embraced it.

I also decided I would at last address the criticisms of insecure male pundits that male nudity in sex scenes was never convincing. We used lifelike dildos that were not only erect but rigged to ejaculate. Most of the sex scenes were played in careful lighting, and the effect was quite convincing. But getting the desired effect did take some work. The first time one of the fake dicks was tested in rehearsal—it was large enough to read at the back of the house—the shot went all the way across the stage at eye level. I laughed so hard I fell off my chair. We tried a number of liquids to suggest semen, but in the end it was plain water that made the most convincing cum when properly ejected under the harsh lights of the stage.

There was a great deal of fuss in the press about the show before the opening, and it wasn't restricted to Toronto. I learned that a tour operator in upstate New York was offering trips to see the show, including B&B accommodation. When I was at the Barn after rehearsal one night, another gay playwright who was opening a show passive-aggressively congratulated me on "sucking up all the publicity." I smiled and flexed my tits at him.

Sarah Stanley and an invited audience watched the first tech/dress run, which is where the production tries to bring all the

elements in the theatre together, lights, set, sound and performers, before opening night. It was a bit of a nightmare. The tempo
I establish for my productions, which is brisk and nuanced,
demands the performers be in control of all elements at all times
in order to tell the story properly. However, any show in front of
a first audience is terrifying, and it always throws the actors into
an adrenaline frenzy, with the result that they race through the
play. This is completely natural, and the actors often need four
or five performances in front of audiences before they become
fully in control of the cadence and rhythm of the overarching
narrative. Sadly, though, we rarely get four or five previews, so
I've had some very rocky opening nights.

In her office afterwards Sarah said, "How does the audience
get in?" I had no idea what she was talking about, and my face
showed it. She gave me that smart, sly smile she's known for and
said, "It's all so fast and hard. There's a lot going on. It never
rests, so in parts it gets tiresome because there's been no space
for me to get on board."

I thanked her and spent a sleepless night thinking about what
she'd said. I'd sat with the audience and could feel exactly what
Sarah was talking about. The audience hadn't been engaging
with the narrative in the way I hoped.

In rehearsal the next day I shared Sarah's note with the cast
and said, "Guys, we're doing a play by one of Canada's queerest
playwrights in the world's queerest theatre. I know it's scary and
I'm so grateful you've all been brave enough to come along, but
we know these people. Sometimes we *are* these people. Don't
judge them. Find the noble, likeable parts of their personalities
and enjoy them, but do the same thing with their selfish, unlikeable side. Just let them be human." The actors, who'd felt the
same response, agreed.

The public preview that night was much smoother and the audience laughed more easily than the night before. The actors became more confident and did indeed open up and let the audience more into their performances.

I sat out the opening performance of the play, as I often did when the demand for tickets exceeded the seats available. Instead I smoked a joint and took half a lorazepam before going to meet the cast, crew and audience at the after-party at the bar/restaurant Byzantium on Church Street. The party was in full swing when I arrived. I moved through the crowd smiling, shaking hands and exchanging cheek kisses with well-wishers as I searched the crowd for Randy. I finally found him at the back of the restaurant talking to the Davids.

"How'd it go?" I asked, searching his eyes, which were evasive. My stomach turned to ice.

He said, "I'm not sure they got it."

"Did they laugh?" I asked.

"Some of us."

"Were they bored?"

"No one was bored. But not everyone was happy."

David Gale handed me a beer and gave me a hug as he told me he loved the play, adding, "I'm Jewish and gay so I understood the concentration camp footage, but not everyone did."

I smiled and kissed him. "Fuck them."

David Wright gave me a dubious smile.

The next morning the *Globe and Mail* was just outside the apartment door, as it always was.

The headline on the Arts section's front page read: "Brad Fraser: Yesterday's Man."

# PART EIGHT

# THRENODY

I HAVE HAD A GREAT MANY bad reviews in my career; I have had reviews that reeked of homophobia and fear, I have had reviews that denounced my existence and denied the exist-ence of the characters on the stage, I have had reviews that commented on my physical appearance, but I had never had a review as toxic as this one. But my greatest sin according to this reviewer was including the concentration camp footage behind Martin's monologue. For daring to make this parallel, I was denounced as I had never been denounced before from a number of quarters.

That a supposedly educated theatre reviewer would not know the history of gay men in Nazi Germany was insulting. I remem-ber seeing Martin Sherman's amazing *Bent* staged in Edmonton, one of the best plays about the incarceration of gay men along with the disabled and other minorities. At the end of the war, when the camps were liberated, everyone was freed—except the homosexuals, who were sent to mental hospitals and prisons. Other people who were incarcerated would insist that, for the homos, that was justified.

In many ways the gay press found me even more problematic, and many of their responses seethed with malice for my having spoken of our darkest secrets in a public place. Barebacking, passing the virus, drug use, sex and substance addiction, depression, despair—these were things they loved to write about in the neighbourhood weekly, but they should not be graphically staged in a place where straight people could judge us.

The *Toronto Star* gave the show a fair but mixed review, although it too was shocked by the concentration camp footage. A few out-of-town papers gave it strong, positive reviews, but the consensus in the city was that I had produced a major flop by going just one step too far in my attempts to shock the public.

On the second night I took a seat in a corner at the back of the house after the audience had been seated and watched the show. At the end of the first act, where the monologue with the concentration camp video happened, I felt a ripple of energy in the audience that pulled many of them out of the play completely. I realized the images made the monologue redundant. Horror stacked on horror creates indifference. I didn't want to appear to be cutting the clip because people disapproved of it, but I also wanted my message to come through. I realized there were some who would never hear what I was saying as long as it was accompanied by that imagery. So I cut that video. I also cut others, to tone down the busyness of the show. It didn't bother me at all to do this, as I often changed distracting or problematic technical aspects of shows after opening night.

I sent an eloquent, informative letter about the history of gays in the Holocaust to the editor at the *Globe*, which they published. I took the reviewer and the Toronto press in general to task for their historical ignorance, then deconstructed the homophobia in the review. While my statement was admired by some, it created a darker backlash from those I'd called to task.

A few days later a series of letters and articles appeared in the press further condemning the play, which was selling out despite the first reviews. There was an article about how lame using video in the theatre had become. There was an article about how nudity and sex in the theatre had become tiresome. "Journalists" called me at home to ask how it felt to fail. *Variety* ran a scathing review by a local reviewer whose closeted but predatory behaviour I'd written about a number of times. *Martin Yesterday* was the talk of the town. But not in a good way.

Three days after opening, Iris Turcott called me. "Come over to my place for coffee, honey," she croaked. "We've gotta talk about this shit."

Iris had been the dramaturge on the play since its inception as a stage piece. When I got to her apartment in a city co-op she was, as always, sucking on a cigarette in her dining room.

"What the fuck?" I asked as I slipped into the chair across from her, pulling a can of Diet Pepsi from my bag and popping it open.

Iris stubbed her half-smoked cigarette out in an ashtray on the table. "That cunt at the *Globe*—that was an attempt to really hurt you with the big-time arts donor crowd. It was dirty."

"You saw my letter?"

"Fucking great. Fuck that cunt." ("Cunt" was one of Iris's favourite words and she applied it liberally to all people.)

"I still don't get it."

Iris pulled another cigarette from her pack and lit it angrily. No one angrily lit cigarettes like Iris Turcott. It was awe-inspiring. "You left us out."

"Who?"

"Straight people, stupid. Everything's gotta fucking be about us. We don't care what queers do. And we certainly don't want to be told their deaths are our fault through our fucking indifference."

It had not been lost on me that *Martin Yesterday* was my first play with an all-male cast. In fact, in all of my earlier plays the queer-identified characters were always outnumbered by the straight-identified characters.

I said, "None of them even mentioned it was at a gay theatre for a gay audience."

"Of course not," she snarled. "Most of them don't know what context is."

We both laugh/coughed heavily, sounding like Joan Rivers and a harbour seal.

"They hate me."

Iris nodded. "They've hated you before."

"Not like this," I said.

"So what're you going to do?"

"I need to rewrite it. Open it up a bit. Tone it down. For Edmonton."

She nodded. "Smart. For Edmonton."

Ben Henderson at Theatre Network had asked me if he could produce the show even before it opened in Toronto. I needed the money and agreed, although I thought the play would be an odd fit and a hard sell in Edmonton with its small queer community.

"Do you think having an all-male cast is an issue?" I asked Iris.

She shrugged. "A lot of your audience are women, so I don't think it helped."

"What if I changed Manny"—the character who was the lead's best friend and artistic partner and the only straight guy in the show—"to a woman and made her Jewish?"

Iris snapped her fingers and laughed. "Great."

"Anything else?"

"Maybe the exploding dicks are unnecessary in future productions."

"Is that as bad as they say it is?"

She lit another cigarette. "Jesus. I don't think anything could be as bad as they're making out—but you enjoy yourself too much, honey. You don't care what they think. You make jokes at their expense. What did you expect?"

I hugged her and left to get to work on the rewrite.

Things had become very quiet since *Martin* opened. Theatre friends who used to call regularly had stopped; guys at the gym who'd formerly engaged me in meaningless conversation now smiled wanly and didn't chat. Then the national press picked up on the fuss and stories began to appear in other cities. "New Fraser Play Bombs" was the consensus, followed by lurid descriptions of the play's sex and emotional violence.

I was surprised by how emotionally affected I was by all this. It wasn't depression so much as a sort of sick realization of just how precarious my success was and how vulnerable it was to elitist, homophobic people.

Every morning when I walked out of the apartment to go about the day's work I'd say to myself, "Stand up straight. Be proud. Keep your head up. You've earned the right to fail."

One morning the phone rang at an hour so early it couldn't have been anyone who knew me.

"Is this Brad Fraser?" A man with an English accent.

"Who's this?"

"My name's Braham Murray. I'm the artistic director of the Royal Exchange Theatre in Manchester."

His accent made him hard to understand. I said, "*What's* your name?"

"Braham. Like Abraham without the A."

This was interesting enough to get me out of bed. "Hi, Braham."

"Is this a bad time?"

"Only in the most general sense," I replied. "What can I do for you?"

He said, "We did *Poor Super Man* at the Exchange last season and it was a tremendous hit. A few years before that we did *Unidentified Human Remains* and it was also a great hit."

I could only vaguely recall hearing about these production. There'd been so many. "Thanks," I said. "I heard great things. How did you get my number?"

"Your agent gave it to me. Are you working on anything new?"

I laughed, perhaps a tad bitterly, and said, "My new play just opened."

"I take it you're not happy with it."

"I'm *quite* happy with it. The press is not."

He laughed and asked me what was going on. I told him the whole story. When I was done he said, "When Joe Orton's *Loot* bombed in the West End I suggested he bring it to Manchester and we'd see if we could improve it."

I said, "Didn't that production go on to be very successful?"

"Yes, it did."

I became even more attentive. I said, "I'm a big Orton fan."

He said, "I can tell. *Remains* and *Poor Super Man* are brilliant plays, mate. Seriously brilliant. I had this urge to call you to say if there's anything you want to write and you need a producing theatre for it, I'd like to offer that to you."

This entire phone call was like a lightning bolt from heaven. "Wow. Thanks, Braham. That's amazing."

He said, "Why don't I come over and see the show. Then we'll meet."

I said, "Why don't you."

Braham arrived in Toronto just a few days before the show was scheduled to close. He was a short, thick-lipped man with a grizzled lower face, sparkling eyes and a confidence I'd rarely encountered in directors. From the start we had an amazing rapport.

After seeing *Martin Yesterday* he said, "It's a wonderful show. Complex and mercurial. Bracingly offensive. They've gone off you after a few years of adoration. It's not unusual."

I said, "Thanks."

Braham said, "What if we do it at the Royal Exchange next season and see what happens?"

I said, "I would be most grateful."

He clapped me on the shoulder. "Then we shall."

He flew back to Manchester, and a few weeks later Shain had closed the deal for the Royal Exchange to produce the British premiere of *Martin Yesterday*.

The final performance of the show at Buddies was a Sunday matinee. I slipped in at the last minute and took a seat at the back of the house. It was the first time I'd been back since instituting the video cuts after the second show. I was uncertain: had the reviewers been right? Would it be that bad? But after the lights went down, the integrity of everyone's work pulled me in and held me for the next two hours. The rear-projection roller-coaster ride worked fabulously. The actors had proven strong in the face of adversity.

Ironically, it would be a newspaper that took me in a new direction.

Kenneth Whyte, editor of the newly launched right-of-centre *National Post* newspaper, and incidentally brother of my boss so many years ago at Walden's, hired me to be a roving arts writer, commenting on whatever was happening across the country. I was paid a good rate. They covered my travel costs when I flew to Edmonton to write about the Fringe Festival and when I went to Stratford to write about the festival there. People I'd known and worked with for years were suddenly treating me like "the press," sucky and obsequious when I was around and they were hoping for a mention, and resentful and cutting when I was out of sight.

Writing about the theatre left me conflicted. On the one hand, it brought more attention to a discipline that was often ignored. On the other hand, it put me in a position where I was forced to judge and qualify the work of my peers, which never turns out well. I was aware of how close I could come to being the thing I hated most. After spending ten days running around the city interviewing celebrities for the Toronto International Film Festival, things felt even more complicated. When I agitated for assignments that were less connected to the arts and pitched political columns or stories, the phone stopped ringing.

Thankfully *Remains* was being produced at a lot of colleges and universities, and they often invited me to speak. After the first two invitations I'd told Shain to accept if they were paying, but to stipulate in my contract that I would not see the show. I was happy to impart whatever wisdom I could and share amusing anecdotes, of which there were many about the show by this point, but I couldn't stand to sit through another production of the script.

One night I was noodling in my sketchbook when the phone rang. The voice on the other end was deeply accented and not one I recognized. I couldn't understand what he was saying, although his tone was very urgent. As I asked him to repeat himself, I realized I was speaking to a friend/fuck buddy of Tad's, a Russian hooker with a huge dick who Tad saw whenever he could. I had gotten a strange vibe when we'd been introduced and tried to steer clear of the guy. He finally slowed down and enunciated well enough to tell me he was calling from Wellesley Hospital, where he'd left Tad in the emergency ward moments earlier. I asked him what happened, if there'd been an accident. I hadn't heard from Tad in months.

The Russian said, "It is AIDS."

I said, "Will you stay until I get there?"

The Russian said, "I want no part of this," and hung up.

Tad was in a glass quarantine cell. A nurse handed me a mask, waited for me to put it on, and let me in.

Tad—or the skeleton of Tad—was sitting up in bed looking at me with a strange, birdlike alertness. There were dark purple rings under his eyes, and his cheeks were dark and hollow. Tad said, "I told Ruskie not to call you."

I shrugged. "He did. How long have you known?"

Tad's eyes gleamed strangely. I was wondering if he had one of the many brain infections that were related to the disease. He said, "I quit my job. Threw my uniforms down the garbage chute. People were knocking on the door but I wouldn't answer."

I sat in the chair by the door. "Did you see a doctor?"

"Why? They can't do anything. They couldn't do anything for Bart." Bart was his ex-model boyfriend who'd died just before Tad had come to New York for the opening of *Remains*.

I said, "There's AZT, the cocktail they're trying—"

He shook his head vehemently. "I'm going to die."

I said, "Tad, people aren't dying so fast anymore. There are all kinds of new treatments—"

"I'm dying," he said. "I want to die."

I stared him, eyes stinging. "You're not going to die."

He let out a long breath and leaned back in the bed. He said, "If you're going to cry you have to go out in the hall to do it."

I said, "I'll cry later then."

Eventually, haltingly, I got most of the story in a disjointed fashion. Tad figured he'd been infected when he was with Bart—"We weren't always careful"—but had refused to see a doctor about it. He dodged all talk of AIDS, even avoiding the nightly news for fear it would be mentioned. When his body started to break down he had no idea what was happening. Then his behaviour got weird and he didn't know how to control it. The Russian, who was the only person Tad saw at the time, grew concerned when he found Tad wandering the hallway of his condo building.

A nurse finally came in and gave him a series of pills. When she left I said, "I'll come back tomorrow."

He said, "Brad, don't—"

I said, "I'm coming back tomorrow," and left.

I was right. Tad didn't die.

In fact, when I went back to see him the next day he was looking considerably better. That crazed gleam had left his eyes. There was an IV in the top of his hand. No one told me I had to wear a mask. His voice was weak but his colour was better. When I asked, the nurse assured me he was responding well to the medications they were giving him. After she was gone I asked him, "Still want to die?"

"Did I say that?"

I nodded. He managed a wan smile. He asked, "Did you bring me here?"

I realized he didn't remember a thing from the day before. "No. The Russian called me. He found you."

"Where'd he go?"

I said, "Don't know. But I don't think he's coming back."

Tears filled his eyes as he thanked me for coming after our not speaking for so long. He never offered an explanation, and I never asked for one.

When I went back the next day, one of his girlfriends from the airline was there. Tad introduced us and we had an instant bond. A few days later Tad's sister from Winnipeg arrived and the three of us spent a week together at the hospital until he was out of the danger zone. After that we took him home and took turns caring for him until, after a few months, he was able to care for himself. By August he was well enough for me to take a trip to Amsterdam with my friend John the lawyer to attend the 1998 Gay Games.

If New York had been Sodom four years earlier when Gordon and I had gone for the Games, Amsterdam was Gomorrah. The sense of doom and perpetual mourning that had informed the New York celebration had dissipated, and these Games were suffused with, if not a sense of optimism, at least a sense of something other than mourning. Deaths from AIDS had slowed down, and in the more privileged demographics infections from HIV had lessened. Those of us who'd been immersed in the plague from the beginning got our first respite in over fifteen years. Realizing I might not have the opportunity again, I decided to see if I could set a record for number of cocks blown at a sex bar in a single evening. I was more popular than I'd expected. If all of the men on the earth had disappeared at that moment, there was enough DNA in my T-shirt to replace many of them.

After Amsterdam I had a month at home in Toronto before flitting off to Edmonton to open *Martin Yesterday* at the Roxy. Journalists across the country were outraged when it was billed as a new play. In interviews I reminded them that I had changed the sex/gender of one character and refocused the entire main conflict in the play, as well as having severely "toned down the sex and violence" for a straight audience. It played to nearly empty houses. I wouldn't work again in Edmonton for a decade.

There was redemption for *Martin Yesterday*, though.

In 1999 I flew to Manchester to take part in rehearsals. The Royal Exchange is a high-tech wonder of glass and metal that sits like a futuristic machine in the centre of a vast Victorian building that was once the Manchester cotton exchange. When the IRA set off the largest bomb on English soil in 1996, it had devastated a large swath of downtown and led to a major rebuild. The upgrade of the theatre had been completed shortly before I arrived.

I'd been dreaming of seeing Manchester since the early eighties, when it was one of the hot spots for new music, introducing some of my favourite bands at the time, including Joy Division, the Happy Mondays and the Smiths. Even though the days of historic dance club the Haçienda were over, the Manc club and music scene was still legendary, and I was eager to explore it. The theatre had put me in a small apartment above a gay pub on Canal Street.

The play was being directed by Marianne Elliott, who went on to win many awards for her exceptional directing, including an Olivier and a Tony for *War Horse* twenty years later. Marianne had already directed *Poor Super Man* for the Royal Exchange and seemed to have a strong sympathy for my work. There was an amazing cast, including Ian Gelder—who'd played David McMillan in the production I'd seen at the Traverse a few years earlier—as Martin and his partner, the highly regarded Ben Daniels, as Matt. They had a wonderful chemistry that elevated the material above either of my productions.

I was amazed at how well the show worked in the Royal's in-the-round configuration. The roller-coaster ride had been changed to one of those "lift you up and drop you down" rides that impressively utilized the advanced tech and three-storey height of the theatre.

It was a beautiful production, imaginatively realized and exquisitely acquitted on every level. When I had directed the show at Buddies I had wanted to make a statement—a proclamation of my queerness and an indictment of those who were hostile to it. Marianne Elliott directed this play. There is a difference.

This was the beginning of a two-decades-long relationship with Braham and the Royal Exchange that would foster some of my best work.

Thanks to the miracle of AOL, the press office was able to get reviews to me as they came out. I'd been terrified to look at them after the show's reception in Canada, but forced myself to now.

They were not all raves. But they were not all denunciations of Brad Fraser, either. They were, for the most part, well thought-out and critically considered. There were homophobic comments, but there was also an acknowledgement that inciting this sort of reaction was exactly what I was going for.

In the Canadian papers there was a grudging smattering of reports about the positive reaction in Britain, but from this point on my relationship with the Canadian press would be deeply altered. I was a much less attractive subject when my international success, which they'd previously applauded so lavishly, contrasted with their own negative reviews. I'd been judged ungrateful, and if there was anything the Canadian elites hated, it was an ungrateful faggot.

It had also been just ten years since Pete had warned me about success and fame not lasting, and I had responded with my wish for at least a decade of it.

New Year's Eve 2000 was approaching. It wasn't technically the end of the millennium, but the world was acting as if it were. While many feared all computers would fail when they were unable to recognize the rolling over of the first digit, most of us were skeptical but excited about the change.

Just before Christmas the phone rang. "Hey, Birdley."

"Randy! What's going on?"

"Coming to Toronto."

"Great. When?"

"I'm on my way to Bangkok but I thought I'd overnight in T.O. and spend New Year's Eve with you."

"Of course. Are you going on a holiday?"

"I might be working over there."

"Great. You can tell me all about it on New Year's Eve."

On the day, when he buzzed me on the intercom from downstairs and I let him into the building, I could feel that familiar flutter of pleasure I got in my stomach whenever I saw Randy. Twenty years on he was still one of my favourite people. We grated on one another if we were together for too long, but we had a million laughs. I opened the door and hugged him, then took a step back with my hands on his shoulders so we could check each other out. He looked great. I looked great. Neither of us looked anything like we'd looked when we met.

We ate pizza with beers as we caught up.

"So what's the plan tonight?" he asked.

"Tad invited us over to his place. His building faces the lake and there's gonna be a huge-ass fireworks display. If you're cool with that."

He was cool with it, and the three of us had a lovely evening mostly talking about Edmonton in the early eighties and how our lives had changed since. Tad was working out again, and except for the hollowness of his cheeks, which was caused by the medications that kept the virus mostly in check inside his body, he looked as healthy as ever.

Just before midnight we took the elevator up to the fortieth floor and joined hordes of other people assembled in the gym, with its tall glass windows, and out on the deck, which is where we headed. It was cold, but Toronto cold, not Edmonton cold where your face would be freezing off. The sky and the water were dark mirrors, the Toronto Islands in the distance creating the only line that differentiated them from one another.

I stood between Randy and Tad. When the fireworks started I put my arms around their shoulders and pulled them into a sideways embrace. They put their arms around me as the sky exploded with fire and thunder, propelling us into the future.

I was feeling many things in that moment, but what I felt most of all was gratitude.

# DISAPPEARING THE QUEER

STRAIGHT PEOPLE disappear queer people. They do it all the time. Often it is done intentionally and with malice, but nearly as often it is completely unconscious. Many so-called progressive straight people would be horrified if they realized how often they do it.

Historically many societies, particularly over the last two thousand years, have disappeared their queers through censure, persecution and death. Every law enacted against queer sex and every enforcement of that law is an attempt to disappear the queer. Nazi Germany is not the only place to have made a concerted effort to obliterate its queer population. Gay people are still punished with discrimination, imprisonment, torture and death in many countries.

Historians have intentionally and systemically attempted to destroy or conceal the rich history of queer relationships and acts in ancient history. If they can convince people queerness never existed previously, it makes it easier to disappear it in the present day. How many priceless artifacts that could comment on our existence were destroyed forever because of Judeo-Christian disapproval?

Every time someone in the popular media chooses to omit or change the queerness of a character in order to make the art palatable to a straight audience, they disappear the queer.

Every person who protests against responsible sexual education for children because they believe children shouldn't know about queer existence disappears the queer.

Every family that has denied or suppressed knowledge of a queer family member has disappeared the queer. Every parent and sibling who rejects a queer family member disappears the queer.

Every person who claims to be accepting of equal rights for all but complains about our public expressions of affection or knowledge of our sexual lives is disappearing the queer.

Disappearing the queer is so pervasive that queers often do it to one another.

We do it when we rush to a fellow queer's home after they have died, to sanitize it of any sign of their queerness so as not to embarrass the family. Some of this, like getting rid of a friend's porn and sex toys, is common sense and done for straight people too; far too often the less publicly embarrassing signifiers of queer—pics with an ex-boyfriend or ex-girlfriend, campy souvenirs from trips abroad, photos in drag—are also eliminated. There was a lot of this during the AIDS years and it still goes on today.

We do it when gays and lesbians claim bisexual people don't really exist.

We do it when we fail to grant authenticity to a trans person's being because it does not match our presumptions about biology.

We do it when we exclude queers of other races and cultures from our spheres of privilege and try to pass that off as the result of an uncontrollable innate sexual preference rather than racism.

We do it when we brag we are straight-acting/looking.

When you are raised in a culture that is racist, homophobic and misogynistic, every citizen will feel each of those things to some degree, even if they are a member of the targeted group. Hatred from the majority works best as a control mechanism if it leads to self-hatred for the minoritarian member as well.

Like all queer people of my generation I struggled with self-hatred. When I was growing up, homosexuality was considered a mental illness. We were all expected to commit suicide or kill ourselves prematurely through our self-destructive lifestyle. I came to realize at quite a young age that, while my queerness was unique to me, many of my desires and experiences were not unique to being queer but were shared by most everyone who's human.

The life I've lived has very little in common with those of my het family members, and I believe that is specifically because of my queerness. Out of necessity, being gay forced me from the world and class I was born into. I had to search for my place in the world and for the people who would genuinely love me for who I am. My survival depended on it.

To my critics, my greatest sin has always been suggesting that being gay might be better than being straight. In truth I don't believe one state is intrinsically superior to the other, but I do love the reaction that comes when I make straight people feel, even for a moment, what it's really like to be diminished for being gay.

I make no apologies for my appetites and I make no apologies for the techniques, conscious nor not, I've developed for coping with being queer in a straight world and being a truth-teller in a world of liars. I've done what I had to not just to survive but to thrive, to tell my truth, to effect the kind of change I feel the world needs. I may not always succeed, but I have never stopped trying.

For fifteen years of the previous century the world saw the biggest disappearance of queer people in human history.

While millions of heterosexuals worldwide were infected with AIDS, in the West it was mostly queer men who were infected and died. In the retrospect of advanced age, fifteen years is not a long time. In the perspective of a young person living through that time, fifteen years was an eternity.

I knew some of those men. Many of them were discarded. Forgotten. Disappeared. This book is for those people, whether they're named in these pages or not.

I have fought having my queerness eradicated for my entire life. I have fought it with my family. I have fought it with my enemies and my friends. I have fought it with society. These battles have scarred me, but they have made me hard. These battles have wounded me, but they have made me strong. These battles have made me resolute.

I will not be disappeared.

## ACKNOWLEDGEMENTS

A book like this doesn't get put together without a great deal of help along the way. I'd like to acknowledge the following people who were integral to the completion of this project.

Bruce Walsh and the University of Regina Press, for getting the ball rolling.

Paul Bellini and Spencer Schunk, who are my most willing and constructive readers; also, David Gale, Kate Newby, Adam Pottle, and Robert Ouellette, for their feedback.

Ali Machum, who provided crucial early editing advice.

Robert Black, who did the genealogy investigation and provided crucial support.

Michael Levine, who consented to represent the book and got it to this publisher.

Tim Rostron, and everyone at Doubleday Canada / Penguin Random House Canada, for their sensitive professionalism and guidance.

Freelance copy editor Shaun Oakey.

Rajiv Maikuri, for facilitating introductions.

The Ontario Arts Council for the financial support that funded the first draft.

Page x: Brad in the saddle (author's collection); page 30: Brad in grade seven (author's collection); page 42: Brad in '76 (author's collection); page 60: *Mutants* clipping (republished with the express permission of *Edmonton Journal*, a division of Postmedia Network Inc.); page 74: Angelo Rizacos and Karen Woolridge in *Wolfboy* at the 25th Street Theatre (author's collection); page 88: Brad circa *Rude Noises* (author's collection); page 100: Carl Marotte and Keanu Reeves in Theatre Passe Muraille's *Wolfboy* (photo: David Hlynsky); page 124: Brad with cast and crew of *Chainsaw Love* (author's collection); page 138: promotional panel by Brad for *Young Art* (author's collection); page 144: inspirational police poster (author's collection); page 152: cover of published play showing Kate Newby in Alberta Theatre Projects' *Unidentified Human Remains* (photo: Trudie Lee); page 182: Brent Carver and Greg Spottiswood in Crow's Theatre's *Unidentified Human Remains* (photo: Michael Cooper); page 204: Unidentified Human Remains program (used by permission, all rights reserved, Playbill Inc.); page 230: poster for the Montreal production of *The Ugly Man* (courtesy of Théâtre de Quat'Sous); page 248: Damian Baldet, Michael J. Blankenship and Annie Fitzpatrick in Ensemble Theater of Cincinnati's *Poor Super Man* (photo: Sandy Underwood); page 264: Brad in a golden shirt (photo: David Hawe); page 286: poster for the Sydney production of *Poor Super Man* (courtesy of Sydney Theatre Company); page 304: Steve Cumyn, Jean-Philippe Cote and Rod Wilson in *Martin Yesterday* (photo: David Hawe); page 318: Cam (photo: Brad Fraser).